USING

microsoft® excel® 2010

Tracy Syrstad
Bill Jelen

800 East 96th Street, Indianapolis, Indiana 46240 USA

Using Microsoft® Excel® 2010

ISBN-13: 978-0-7897-4290-2
ISBN-10: 0-7897-4290-X

Library of Congress Cataloging-in-Publication Data
Syrstad, Tracy.
  Using Microsoft Excel 2010 / Tracy Syrstad, Bill Jelen.
    p. cm.
  Includes bibliographical references and index.
  ISBN-13: 978-0-7897-4290-2
  ISBN-10: 0-7897-4290-X
  1. Microsoft Excel (Computer file) 2. Business—Computer programs. 3. Electronic spreadsheets. I. Jelen, Bill. II. Title.
  HF5548.4.M523S97 2011
  005.54--dc22
                        2010028386

Printed in the United States of America
Second Printing: October 2010

Trademarks

Warning and Disclaimer

Bulk Sales

Que Publishing offers excellent discounts on this book when ordered in quantity for bulk purchases or special sales. For more information, please contact

U.S. Corporate and Government Sales
1-800-382-3419
corpsales@pearsontechgroup.com

For sales outside of the U.S., please contact

International Sales
international@pearson.com

Associate Publisher
Greg Wiegand

Acquisitions Editor
Loretta Yates

Development Editor
The Wordsmithery LLC

Managing Editor
Sandra Schroeder

Project Editor
Mandie Frank

Copy Editor
Barbara Hacha

Indexer
Erika Millen

Proofreader
Dan Knott

Technical Editor
Bob Umlas

Publishing Coordina-tor
Cindy Teeters

Interior Designer
Anne Jones

Cover Designer
Anna Stingley

Compositor
Mark Shirar

Contents at a Glance

Introduction

1   Getting to Know the Excel Interface

2   Introducing the Excel Web App

3   Entering Data in Excel

4   Data Formatting

5   Using Formulas

6   Using Functions

7   Sorting

8   Filtering and Consolidating Data

9   Subtotals and Grouping

10   Pivot Tables

11   Creating Charts

12   SmartArt, WordArt, and Pictures

13   Macros and UDFs

        Index

Media Table of Contents

To register this product and gain access to the free web edition and the audio and video files, go to quepublishing.com/using.

Chapter 1:   **Getting to Know the Excel Interface**

Show Me **Media 1.1**—Adding a Command to the
Quick Access Toolbar 13
Show Me **Media 1.2**—Freezing Columns 21

Chapter 2:   **Introducing the Excel Web App**

Show Me **Media 2.1**—Creating a Windows Live ID 31
Tell Me More **Media 2.2**—SkyDrive 35

Chapter 3:   **Entering Data in Excel**

Show Me **Media 3.1**—Using the Fill Handle to Fill in a Series 43
Show Me **Media 3.2**—Converting Formulas to Values 50
Tell Me More **Media 3.3**—Pasting and Delimited Text 51

Chapter 4:   **Data Formatting**

Show Me **Media 4.1**—Creating a Custom Style 74
Show Me **Media 4.2**—Using Format Painter 86
Show Me **Media 4.3**—Creating a New Theme 89
Show Me **Media 4.4**—Applying Conditional Formatting 91
Tell Me More **Media 4.5**—Using Preset Conditional Formatting Rules ... 93

Chapter 5:   **Using Formulas**

Show Me **Media 5.1**—Entering a Basic Formula 101
Tell Me More **Media 5.2**—Typing an Array Within an Array 114
Show Me **Media 5.3**—Evaluating a Formula 119

Chapter 6:   **Using Functions**

Show Me **Media 6.1**—Using the AutoSum Functionality 125
Tell Me More **Media 6.2**—Using the INDEX Function 130
Show Me **Media 6.3**—Calculating Times Over 24 Hours 142
Show Me **Media 6.4**—Using Goal Seek to Return a Value 144

Chapter 7:   **Sorting**

Show Me **Media 7.1**—Sorting Values with the Sort Dialog 148
Show Me **Media 7.2**—Using the Quick Sort Buttons to
Sort Multiple Columns 152
Tell Me More **Media 7.3**—Creating Custom Lists 155
Show Me **Media 7.4**—Rearranging Columns Using
the Sort Dialog 155

Chapter 8:   **Filtering and Consolidating Data**

Show Me **Media 8.1**—Using the Search Function
to Include and Exclude Items in the Filtering Listing 165
Show Me **Media 8.2**—Using the Search Function
to Filter for Specific Dates 168
Show Me **Media 8.3**—Using the Advanced Filter with
Various Criteria 175
Tell Me More **Media 8.4**—Finding Duplicates 178

Chapter 9:   **Subtotals and Grouping**

Tell Me More **Media 9.1**—Adding Grand Totals
When the Subtotals Were Manually Entered 181
Show Me **Media 9.2**—Using the Subtotal Tool 183
Show Me **Media 9.3**—Subtotaling by Multiple Columns 191
Show Me **Media 9.4**—Inserting Blank Rows Between
Subtotal Groups 195

Chapter 10:   **Pivot Tables**

Show Me **Media 10.1**—Creating a Pivot Table 202
Tell Me More **Media 10.2**—Using Other Data Sources 204
Show Me **Media 10.3**—Grouping Dates into Months
and Years 212
Show Me **Media 10.4**—Adding Slicers to
a Pivot Table 226

Chapter 11:   **Creating Charts**

Tell Me More **Media 11.1**—The Importance of Choosing the
Right Chart Type 234
Show Me **Media 11.2**—Creating a Chart 234
Show Me **Media 11.3**—Assigning a Series to the Secondary Axis 242
Show Me **Media 11.4**—Creating Sparklines 250

Chapter 12:   **SmartArt, WordArt, and Pictures**

Show Me **Media 12.1**—Inserting SmartArt 257
Show Me **Media 12.2**—Inserting SmartArt That Includes Images 258
Show Me **Media 12.3**—Linking SmartArt to Cells 262
Tell Me More **Media 12.4**—Applying Styles 267

Chapter 13:   **Macros and UDFs**

Tell Me More **Media 13.1**—Creating a Trusted Location 272
Show Me **Media 13.2**—Getting the Most Out of the
Macro Recorder by Using the Keyboard 275
Show Me **Media 13.3**—Recording a Macro Using
Relative Referencing 277
Show Me **Media 13.4**—Creating a Simple UDF 285

Table of Contents

Introduction 1

1   Getting to Know the Excel Interface 7

Customizing the Ribbon 7
    Removing Default Tabs and Groups .7
    Creating a Custom Tab 8
    Adding a New Group 9
    Adding a New Button 9
    Minimizing the Ribbon 10

Customizing the Quick Access Toolbar 11
    Move the Quick Access Toolbar 11
    Adding Commands to the Quick Access Toolbar 11
    Customizing the Quick Access Toolbar for the
        Current Workbook 14
    Removing Commands from the Quick Access Toolbar 15

Dialog Launchers 15

Zoom 16

Page Break Preview 17
    Changing a Page's Column Break 17

Page Layout 18
    Inserting the Filename and Date into the Header 18

Page Numbering 19
    Inserting *Page* of *Pages* Page Numbering 19

Repeating Rows or Columns When Printing 20
    Repeating a Header Row 20

Freezing Panes 20
    Freezing Columns and Rows at the Same Time 21

Working with Custom Views 22
    Creating a Custom View of Filtered Data 22

Arranging Windows 23

Inserting Rows & Columns 23
    Inserting a Row 24

Renaming a Sheet 24

Moving or Copying Sheets 24
    Within the Workbook 25
    Between Workbooks 25

Change Multiple Worksheets at One Time 25
    Changing Multiple Sheets 26

Setting Workbook and Sheet Protection 26

    Setting Workbook Protection 26

    Setting Sheet Protection 27

    Unlocking Cells 27

Recent Documents 27

Saving as PDF 28

Opening Templates 28

Troubleshooting Excel Options 29

2   Introducing the Excel Web App **31**

Requirements 31

Acquiring a Windows Live ID 31

    Creating a Windows Live ID 32

Uploading and Downloading Workbooks 33

    Accessing the SkyDrive 34

    Uploading with Windows Live 34

    Saving to SkyDrive from Excel 35

    Creating a New Workbook 36

    Opening a Workbook 37

    Saving a File to Your Local Drive 37

Sharing a Workbook 38

    Creating a New Folder 38

    Setting Folder Permissions 39

    Simultaneous Editing 40

Interacting with a Sheet Online 41

3   Entering Data in Excel **43**

Dragging the Fill Handle to Extend a Series 43

    Extending a Series Containing Text 44

    Extending a Numerical Series 44

Creating Your Own Series 44

    Creating a Custom List 45

Joining Text 45

    Joining a First Name and Last Name 46

Joining Dates and Text 46

Fixing Numbers as Text 47

    Using Convert to Number on a Range 48

    Using Paste Special to Force a Number 48

Convert Text Case 48

Copying Formulas Rapidly 49
 Filling a Formula Down a Column 49

Converting Formulas to Values 50
 Quickly Replacing Formulas with Values 50

Using Text to Columns 51
 Working with Delimited Text 51
 Working with Fixed Width Text 53
 Using Text to Columns to Convert Text to Numbers 55

Controlling the Next Cell Selection 55
 Enter Versus Tab 55
 Moving Cell Pointer Direction 56
 Preselecting the Data Range 56
 Entering Data in a Circle 56

Working with Tables 57
 Defining a Table 57
 Expanding a Table 59
 Adding a Total Row to a Table 60

Data Validation 61
 Limiting User Entry to a Selection from a List 62

4   Data Formatting **65**

Cell Formatting 65
 Font Group 65
 Alignment Group 69

Justifying Text in a Range 72
 Reflowing Text in a Paragraph 73

Cell Styles 74
 Creating a Custom Style 74

Using Number Formats in Excel and Excel Starter 74
 General 75
 Number 75
 Currency 75
 Accounting 76
 Date 76
 Time 76
 Percentage 76
 Fraction 77
 Scientific 77
 Text 77
 Special 78
 Custom Formats 78

Dealing with Formatting Issues 84

Using Number Formats in Excel Web Apps 84
Using the Number Format Drop-down 84
Using Increase and Decrease Decimal 84

Using Format Painter 85
Copying the Formatting of a Range 86

Adjusting Row Heights and Column Widths 87
Applying One Column's Width to
    Other Columns 88

Using Themes 88
Applying a New Theme 89
Creating a New Theme 89
Sharing a Theme 90

Using Conditional Formatting 91
Applying a Custom Icon Set 92
Using Rules 93
Clearing Conditional Formatting 98

5   **Using Formulas** **99**

The Importance of Laying Data Out Properly 99

Adjusting Calculation Settings 100

Formulas Versus Values 100

Entering a Formula 101
Enter a Formula 101
Relative Versus Absolute Formulas 101
R1C1 Notation 102
Using F4 to Change the Cell Referencing 103

Entering Formulas 104

Copying a Formula 104
Copying a Formula by Using Ctrl+Enter 105
Copying a Formula by Dragging the
    Fill Handle 105

Formula Operators 106
Order of Operations 107

Using Names To Simplify References 107
Applying and Using a Name in a Formula 108

Inserting Formulas into Tables 109
Entering a Formula in a Table 109

Table References in Formulas 110

Writing Formulas That Refer to Tables 111

Using Array Formulas 111

Example 1 112

Example 2 112

Example 3 113

Editing Array Formulas 114

Deleting Array Formulas 115

Troubleshooting Formulas 115

Error Messages 116

Trace Precedents and Dependents 116

Watch Window 118

Evaluating Formulas 119

6   Using Functions **121**

Breaking Down a Function 121

Finding Functions 121

Entering Functions 122

The Formula Wizard 122

Using In-Cell Tips 124

AutoSum 125

Other Auto Functions 126

Lookup Functions 127

CHOOSE 127

VLOOKUP 127

MATCH and INDEX 129

INDIRECT 130

SUMIFS 131

SUMPRODUCT 132

Logical Functions 133

IF/AND/OR/NOT 134

Nested IF Statements 135

IFERROR 135

Date and Time Functions 136

Convert and Breakdown Dates 136

Convert and Breakdown Times 138

Date Calculation Functions 138

Troubleshooting: Calculating with Dates 140

Data Analysis Tools 142

Goal Seek 144

Using Goal Seek 145

Using the Wizard to Troubleshoot Formulas 145

    Troubleshooting a Formula 145

7   **Sorting** **147**

Preparing Data 147

Sorting in the Web App 147

The Sort Dialog 147

    Sorting by Values 148

    Sorting by Color or Icon 149

    Doing a Case-Sensitive Sort 151

Using the Quick Sort Buttons 151

    Quick Sorting Multiple Columns 151

Random Sort 152

    Randomizing Data 152

Sorting with a Custom Sequence 153

    Using a Custom List 153

Rearranging Columns 155

    Using the Sort Dialog 155

    Using the Mouse 156

Fixing Sort Problems 157

8   **Filtering and Consolidating Data** **159**

Preparing Data 159

Applying a Filter to a Dataset 159

    Clearing a Filter 160

    Reapplying a Filter 161

    Filtering in the Web App 161

    Turn Filtering on for One Column 161

Filtering Options 162

    Filter Listing for Listed Items 162

    Grouped Dates Filter Listing 163

    Searching Functions for Listed Items 165

    Using the Search Function for Grouped Dates 167

    Using Text, Number and Date Special Filters 169

    Filtering by Color or Icon 171

Filtering By Selection 172

    Using Filter Selection 172

Allow Filtering on a Protected Sheet 172

Using the Advanced Filter 173

Using the Criteria Range 174
Filtering for Unique Items 176

Removing Duplicates 177
Removing Duplicates from a Dataset 177

Consolidating Data 178
Consolidating Duplicate Data by Category 179

9   Subtotals and Grouping **181**

SUBTOTAL Function 181

Subtotal Tool 182
Summarizing Data Using the Subtotal Command 183
Placing Subtotals Above Data 184
Remove Subtotals or Groups 184

Expanding and Collapsing Subtotals 184

Copying Subtotals 185
Copying Only the Totals to a New Location 185

Formatting Subtotals 186
Applying Formatting to Only the Totals 186

Applying Multiple Subtotal Function Types 187
Applying Multiple Subtotal Function Types 187
Combining Multiple Subtotals to One Row 188

Subtotaling by Multiple Columns 190
Subtotaling by Multiple Columns 191

Sorting Subtotals 192
Sorting a Subtotaled Column 192

Inserting Blank Rows 192
Separating Subtotaled Rows for Print 193
Separating Subtotaled Rows for
    Distributed Files 194

Grouping and Outlining 196
Manually Grouping Rows 198

10   Pivot Tables **199**

Data Preparation 199

Pivot Table Limitations 200
Pivot Table Compatibility 201

PivotTable Field List 201

Creating a Pivot Table 202
Creating a Pivot Table 203

Moving Fields in a Pivot Table 205
Remove a Field 205

Rename a Field 205

Change Calculation Type 206
Change the Calculation Type of a Field Value 206

Show Values Based on Other Items 206

Pivot Table Sorting 208
Pivot Table Quick Sort 208
Pivot Table Sort (*Fieldname*) Dialog 208

Expanding and Collapsing Fields 211

Drill Down 211

Grouping Dates 212
Group a Date Field into Months and Years 213
Summarize Weeks 213

Filtering Options 214
Filter Listing for Listed Items 214
Search Function for Listed Items 215
Special Filters 218

Filter By Selection 221
Filter by Manual Selection 221
Clearing Filters 221

Calculated Fields 222
Create a Calculated Field 223

Adding Color and Lines to a Pivot Table 223

Hiding Totals 223

Formatting Values 224

Pivot Table Views 225

Slicers 226
Add a Slicer to a Pivot Table 227

Making Data Suitable for Pivot Tables 227

11 Creating Charts **231**

Components of a Chart 231

Preparing Data 232

Types of Charts 233

Creating a Chart 234
Creating a Chart 235
Chart Styles 236

Chart Layouts 237
Adding a Chart Title 237
Adding an Axis Title 238
Adding or Moving the Chart Legend 238
Moving or Resizing a Chart 239
Changing a Chart's Type 239

Mixing Chart Types 240
Creating a Chart with Multiple Chart Types 240

Showing Numbers of Different Scale 241
Chart Data of Vastly Different Scales 242

Updating Chart Data 242
Pasting New Data onto Existing Series 243

Switching Rows and Columns 243

Trendlines 244
Adding a Forecasting Trendline 245

Stock Charts 246
Creating a Stock Chart 246

Bubble Charts 247

Pie Chart Issue: Small Slices 247
Rotating the Pie 248
Create a Bar of Pie Chart 248

Sparklines 250
Creating Sparklines 250
Adding Points to a Sparkline 250
Spacing Markers in a Sparkline 251
Delete Sparklines 252

Saving a Chart as a Template 252
Creating a Chart Using a User-Created Template 253

12   **SmartArt, WordArt, and Pictures** **255**

SmartArt 255
Inserting SmartArt 256

Inserting SmartArt Images 257
Selecting SmartArt 259
Adding and Deleting Shapes 259
Reorder Components 260
Formatting the Selected Layout 261
Changing the Selected Layout 261
Changing an Individual Component 261

Linking a Cell to Smart Art 262

Inserting WordArt 264

Inserting Pictures 265

    Inserting a Picture 265

    Resizing and Cropping Pictures 265

    Corrections, Color, and Artistic Effects 267

    Arranging Pictures 268

    Reducing a Picture's File Size 270

13   Macros and UDFs **271**

Enabling VBA Security 271

    Developer Tab 273

Introduction to the Visual Basic Editor 273

    Project Explorer 274

Understanding How the Macro Recorder Works 275

    Navigating While Recording 275

    Relative References in Macro Recording 276

    Avoid the AutoSum Button 278

Recording a Macro 279

    Filling in the Record Macro Dialog 279

Running a Macro 281

    Running a Macro from the Ribbon 281

    Running a Macro from the Quick Access Toolbar 282

    Running a Macro from a Form Control, Text Box, or Shape 283

User-Defined Functions 284

    Structure of a UDF 285

    How to Use a UDF 287

    Sharing UDFs 287

    Using Select Case to Replace Nested IF 288

Index **291**

About the Authors

Tracy Syrstad is the project manager for the MrExcel consulting team and also handles many of the tech support phone calls. If you have a problem with Excel or another Microsoft Office product, she's there to listen and provide a solution.

Bill Jelen is the host of MrExcel.com. You will frequently find Bill on the road, entertaining people with his Power Excel seminars. He is the author of many books about Microsoft Excel and is the voice of the Learn Excel from MrExcel podcast.

Dedications

Tracy: *To John Syrstad*

Bill: *To Leo Laporte*

Acknowledgments

Tracy: Thanks to Bill Jelen and Loretta Yates for the chance to write this book. It really helped strengthen my confidence in my Excel knowledge and abilities. Kristy Sharpe, Kathryn Riley, and Juan Pablo González Ruiz were vital in helping me maintain a positive attitude through the very long days it took to get this book done so quickly. And thank you to all the MrExcel clients over the years who have asked me how to do something in Excel. Those questions helped guide me in choosing the subjects to cover.

Bill: Thanks to Tracy Syrstad for developing the content for this book. I am thrilled to be her co-author again after our successful Excel VBA books. I appreciate Bob Umlas being a great tech editor. Loretta Yates at QUE is always a pleasure to work with. At MrExcel.com, thanks to Scott Pierson, Barb Jelen, and Schar Oswald. At home, I appreciate the support and understanding of Josh, Zeke, and Mary Ellen.

We Want to Hear from You!

As the reader of this book, *you* are our most important critic and commentator. We value your opinion and want to know what we're doing right, what we could do better, what areas you'd like to see us publish in, and any other words of wisdom you're willing to pass our way.

As an associate publisher for Que Publishing, I welcome your comments. You can email or write me directly to let me know what you did or didn't like about this book—as well as what we can do to make our books better.

Please note that I cannot help you with technical problems related to the topic of this book. We do have a User Services group, however, where I will forward specific technical questions related to the book.

When you write, please be sure to include this book's title and author as well as your name, email address, and phone number. I will carefully review your comments and share them with the author and editors who worked on the book.

Email: feedback@quepublishing.com

Mail: Greg Wiegand
         Associate Publisher
         Que Publishing
         800 East 96th Street
         Indianapolis, IN 46240 USA

Reader Services

Visit our website and register this book at quepublishing.com/using for convenient access to any updates, downloads, or errata that might be available for this book.

Introduction

Familiarity with Microsoft Excel is a requirement for most jobs today. Workers in every office use Excel to track and report information. Sales reps track leads, prospects, commissions, and travel expenses in Excel. Workers on the factory floor log schedules and quality data in Excel.

Excel is an amazingly flexible program. A new Excel worksheet offers a seemingly endless blank canvas of rows and columns where you can enter, summarize, and report data of any type. Charts and other data visualization tools can convert a page full of numbers to a visual snapshot. Pivot tables can summarize thousands of detailed records to a one-page summary in a few mouse clicks.

If you've never opened Excel, or if you've used Excel only to neatly arrange lists in columns, this book will get you up to speed with the real-life skills needed to survive in a job that requires familiarity with Excel.

Excel Comes in Many Flavors

When a potential employer asks if you know Excel, you need to ask which version of Excel. There are a lot of products available that have Excel in the name, but offer a different subset of commands.

- **Excel 2010** is the most recent version of the full-featured Excel program. The full version of Excel is what you will find in use in most job environments.

- **Excel Starter** is a new version of Excel that ships with new PCs. This free version of Excel offers the core Excel functionality, such as formatting, formulas, sorting, and filtering. It does not offer advanced commands such as pivot tables. Before 2010, the entry-level spreadsheet program from Microsoft was called Microsoft Works, and it created nonstandard spreadsheet files. The Excel Starter version of Excel can create true Excel files. If you create a file in Excel Starter and send it to someone with Excel 2010, the recipient will be able to open and use the file in Excel 2010.

- **Excel WebApp** is a new browser-based version of Excel. Whereas the browser is great for displaying existing Excel worksheets, the Excel 2010 WebApp allows users to enter new data and formulas in an Excel workbook while online. Those users do not need to have Excel installed on their computers. Mobile workers today might use Excel WebApp to access their Excel data while they are out of the office. You also might expect college students to use Excel WebApp to collaborate on group projects using this free version of Excel.

- **Excel 2007** is similar to Excel 2010. If you learned how to use Excel 2010 and begin work where the company uses Excel 2007, you will be able to transfer most of your skills. Some new features, such as sparklines, are missing. The File menu offers far fewer choices than the Excel 2010 File menu. (In Excel 2007, the word "File" was replaced with an Office logo inside a round circle in the top-left corner of the program. This was a bad idea and Microsoft went back to the word "File" in 2010.) For the most part, you should find yourself comfortable working in Excel 2007 using the knowledge that you learn about Excel 2010 using this book.

- **Excel 2003, Excel 2002, Excel 2000, and Excel 97** are collectively known as the legacy versions of Excel. Although the concepts of entering data and formulas in the worksheet are the same, the entire command structure is different in these versions of Excel. Instead of the intuitive Ribbon interface, you will find long text lists of commands organized on menus, such as File, Edit, View, Insert, and so on. Although the menu system is harder to learn, hundreds of millions of people originally learned about Excel using these menus. Nearly half of office computers are still hanging on to their legacy installations of Excel. Be prepared to have a steep learning curve as you try to find where the Excel 2010 commands are located in the old Excel menus.

If this is your first experience with Excel, going to work in an office that is still using Excel 2003 is going to present some frustrations for you and the employer as you try to adjust to the older version of Excel. If the company is still using Excel 2003, it either means that they didn't have the money to upgrade or that the people at the company are firmly entrenched with and know the old Excel very well. Be up front with your manager. Explain that you learned Excel using Excel 2010. That manager resisted upgrading to Excel 2010 because he or she didn't want to take the time to get up the learning curve to learn the new Ribbon interface. As someone who learned on Excel 2010, it will be just as intimidating to learn where familiar commands are in the old Excel environment.

This book allows you to customize your own learning experience. The step-by-step instructions in the book give you a solid foundation in using Excel 2010, and rich and varied online content, including video tutorials and audio sidebars.

How This Book Is Organized

This book teaches you the important functions and uses for Microsoft Excel. You should be able to turn to any page and learn a task that will help you in your job using Excel.

Additional content, such as video tutorials, demonstrate key concepts.

Using Excel 2010 will teach you the following:

- How to tell the difference between Excel 2010, Excel Starter, and Excel Web Apps.

- How to use the Excel Ribbon Interface.

- Faster ways to enter data in Excel.

- Formatting your data in Excel.

- Entering formulas to perform calculations in Excel.

- Using Excel functions to perform special calculations such as loan payments.

- How to sort your data so that you can see the earliest, latest, largest, or smallest items at the top of your report.

- How to filter your data so that you can find records that match a certain value.

- How to summarize data with subtotals or pivot tables.

- Creating charts and other visualizations from your data.

- Using Excel's presentation layer to add pictures and diagrams to your reports.

- Learn about the macro recorder so that you can start to build new commands in Excel.

- Many other tips and tricks to make your use of Excel more efficient.

The concepts in this book will allow you to get started by entering data and formulas in Excel. However, the later chapters on pivot tables and charting will provide you with enough advanced techniques to allow you to thrive in any job requiring Excel.

After you get up to speed with entering data and formulas in Excel, you might have a tendency to leave this book on the shelf. As your experience with Excel grows, you should come back to peruse the later chapters. Remember that there are usually five ways to accomplish every task in Excel. While you could successfully add subtotals to a data set using the formula skills from Chapter 5, "Using Formulas," there is a good chance that using the Subtotal function from Chapter 9, "Subtotals and Grouping," will allow you to accomplish the same task in a fraction of the time. Although you might not realize that you have a need for pivot tables at this moment, as you begin doing more tasks in Excel, it is likely that you will discover that Chapter 10, "Pivot Tables," can dramatically simplify an otherwise tedious task. By revisiting this book once every few weeks, you may discover faster ways to solve real tasks that you encounter at work.

Using This Book

This book allows you to customize your own learning experience. The step-by-step instructions give you a solid foundation in using Excel 2010, and rich and varied online content, including video tutorials and audio sidebars, provide the following:

- Demonstrations of step-by-step tasks covered in the book
- Additional tips or information on a topic
- Practical advice and suggestions
- Direction for more advanced tasks not covered in the book

Here's a quick look at a few structural features designed to help you get the most out of this book.

- **Chapter objective**—At the beginning of each chapter is a brief summary of topics addressed in that chapter. This objective enables you to quickly see what is covered.
- **Notes**—Notes provide additional commentary or explanation that doesn't fit neatly into the surrounding text. Notes give detailed explanations of how something works, alternative ways of performing a task, and other tidbits to get you on your way.
- **Tips**—This element gives you shortcuts, workarounds, and ways to avoid pitfalls.
- **Cross-references**—Many topics are connected to other topics in various ways. Cross-references help you link related information, no matter where that information appears in the book. When another section is related to one you are reading, a cross-reference directs you to a specific page in the book on which you can find the related information.

Let Me Try It

Tasks are presented in a step-by-step sequence so you can easily follow along.

Show Me

Video walks through tasks you've just got to see—including bonus advanced techniques.

Tell Me More

Audio delivers practical insights straight from the experts.

Special Features

More than just a book, your USING product integrates step-by-step video tutorials and valuable audio sidebars delivered through the free web edition that comes with every USING book. For the price of the book, you get online access anywhere with a web connection—no books to carry, content is updated as the technology changes, and you benefit from video and audio learning.

About the USING Web Edition

The web edition of every USING book is powered by Safari Books Online, allowing you to access the video tutorials and valuable audio sidebars. Plus, you can search the contents of the book, highlight text and attach a note to that text, print your notes and highlights in a custom summary, and cut and paste directly from Safari Books Online.

To register this product and gain access to the free web edition and the audio and video files, go to quepublishing.com/using.

This chapter shows you how to customize the ways you interact with and see your work in Excel, both online and on paper.

1

Getting to Know the Excel Interface

Customizing the Ribbon

When Microsoft released the new Ribbon interface in Excel 2007, users couldn't make changes to the tabs as they could the menus in legacy Excel. If there was a function you wanted quick access to in Excel 2007, you had to add it to the Quick Access toolbar.

With the release of Excel 2010, Microsoft returned the capability to customize the Ribbon. You can modify the existing tabs or create your own.

Removing Default Tabs and Groups

You can customize the Ribbon by hiding tabs or removing groups you don't think you need.

 LET ME TRY IT

Hiding a Tab

To hide a tab, follow these steps:

1. Right-click any tab and select Customize the Ribbon.

2. The list of existing tabs is on the right side of the Customize the Ribbon dialog (see Figure 1.1).

3. Unselect the tab(s) you want hidden from view and click OK.

Figure 1.1   *Use the Customize the Ribbon dialog to make changes to the Ribbon.*

LET ME TRY IT

Removing a Group

You can't customize the default groups, but you can remove them, making room for your own custom group. To remove a group, follow these steps:

1. Right-click any tab and select Customize the Ribbon.

2. The list of existing tabs is on the right side of the Customize the Ribbon dialog (refer to Figure 1.1).

3. Expand the tab containing the group you want to remove.

4. Select the group to remove and click Remove.

> If you remove a group and later decide you want it back, you have two choices: use the Reset option on the Customize the Ribbon dialog, or add the group using the steps from the section "Adding a New Group."

Creating a Custom Tab

The default tabs and groups in Excel may not be the ones best for you or for a particular situation you are working in. You can insert a custom tab into the Main Tabs group or the Tool tabs group. After the tab has been added, you can add the groups and buttons most useful to you.

 **LET ME TRY IT**

Inserting a New Tab

To create a custom tab in Excel to which you can add groups and buttons that you find most useful, follow these steps:

1. Right-click any tab and select Customize the Ribbon.

2. Select where you want your tab to be from the list on the right side of the dialog. The new tab will be placed below your selection.

3. Click New Tab. Excel creates a new tab with a new group, both with (Custom) after the name.

4. Highlight the new group and click Rename to rename the group.

5. Highlight the new tab and click Rename to rename the tab.

Adding a New Group

Although not required, grouping similar buttons together can make them easier to find, especially if you're helping someone else find a specific function. When you create a new tab, Excel automatically adds a new group for you, but you may need another group. A custom group is the only way to add buttons to a default tab.

You can also add one of the predefined groups found on the default tabs. These predefined groups are located under the Main Tabs and Tool Tabs commands in the list on the left side of the dialog.

 LET ME TRY IT

Adding a Group to an Existing Tab

To add a custom group to an existing tab, follow these steps:

1. Right-click any tab and select Customize the Ribbon.

2. In the list on the right side of the dialog, navigate to where you want to add a new group. The new group will be placed below your selection.

3. Click New Group. Excel creates a new group.

4. Highlight the new group and click Rename to rename the group.

Adding a New Button

Excel won't allow you to add a button to any of the default groups, but no such limitations exist for the custom groups you create.

 **LET ME TRY IT**

Adding a New Button to a Custom Group

To add a new button to a custom group, follow these steps:

1. Right-click any tab and select Customize the Ribbon.

2. In the list on the right side of the dialog, navigate to the custom group where you want to add the new button. The new button will be placed below your selection, as shown in Figure 1.2.

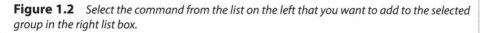

Figure 1.2   *Select the command from the list on the left that you want to add to the selected group in the right list box.*

3. In the list on the left side of the dialog, find the button you want to add.

4. Click Add to add the button to the group.

Minimizing the Ribbon

If you're working on a system with a small screen, the Ribbon probably takes up too much space. You can minimize the Ribbon, showing only the tab names, as shown in Figure 1.3.

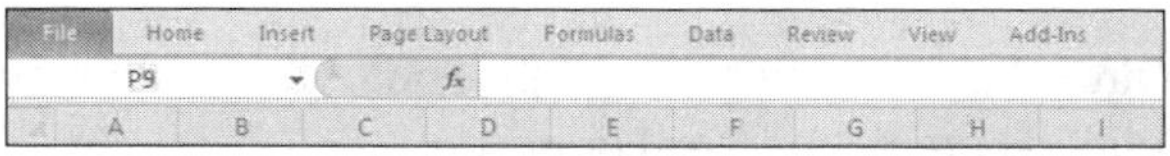

Figure 1.3   *When you minimize the Ribbon, only the tab names are visible.*

To toggle the Ribbon between being minimized and normal, press Ctrl+F1 on the keyboard or click the up/down arrow by the Help button in the upper-right corner of the screen (see Figure 1.4).

Figure 1.4   *Click the arrow by the Help button to minimize the Ribbon. Click it again to make the Ribbon normal again.*

Customizing the Quick Access Toolbar

The Quick Access toolbar is located in the upper-left corner of Excel, above the Ribbon. It is always visible, even when the Ribbon is minimized and, unlike the Ribbon, the commands aren't dependent on what you are doing in Excel, such as working with a chart.

Move the Quick Access Toolbar

You can move the Quick Access toolbar below the Ribbon by right-clicking the toolbar and selecting Show Quick Access Toolbar Below the Ribbon, as shown in Figure 1.5.

Figure 1.5   *You can place the Quick Access toolbar above or below the Ribbon.*

Adding Commands to the Quick Access Toolbar

Almost any command can be added to the toolbar, and you can also add *some* selections from within drop-downs.

You can customize the Quick Access toolbar in three ways:

- Click the drop-down arrow on the right end of the toolbar and select from the predefined commands (see Figure 1.6).

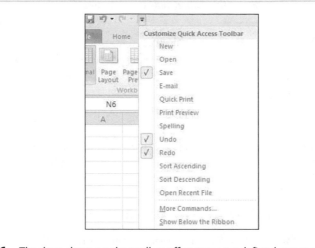

Figure 1.6 *The drop-down on the toolbar offers some predefined commands you can use to customize your Quick Access toolbar*

- Right-click a button on the toolbar and select Customize Quick Access Toolbar to bring up the Customize the Quick Access Toolbar dialog shown in Figure 1.7.

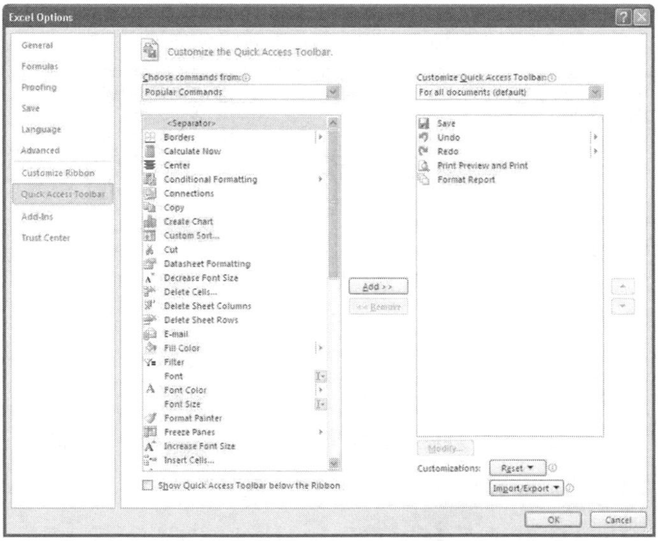

Figure 1.7 *Customize the Quick Access toolbar through the Customize the Quick Access Toolbar dialog.*

- Right-click a command or drop-down item in the Ribbon, as shown in Figure 1.8. If the option Add to Quick Access Toolbar appears, select it to add the item to the toolbar

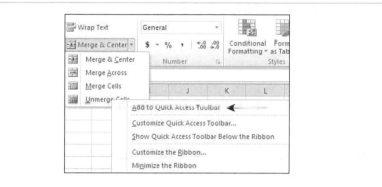

Figure 1.8 *If you see Add to Quick Access Toolbar when you right-click a Ribbon item, the command can be added to the Quick Access toolbar.*

SHOW ME   Media 1.1—Adding a Command to the Quick Access Toolbar
You can watch a free video of this task when you log on to my.safaribooksonline.com/9780132182287/media.

LET ME TRY IT

Adding a Command to the Quick Access Toolbar

Follow these steps to add a command to the Quick Access toolbar:

1. Right-click a button on the toolbar and select Customize Quick Access Toolbar.

2. Navigate the list on the left side of the dialog box to find the command you want to add to the toolbar.

3. Select the Command and click Add to copy the command over to the Quick Access toolbar.

Customizing the Quick Access Toolbar for the Current Workbook

You can add commands to the Quick Access toolbar that will appear only when a specific workbook is open. This can be especially useful if your workbook contains macros you want to activate with buttons.

 **LET ME TRY IT**

Add a Macro Button That Appears Only in the Current Workbook

Follow these steps to add a macro button to the Quick Access toolbar that only appears when the current workbook is open:

1. Right-click a button on the toolbar and select Customize Quick Access Toolbar.

2. Select the current workbook from the drop-down on the right side of the dialog, as shown in Figure 1.9.

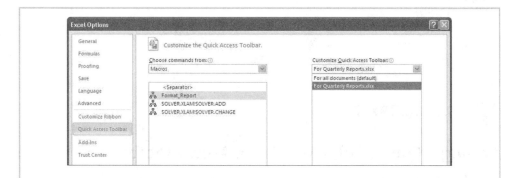

Figure 1.9   *Select the workbook you want the custom button for.*

3. Select Macros from the drop-down on the left side of the dialog.

4. Select the macro you want to assign to the toolbar and click Add.

5. With the macro selected in the list on the right side of the dialog, click Modify.

6. Select a Symbol for the button and change the Display Name that will appear when the cursor hovers over the button. Click OK.

7. Your custom macro button will appear in the toolbar, as shown in Figure 1.10.

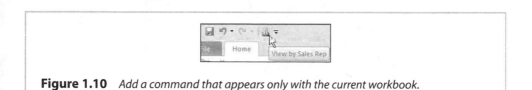

Figure 1.10 *Add a command that appears only with the current workbook.*

Removing Commands from the Quick Access Toolbar

You can remove a command from the Quick Access toolbar in three ways:

- Click the drop-down arrow on the right end of the toolbar and deselect the command from the list of predefined commands.

- Right-click any button on the toolbar or Ribbon and select Customize Quick Access Toolbar to bring up the Customize the Quick Access Toolbar dialog. Select the command from the list on the right side of the dialog and click Remove.

- Right-click the command button itself in the Quick Access toolbar and select Remove from Quick Access Toolbar.

Dialog Launchers

In legacy Excel, when you selected a menu option, such as File, Format Cells, a dialog would appear for you to interact with. With the Ribbon, many, but not all, of the options from the dialog appear on a Ribbon. It can be frustrating trying to find one of those missing commands. You can find the other commands that you knew were with it in legacy Excel, but it's not in that group on the Ribbon.

You could customize the Ribbon to show the command you are looking for, but there may be another way. Some groups on the Ribbon have a little extra image in the lower-right corner, as shown in Figure 1.11. Click that little arrow, and the dialog you were used to from legacy Excel will appear.

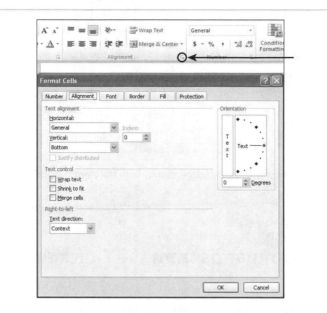

Figure 1.11   *Interact with the dialogs you used in legacy Excel to avoid some of the frustration of hunting down hard-to-find or missing commands.*

Zoom

The capability to zoom in and out on a sheet is an often-forgotten functionality in Excel. Instead, large fonts are used when designing a sheet; then the designer later wonders why problems occur, such as the validation text being too small to see. Instead of relying on font size to make text on the sheet larger, zoom in on the sheet.

You can use three ways to change the zoom on a sheet:

- **View, Zoom**—On the View tab, the Zoom group contains three options for zooming on a sheet:

    - **Zoom**—Brings up the Magnification dialog.

    - **100%**—Sets the zoom to 100%.

    - **Zoom to Selection**—Zooms in on the selected range.

- **Wheel Mouse**—While holding down the Ctrl key, use the scroll button on your mouse to zoom in and out.

- **Zoom Slider**—In the lower-right corner of the Excel window is the Zoom Slider, shown in Figure 1.12. You can use the slider or the - and + buttons to change the zoom of the active sheet.

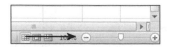

Figure 1.12   *The Zoom Slider is a new way of zooming in and out on a sheet.*

Page Break Preview

With Page Break Preview, you can see where columns and rows will break to print onto other pages. Dashed lines signify automatic breaks that Excel places based on settings, such as margins. Solid lines are manually set breaks.

 LET ME TRY IT

Changing a Page's Column Break

Follow these steps to change the location of a column break:

1. Select Page Break Preview from the View tab.

2. Place your cursor over the blue column line you want to move until it becomes a double arrow, as shown in Figure 1.13.

Figure 1.13   *Place your cursor over the dashed blue line so it becomes a double arrow.*

3. Hold down the left mouse button and move the blue line to where you want the column break to be.

4. Release the mouse button. The dashed blue line becomes a solid blue line, as shown in Figure 1.14.

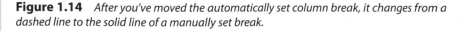

13	Taylor Sw	3:37
6	Finger Ele	3:28
26	Paramore	3:31
37	Billy Ray C	4:04
25	Good Cha	4:04
12	Wyclef Je	4:02
16	Taylor Sw	3:24
56	Seether	3:16
70	Last Good	3:10

Figure 1.14   *After you've moved the automatically set column break, it changes from a dashed line to the solid line of a manually set break.*

Page Layout

The Page Layout viewing mode is like an editable Print Preview—you can see what your page will look like when it prints out, but you can still enter data and make other changes. Columns and rows will move between pages as you adjust their widths or the margins of the page. You can also enter information directly into the header and footer of a page.

 **LET ME TRY IT**

Inserting the Filename and Date into the Header

Follow these steps to enter the filename in the left header and date in the right header while in Page Layout view mode:

1. Go to View, Page Layout.

2. Move your mouse to the top of the page where it says Click to Add Header. As you move your mouse left and right, the different parts of the header will be highlighted, as shown in Figure 1.15

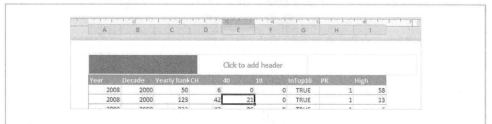

Figure 1.15   *You can edit the header directly while in Page Layout mode.*

3. Click the left header field.

4. Go to Header & Footer Tools, Design and select File Name. The code for File Name, &[File], will be placed in the header field.

5. Click the right header field.

6. Go to Header & Footer Tools, Design, and select Current Date. The code for Current Date, &[Date], will be placed in the header field.

7. Click anywhere on your sheet to leave the header. The codes will update to show the actual filename and date (see Figure 1.16)

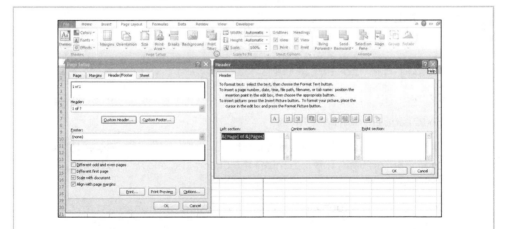

Figure 1.16   *Insert the file name and date in the header.*

Page Numbering

Page numbering is set up in the header or footer of a sheet. To access the Page Setup dialog, go to File, Print and click the Page Setup link at the bottom of the Settings or go to the Page Layout tab and click the dialog launcher in the lower right corner of the Page Setup group, circled in Figure 1.17. From the Page Setup dialog, select the Header/Footer tab. When you customize the header or footer, the options for inserting page numbering will be available.

Figure 1.17   *Use the dialog launcher (circled) to open the Page Setup dialog and access the Header/Footer dialog to insert page numbering.*

 **LET ME TRY IT**

Inserting *Page* of *Pages* Page Numbering

To insert page numbering based on the total number of pages, follow these steps:

1. Go to Page Layout, Page Setup and click the dialog launcher in the lower-right corner of the group.

2. Select the Header/Footer tab from the Page Setup dialog.

3. Click Custom Header or Custom Footer.

4. From the Header or Footer dialog that appears, place your cursor in the section you want the page numbering to appear.

5. Click Insert Page Number, which is the second button.

6. Type "of" (space *of* space).

7. Click Insert Number of Pages, which is the third button.

8. Click OK twice

Repeating Rows or Columns When Printing

When you have a report that spans several pages, you probably want to repeat your row or column headers on all the pages.

 LET ME TRY IT

Repeating a Header Row

Follow these steps to have your header row repeat at the top of each printed page:

1. Go to Page Layout, Print Titles.

2. Click the Collapse Dialog button on the far right side of the Rows to Repeat at Top field. This minimizes the dialog and allows you to interact with the sheet.

3. Select the row(s) you want to repeat by clicking the numbered row header(s).

4. Click the button on the far right side of the Rows to Repeat at Top field to return to the dialog.

5. Click OK. The selected row(s) will now repeat at the top of each printed page.

Freezing Panes

If you've set up your data in a Table, Excel places the headers into the column headings when you scroll down the sheet, as shown in Figure 1.18. But normally, when you scroll through a sheet, your row and column headers disappear. This can be inconvenient when you have a lot of data and need the identifying headers. With the Freeze Panes options, you can force the top rows, leftmost columns, or both to remain visible as you scroll around the sheet.

	A8		▾	fx	2008				
	Year	Decade	Yearly Rank		CH	40	10	InTop10
4	2008	2000			233	42	26	9	TRUE
5	2008	2000			258	30	11	0	TRUE
6	2008	2000			284	13	4	0	TRUE
7	2008	2000			310	21	12	0	TRUE
8	2008	2000			319	28	17	0	TRUE
9	2008	2000			332	26	22	0	TRUE

Figure 1.18   *Table column headers become part of the column headings so that they are always visible when you scroll down the sheet.*

Three options are available under Freeze Panes:

- **Freeze Panes**—Rows and/or columns are frozen depending on the cell you have selected at the time. This option changes to Unfreeze Panes if any rows or columns are already frozen.

- **Freeze Top Row**—Freezes the first *visible* row of the sheet.

- **Freeze First Column**—Freezes the first *visible* column of the sheet.

When using Freeze Top Row or Freeze First Column, the selection of one will automatically undo the selection of the other. So, if you want to freeze the top row and first column, you must use Freeze Panes.

 SHOW ME   Media 1.2—Freezing Columns
You can watch a free video of this task when you log on to my.safaribooksonline. com/9780132182287/media.

LET ME TRY IT

Freezing Columns and Rows at the Same Time

To freeze columns and rows at the same time, follow these steps:

1. Select the leftmost and topmost cell that you do NOT want frozen.

2. On the View tab, select Freeze Panes, Freeze Panes.

Working with Custom Views

Custom Views allow you to save the way you have a workbook set up. The hidden rows and columns, filter settings, and print settings are all saved, making it easy to switch between Data Entry mode, which shows all your data, and a Presentation mode, which hides your calculation columns and rows.

Custom views will not work if there's a Table in the workbook.

 LET ME TRY IT

Creating a Custom View of Filtered Data

Follow these steps to create a custom view with a preset filter:

1. Select a cell in your data.
2. Go to Data, Filter.
3. Set up the filters the way you want them.
4. Go to View, Custom Views, and click Add.
5. Enter the name of the view in the Name field.
6. Deselect Print Settings if you do not want the print setup saved with the view.
7. The next time you want to view your data in this configuration, go to View, Custom Views, select the view from the list, and click Show.

You may want to add an All Data view to quickly return to a clean sheet.

Arranging Windows

Excel offers two methods for viewing data side by side In the Window group on the View tab, Arrange All opens the Arrange Windows dialog, allowing you to arrange all the current windows in a Tiled, Horizontal, Vertical, or Cascade View. In Excel 2007, View Side by Side was introduced to users. It provides a quick way of viewing two windows horizontally. You can then select Synchronous Scrolling to lock the scrollbars together and move the data on both sheets at the same time.

Inserting Rows & Columns

To insert a new row or column within an existing dataset, select the row or column where you want the insert to go and go to Home, Cells. From the Insert drop-down select to Insert Sheet Rows or Insert Sheet Columns. For a shortcut, you can right-click on the row or column header and select Insert, as shown in Figure 1.19.

Figure 1.19   *To insert a new row 10, right-click on the row header (the 10) and select Insert from the menu. The current row 10 and all the data after it will shift down.*

If you don't have the entire row or column selected, Excel will display the Insert dialog, prompting you to specify whether you want to shift the selected cells right or down, or if you want to insert an entire row or column.

LET ME TRY IT

Inserting a Row

To insert a new row within an existing dataset, follow these steps. To insert the row through the Ribbon options, start at step 3, else continue to step 1 to insert a row using the right-click option.

1. Right-click over the row number's header where you want to insert a blank row. In Figure 1.19, a blank row will be inserted in row 10, so the cursor is placed over the header 10.

2. Select Insert. The new row is inserted and the existing data moved down.

3. To insert a row through the Ribbon options, select a cell in the row where you want a new blank row to be inserted.

4. Go to Home, Cells, Insert and select Insert Sheet Rows. The new row is inserted and the existing data moved down.

Renaming a Sheet

To rename the active sheet, go to Home, Cells, Format and select Rename Sheet from the drop-down. Excel will select the current sheet name in the sheet's tab and you can then type in the new name. You can also rename a sheet by right-clicking on a sheet's tab and selecting Rename.

Moving or Copying Sheets

You can reorganize sheets within the current workbook or move them to a new workbook using the Move or Copy Sheet option found under Home, Cells, Format. The dialog can also be accessed by right-clicking on a sheet tab, as shown in Figure 1.20.

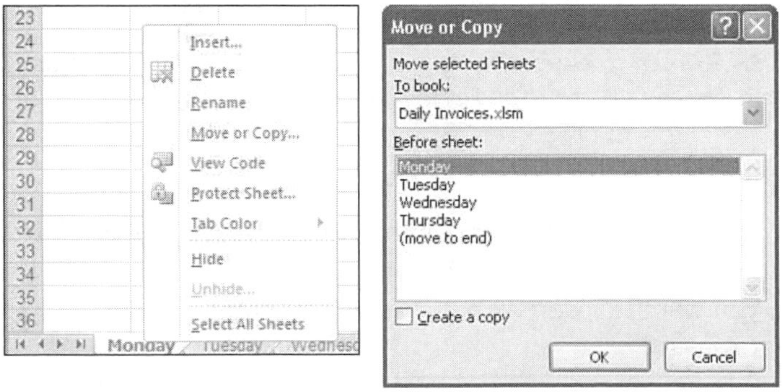

Figure 1.20 *Use the Move or Copy dialog, quickly accessed by right-clicking on a sheet tab, to move or copy sheets within a workbook or to a new workbook.*

Within the Workbook

To move or copy the active sheet to a new location within the same workbook using the Move or Copy dialog, make sure the To Book field is the current workbook. If you're making a copy of the sheet, check the Create a Copy box. Then, in the Before Sheet dialog, select the sheet you want the active sheet to be placed in front of (to the left of). You can also reorganize the sheets in a workbook by clicking and dragging the sheet's tab to a new location. If you want to copy the sheet, hold down the Ctrl key as you move the sheet tab.

Between Workbooks

To move or copy a sheet to another workbook, the second workbook must already be open. Then, using the Move or Copy dialog, select the workbook to move or copy the sheet to from the To Book field. If you're making a copy of the sheet, check the Create a Copy box. In the Before Sheet dialog, select the sheet you want the active sheet to be placed in front of (to the left of).

When you move or copy a sheet from one workbook to another, any formulas on that sheet linked to the original workbook will remain linked.

 LET ME TRY IT

Copying a Sheet to a New Workbook

To copy a sheet to a new workbook, follow these steps:

1. Open both workbooks.

2. Go to the sheet you want to copy.

3. Go to Home, Cells, Format, Move or Copy. The Move or Copy dialog appears.

4. In the To Book field, select the workbook to copy the sheet to.

5. Check the Create a Copy button.

6. Select the sheet you want to copy the sheet in front of (to the left of).

7. Click OK.

Change Multiple Worksheets at One Time

You can change the exact same range on multiple sheets at a time by grouping the sheets and making the change to one of the sheets. For example, you can enter the word "Sales" in A1 of all the selected sheets. Or you can apply a bold format to cell C2 in a group of sheets.

To group sheets together, select one sheet that will be in the group, then, while holding down the Ctrl key, select the other sheets. To ungroup the sheets, either select a sheet not in the group, or right-click on any sheet tab in the group and select Ungroup Sheets.

 **LET ME TRY IT**

Changing Multiple Sheets

To make a change to multiple sheets by just changing one sheet, follow these steps:

1. Go to one of the sheets you need to change.

2. While holding down the Ctrl key, select the sheet tabs of the other sheets you want to make the same change to. This will group the sheets together.

3. Make the changes to the active sheet.

4. To ungroup the sheets, select a sheet not in the group, or right-click on a sheet tab and select Ungroup Sheets.

Setting Workbook and Sheet Protection

Depending on what part of a workbook you want to protect from changes, you should protect the workbook or the worksheet.

Setting Workbook Protection

Protecting a workbook prevents users from adding, deleting or moving sheets. It can also prevent the user from resizing the workbook, though you can still resize the Excel window. To protect a workbook, go to Review, Protect Workbook. There are two options available:

*   **Structure**—Prevents users from adding, deleting, hiding, unhiding, moving, renaming, inserting or copying sheets.

*   **Windows**—Prevents the user from moving or resizing windows of the workbook.

If you want, you can also enter a password. You will have to enter it twice.

Setting Sheet Protection

Protecting a sheet prevents users from changing the content of locked cells. By default, all cells have the locked option selected and you purposefully unlock them. Sheet protection must be applied to each sheet individually.

To protect a sheet, go to Home, Format, Protect Sheet. The Protect Sheet dialog will appear from which you can select what actions a user can do to the sheet. You can also enter a password. You will have to enter it twice.

Unlocking Cells

While a sheet is still unprotected, you can unlock specific cells so that when the sheet is protected, users can still enter information in the cells you want. To change the protection of selected cells, go to Home, Cells, Format, Format Cells. In the Format Cells dialog, go to the Protection tab and unselect the Locked option.

Recent Documents

Under File, Recent, you can see the last several workbooks that were opened. The number of workbooks listed is an option set under File, Options, Advanced, Display, Show This Number of Recent Documents.

To the right of each listed workbook is a stickpin. The pin is gray when not in use, but select a pin and it will change color, direction, and be moved to the top section of the list, as shown in Figure 1.21. A workbook with a colored pin is *stuck*—that is, the workbook will not be removed from the list of recent documents until you unstick it by clicking the pin again.

Figure 1.21 *You can stick the workbooks you use often and place them at the top for easy opening.*

Saving as PDF

Even with the ease of sharing workbooks using Excel Web Apps, PDFs are still a great option because they don't require a connection to the Internet, and users don't have access to your workbook.

You can create a PDF from within Excel simply by saving your workbook. PDF is now a file type in the Save as Type drop-down of the Save As dialog. After you select the Save as Type, you can choose from a variety of options, as shown in Figure 1.22.

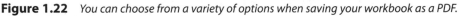

Figure 1.22   *You can choose from a variety of options when saving your workbook as a PDF.*

Opening Templates

Templates are a great way for keeping data in a uniform design. You could simply design your workbook and re-use it as needed, but if you accidentally save data before you have renamed the file your blank workbook is no longer clean. When using a template, there's no risk of saving data in the template because you are working with a copy of the original file, not the file itself.

There are two possible meanings to the words "opening a template." Depending on what you want to do with the template, the methods for opening the file differ:

- Open a template copy for creating a new workbook.

  - Double-click the file from its saved location.

  - Right-click the file and select New.

  - Go to File, New, and select the template from the list of templates. If the template isn't listed, select New from Existing and browse to the template.

- Open the template original to make changes.

  - Right-click the file and select Open.

  - Go to File, Open.

Troubleshooting Excel Options

Nothing is more frustrating than opening Excel and finding out something strange has happened to the way Excel works. Table 1.1 reviews possible scenarios and the settings under File, Options that could be the source of the problem.

Table 1.1   Possible Situations and Solutions

Situation	Check This Setting
The minitoolbar is missing or you need to hide the minitoolbar.	General, User Interface Options, Show Mini Toolbar on Selection
Column headings A, B, C have been replaced with 1, 2, 3.	Formulas, Working with Formulas, R1C1 Reference Style
You are unable to drag cell contents; the Fill handle is gone.	Advanced, Editing Options, Enable Fill Handle, and Cell Drag-and-Drop
You are unable to edit directly in a cell; you can edit only in the formula bar.	Advanced, Editing Options, Allow Editing Directly in Cells
AutoComplete no longer appears when you enter data in a cell.	Advanced, Editing Options, Enable AutoComplete for Cell Values; also ensure there are no blank rows separating your new entry and previous entries
Instead of moving the sheet up/down when you scroll the mouse, the sheet zooms in/out. You want the sheet to zoom in/out when you use the wheel on the mouse.	Advanced, Editing Options, Zoom on roll with the IntelliMouse
Multiple workbooks are open, but only one Excel item shows in the task bar.	Advanced, Display, Show All Windows in the Taskbar
The formula bar has disappeared, or you want to hide the formula bar.	Advanced, Display, Show Formula Bar or View tab, Formula Bar
Instead of the calculated values, the formulas are showing in the cells.	Advanced, Display Options for This Worksheet, Show Formulas in Cells Instead of Their Calculated Results or press Ctrl+~
When you double-click to open a workbook, Excel opens, but remains blank.	Advanced, General, Ignore Other Applications That Use Dynamic Data Exchange (DDE)

Introducing the Excel Web App

This chapter will help you get started working on and sharing your Excel files online. For a more in-depth coverage of Microsoft Office Web Apps and using SkyDrive, refer to *Using the Microsoft Office Web Apps* (ISBN 0-7897-4486-4) by Paul McFedries.

Requirements

You don't need much to get started with the Excel Web App:

- A current browser (minimum: Internet Explorer 7, Mozilla Firefox 3, or Safari 3)
- A Windows Live ID
- An Internet connection

With these three items, you can view your Excel workbooks anywhere in the world where you can access Windows Live.

Acquiring a Windows Live ID

With a Windows Live ID, you can access the Windows Live SkyDrive online storage where you can store, view, edit, and share your Excel workbooks.

You don't need a Windows Live ID if you are accessing someone else's SkyDrive and it's set up to not require a login. But if you want to upload your own files or access a SkyDrive requiring login, you will need a Windows Live ID.

SHOW ME   Media 2.1—Creating a Windows Live ID
You can watch a free video of this task when you log on to my.safaribooksonline. com/9780132182287/media.

LET ME TRY IT

Creating a Windows Live ID

A Windows Live ID enables you to log in to a variety of websites, such as Windows Live, Hotmail, and Xbox Live, using one account. If you already log into a Microsoft-owned site, it is possible you already have a Windows Live ID. You can create the account using an existing email address or obtain a new email address through the live.com or hotmail.com domains, as shown in Figure 2.1. Follow these steps to create a Windows Live ID:

1. User your browser to navigate to https://signup.live.com. If you don't see a webpage similar to the one in Figure 2.1, it's possible you already have a Windows Live ID. In that case, you may see a page similar to Figure 2.2 with your login name in the upper-right corner. If that's the case, you don't need to create a Windows Live ID because you already have one.

Create your Windows Live ID

It gets you into all Windows Live services—and other places you see
All information is required.

⊕ Already using **Hotmail**, **Messenger**, or **Xbox LIVE**? Sign in now

Windows Live ID: [   ] @ [hotmail.com ▾]
[Check availability]
Or use your own e-mail address

Create a password: [   ]
6-character minimum; case sensitive

Retype password: [   ]

Alternate e-mail address: [   ]
Or choose a security question for password reset

First name: [   ]

Last name: [   ]

Country/region: [United States ▾]

State: [Select one ▾]

ZIP code: [   ]

Gender: ○ Male ○ Female

Birth year: [Example: 1990]

Characters: [   ]
Enter the 8 characters you see

Figure 2.1   *Go to https://signup.live.com to create your Window Live ID account.*

2. If you have an existing email address you want to use, type it into the Use Your E-Mail Address field, press the Tab key, and skip to step 6. Otherwise, click the Or Get a Windows Live E-Mail Address link to create a new email address and continue to step 3.

3. In the Windows Live ID domain list drop-down, select the domain you want to have the address for (live.com or hotmail.com).

4. In the Windows Live ID text field, type the username you want.

5. Click Check Availability to see if your username and domain combination is available.

6. If Windows Live informs you that the ID isn't available, repeat steps 3–5; otherwise, if the ID is available, continue to step 7.

7. Type your password into the Create a Password field.

8. Type the same password again into the Retype Password field.

9. If you aren't using an existing email address to create the Live ID account, tell Windows Live what you want to do in case you forget your password:

    • Use the Alternate E-Mail Address if you want Windows Live ID to email you password reset information. The email address must be different from your Windows Live ID.
    • Select the Or Choose a Security Question for Password Reset link if you want to verify your identity online. Select a predefined question from the Question list and enter the correct response in the Secret Answer field. The response must be at least five characters.

10. Fill in the rest of the requested information: name, location, gender and birth year.

11. In the Characters field, type the characters you see in the image.

12. Click I Accept. Windows Live will create your new ID.

Uploading and Downloading Workbooks

You no longer have to remember to move those important files to a USB flash drive and have that flash drive with you. From almost anywhere in the world, you can handle your boss's desperate call to fix the department budget numbers for his 11 A.M. presentation to corporate. All you need is a computer with access to the

Internet. After you've logged into your Windows Live account, you can upload your own workbooks or create new ones for viewing, editing, and sharing.

Only unprotected workbooks can be opened online.

Accessing the SkyDrive

You can sign into your Windows Live account from any site that supports the accounts, such as MSN.com or Bing.com, but to quickly get to your SkyDrive, go to skydrive.live.com. After you're signed in, you're brought to your SkyDrive.

If you don't see your SkyDrive, select More, SkyDrive from the Windows Live page as shown in Figure 2.2.

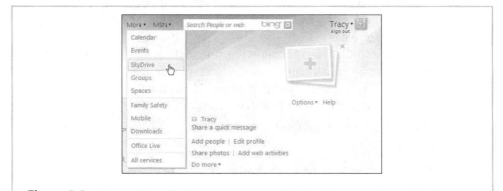

Figure 2.2   *Choose More, SkyDrive to access your SkyDrive from anywhere in Windows Live.*

Uploading with Windows Live

You can upload a workbook viewable by just you, selected individuals, your network, or everyone. The folder where you place the workbook determines this viewing level. After it is uploaded, you can view, edit, and share the workbook.

LET ME TRY IT

Uploading a Workbook

Follow these steps to upload your workbook:

1. Select the folder to which you want to add your workbook. Note that the Favorites and Shared Favorites folders aren't used for file sharing, but for website shortcuts.

2. Select Add Files, shown in Figure 2.3

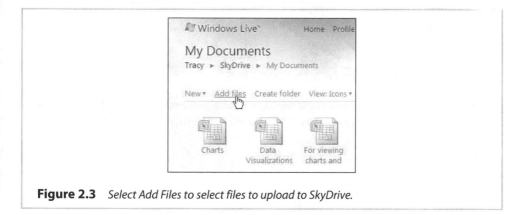

Figure 2.3   *Select Add Files to select files to upload to SkyDrive.*

3. Browse to the location of the file you want to upload and select it.

4. Click Open.

5. Click Upload to upload the file to your SkyDrive.

Saving to SkyDrive from Excel

Save a file from Excel directly to your SkyDrive by choosing File, Save & Send, Save to Web. Excel attempts to log you in automatically, but if it can't, click the Sign In button, shown in Figure 2.4, to bring up the .NET Passport Wizard, which will take you through the steps to associate your Windows Live ID to your Windows User Account. After following the wizard the first time, you will always be linked to your SkyDrive.

TELL ME MORE   **Media 2.2—SkyDrive**

You can listen to a free audio recording about the usefulness of SkyDrive, even if the computer you are at does not have Excel installed. When you log on to my.safaribooksonline.com/9780132182287/media.

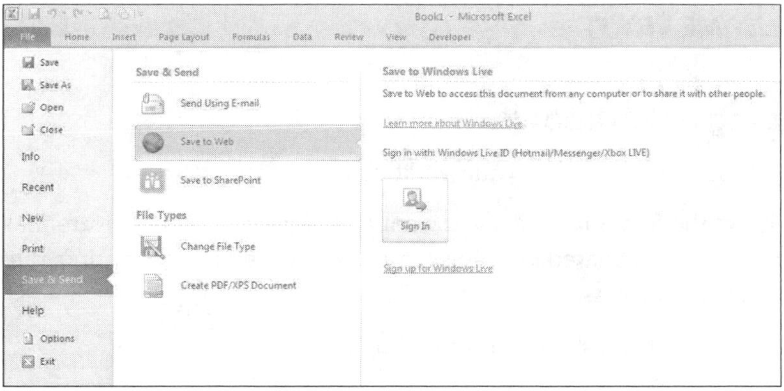

Figure 2.4 *Upload the active workbook to SkyDrive directly from Excel.*

Creating a New Workbook

You aren't limited to workbooks created previously in Excel on your desktop. You can create a new workbook online and download it when you return to the office.

LET ME TRY IT

Creating a New Workbook

To create a new workbook on your SkyDrive, follow these steps:

1. Click the folder you want the workbook in.
2. Click New, Microsoft Excel Workbook (see Figure 2.5).

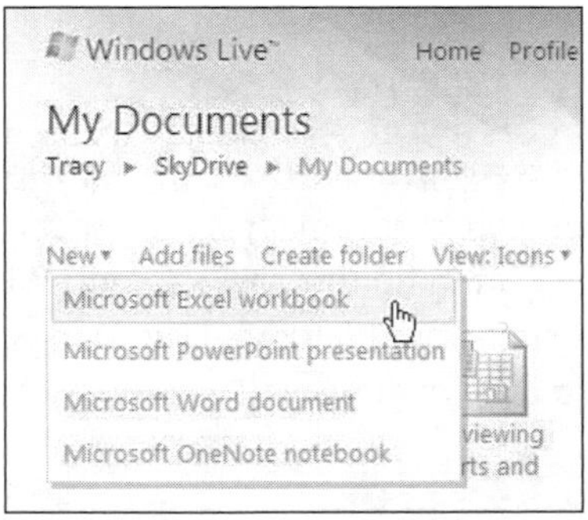

Figure 2.5 *Create a new workbook directly online.*

3. Enter the name of the workbook and click Create. Windows Live automatically appends the file extension (xlsx) for you.

Opening a Workbook

When you select a folder, you'll see all the workbooks in the folder. Select a workbook to see the available options.

When you select to View a workbook, it's opened as a read-only file. Unlike read-only mode on the desktop version of Excel, where you can make changes and not save them to the original file, you cannot make changes while in View mode. You can only look at the workbook, as shown in Figure 2.6.

Figure 2.6   *The View option opens a workbook in Read-only mode with a limited ribbon.*

Select Edit to access the full Excel Web App functionality and make changes to a workbook, as shown in Figure 2.7. Changes are automatically saved as they are made.

Figure 2.7   *Open a workbook using the Edit option to access all editing features.*

Saving a File to Your Local Drive

Eventually, you will want to work on a workbook saved locally. This can be done in several ways:

- Before you open the workbook, select Download from the menu.

- While viewing or editing the workbook, select the File tab to reveal the following options (see Figure 2.8):
  - **Open in Excel**—Open the workbook locally in Excel.
  - **Download a Snapshot**—Download a copy of the workbook containing only its values, formatting, and charts.
  - **Download a Copy**—Download the entire workbook.

The options Save As and Save a Copy create an online copy of the workbook with a new name in the same folder as the original.

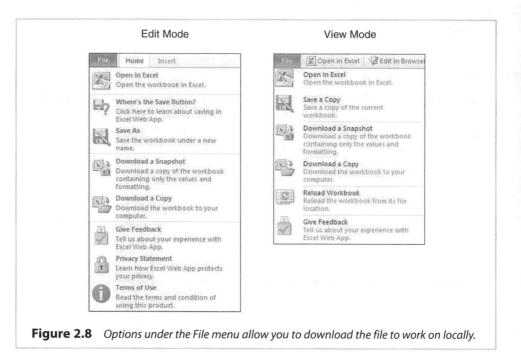

Figure 2.8 *Options under the File menu allow you to download the file to work on locally.*

Sharing a Workbook

SkyDrive doesn't just provide you with the convenience of being able to work with your workbooks wherever you are. It's also set up to help you share your workbooks with other people.

Creating a New Folder

When you create an account, SkyDrive provides two folders for storing your documents: My Documents, a protected folder only you can access, and Public, a folder available to anyone. You cannot change the permissions of these two folders, but you can create new folders and set the permissions you want for them.

 **LET ME TRY IT**

Creating a New Folder

To create a folder from your SkyDrive main page, follow these steps:

1. Select Create Folder.

2. Enter the name of the folder in the Name field

3. Choose who you want to share the folder with: Everyone (Public), My Network, Just Me, Select People (see Figure 2.9).

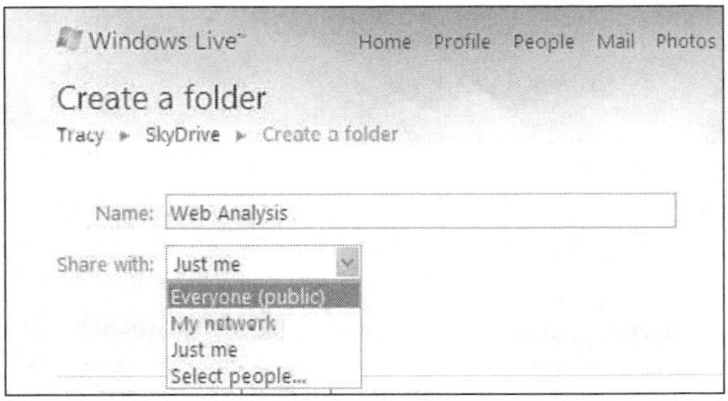

Figure 2.9 *When creating a new folder online, you can choose who you want to be able access it.*

4. Click Next, and you have the option of uploading new files or clicking Cancel to add files at a later time.

Setting Folder Permissions

When you created the preceding folder, Windows Live provided the basic permission settings. For the additional options shown in Figure 2.10, choose More, Edit Permissions while viewing the contents of a folder:

- **Public and Networks**—Select Everyone (Public) and anyone can view the contents of the folder. Select My Network and you can choose between Can View Files if network members can only view your files or Can Add, Edit Details, and Delete Files to give members full permission to modify your folder contents. When you choose My Network, you can also select My Extended Network, allowing networks of your networks (friends of your friends) to View the contents of the folder.

- **Categories**—A listing of the available categories. Select the category and choose Can View Files to allow members to only view files or choose Can Add, Edit Details, and Delete Files to give members full permission to modify your folder contents.

- **Individuals**—Share the folder with select individuals. For each name or email address entered, you can choose to allow the individual to only view files (Can View Files) or give full access to the folder (Can Add, Edit Details, and Delete Files).

Edit permissions for Dept. Budget

Tracy_temp ▸ SkyDrive ▸ Dept. Budget ▸ Edit permissions

You're sharing this folder. Clear these settings

Public and networks

☑ Everyone (public)   Can view files ⌄

☐ My network (2)

Categories

☑ Excel people (3)   Can add, edit details, and delete files ⌄

☐ Favorites (2)

☐ Friends (1)

Individuals

Enter a name or an e-mail address: Select from your contact list

[   ]

[Save] [Cancel]

Figure 2.10   *The Dept. Budget folder is configured to allow anyone to view the files, but people in the Excel People custom category can also edit details.*

Simultaneous Editing

If you're allowing others to edit your workbook, eventually you will be editing the workbook at the same time as another person. When you are the sole person editing the workbook, the text in the lower-right corner of your browser window reads 1 Person Editing. If other people are editing at the same time, the text will update to reflect the number of people.

To see who else is in the workbook with you, click the arrow and a window will open up, showing everyone in the workbook, including you, as shown in Figure 2.11.

People editing this workbook

pandoramod@yahoo.com

tystemp@live.com

2 people editing ⌄

100% ⌄

Figure 2.11   *You can see who else is editing the workbook with you.*

Because changes to workbooks are automatically saved, you can see what the other person is doing almost right away. There is no hierarchy of permissions or way to verify changes, so another user can change your changes as quickly as you can make them.

Interacting with a Sheet Online

Even though the page in your browser looks a lot like the desktop version of Excel, it's not. It's still just a web page, and the navigation methods you're used to from desktop Excel won't work.

The following navigation methods do not work in the Excel Web App:

- There's no right-click context menu.

- There's no fill handle, so you can't drag to fill in a series or copy formulas.

- You can't double-click to autofit rows or columns.

- You can't double-click a cell to edit it. You'll have to make changes directly in the formula bar.

- If you have data/text in one cell bleeding into the one next to it, you can't select the other cell until you make the first column wide enough so it doesn't overlap into the other column.

- You can't click and drag to move cells, rows, or columns.

The following methods still work in the Excel Web App:

- Keyboard shortcuts

- Adjusting the row and column widths manually

- Dragging to select a range

- Clicking row and column headings to select the entire row or column

This chapter shows you tricks for quickly entering data and fixing data that doesn't look right.

Entering Data in Excel

Data entry is one the most important functions in Excel—and one of the most tedious, especially when the data is repetitive. This chapter will show you tricks for copying down data, fixing entered data, and helping your users enter data correctly by providing a predefined list of entries.

Dragging the Fill Handle to Extend a Series

The fill handle, shown in Figure 3.1, can speed up data entry by completing a series for you. Excel comes with several preconfigured series, such as months, days of week, and quarters. You can also add your own series, as described in the "Creating Your Own Series" section later in this chapter.

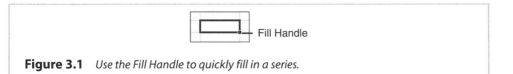

Figure 3.1   *Use the Fill Handle to quickly fill in a series.*

SHOW ME   Media 3.1—Using the Fill Handle to Fill in a Series
You can watch a free video of this task when you log on to my.safaribooksonline.com/9780132182287/media.

Extending a Series Containing Text

To extend a series containing text, enter the text you want the series to start with and drag the fill handle. You don't need to start at the beginning of the series. You can start anywhere in the series and Excel will continue it, starting over if you drag the handle long enough. For example, if you begin a series in A1 with Sunday and drag the fill handle to A8, Sunday will appear again, repeating the series.

If the text series contains a numerical value, Excel will also extend the numerical portion.

Extending a Numerical Series

If you try to fill numerical series based off of a single cell entry, Excel will copy the value instead of filling the series. There are four ways to get around this:

- Enter at least the first two values of the series before dragging the fill handle.

- Hold down the Ctrl key while dragging the fill handle.

- If there is a blank column to the left or right of the numerical column, include that column in your selection when dragging the fill handle down. For example, if you enter 1 in A1 then select A1:B1 (B1 is blank), when you drag the fill handle down, the series in column A will be filled down.

- Hold the right mouse button down while dragging the fill handle and select Fill Series from the context menu that appears when you release the mouse button.

If you hold the Ctrl key while trying to extend a text series, Excel will copy the values instead of filling in the series.

Creating Your Own Series

You can teach Excel the lists that are important to you so that you can take advantage of the series capabilities in Excel. You can take almost any list of items on a sheet and create a custom list for use in filling or sorting.

LET ME TRY IT

Creating a Custom List

Follow these steps to create a custom list:

1. Create your list on the sheet and select the range.

2. Go to File, Options, Advanced, General, Edit Custom Lists.

3. The range you selected is already in the Import List from Cells field, so click Import.

4. The list will be added to both the Custom Lists and List Entries list boxes, as shown in Figure 3.2. The next time you type an item from your list and drag the fill handle, Excel will fill in the rest of the series for you.

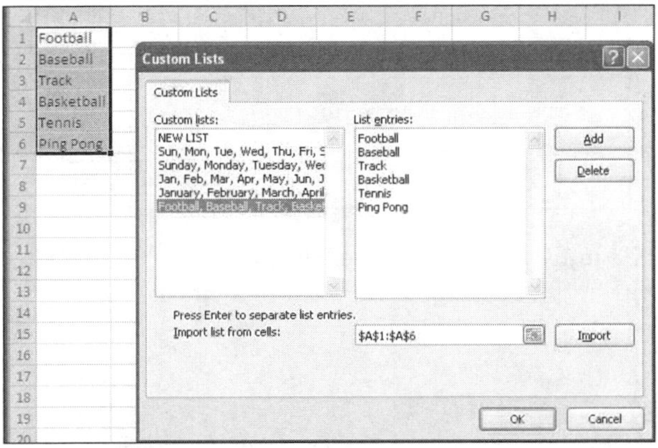

Figure 3.2   *Create a custom list for use in filling in series.*

Unlike the built-in text series, if you include a number with your custom list and extend the series, Excel will copy the text entered and extend only the numerical value.

Joining Text

You can create a formula to join text values from separate columns into another column using the ampersand (&) to link the values together. You can also include additional characters, such as a space, to separate the two values.

LET ME TRY IT

Joining a First Name and Last Name

Follow these steps to join a first name from one column and a last name from another column as the full name in the third column:

1. Type an equal sign in the cell where you want the full name to appear.

2. Select a cell from the first name column.

3. Type & "" &. Note that there is a space between the double quotes.

4. Select a cell from the last name column. Make sure the selection is in the same row as the cell selected in step 2.

5. Press Enter. You should have a formula similar to what's shown in the formula bar in Figure 3.3.

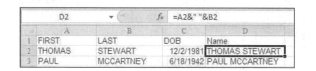

Figure 3.3   *Use & to join text from multiple columns.*

Joining Dates and Text

In Excel, dates are stored as serial numbers. So when you type in a date, such as 4/4/2010, you may see the date like this, but in reality, Excel is storing 40272. If you were trying to join text from a cell containing a date, instead of "Today is 4/4/2010," you would get "Today is 40272."

To get the actual date to appear, wrap the TEXT function around the date. For the example of 4/4/2010, the function would be TEXT(TODAY(), "mm/dd/yyyy"), as shown in Figure 3.4. The TEXT function converts a value to text in the specified number format. It has two arguments. The first argument is the cell containing the numerical value; the second argument is the number format you want applied to the number.

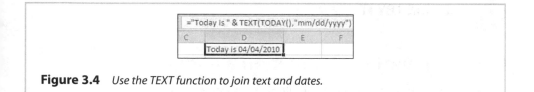

Figure 3.4   *Use the TEXT function to join text and dates.*

Fixing Numbers as Text

When numbers in a sheet are being stored as text, Excel lets you know by placing a green triangle in the cell (if Background Error Checking is enabled). When you select the cell and click the warning sign that appears, Excel informs you that the number is being stored as text, as shown in Figure 3.5. It then gives you options for handling the number, such as Convert to Number or Ignore Error.

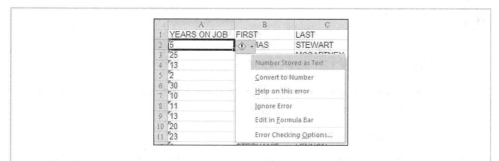

Figure 3.5   *With Background Error Checking enabled, Excel will inform you if a number is being stored as text.*

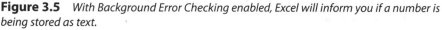

Background Error Checking is found under File, Options, Formulas.

If you have a worksheet with thousands of cells, it will take a long time to convert them all to numbers. Two options for doing a larger-scale conversion are covered in the next sections. If you are using normal Excel, you have a third option available, which is discussed in the "Using Text to Columns to Convert Text to Numbers" section.

 **LET ME TRY IT**

Using Convert to Number on a Range

Here's one option for converting multiple cells into numbers:

1. Select the range consisting of all the cells you need to convert (making sure that the first cell in the range needs to be converted). The range can include text and other numerical values, as long as it doesn't include cells you do not want to be converted to numbers.

2. Click the warning symbol in the first cell.

3. From the drop-down, select Convert to Number, and all cells in the selected range will be modified.

 LET ME TRY IT

Using Paste Special to Force a Number

If you have the Background Error Checking disabled and don't see the green warning triangle, try this method for converting cells to numbers:

1. Enter a 1 in a blank cell and copy it.

2. Select the cells containing the numbers, right-click and select Paste Special, Paste Special.

3. From the dialog that appears, select Multiply and click OK.

The act of multiplying the values by 1 forces the contents of the cells to become their numerical values.

You can also copy a blank cell and use the Add function.

Convert Text Case

Although Excel doesn't provide the ease Word does in changing the case of selected text, the capability is there in the form of functions:

- **PROPER**—Convert the text to proper case. This doesn't work well with names such as "McCartney"—Excel will return "Mccartney" instead, in which case you can use PROPER and then use a Find & Replace of the text "Mcc" to "McC" with the Match Case option selected.

- **UPPER**—Convert the text to all uppercase.
- **LOWER**—Convert the text to all lowercase.

Each of the functions has a single argument—the cell containing the text to be converted. After It Is converted, you can use Paste Special, Values to replace the original text with the converted text.

Copying Formulas Rapidly

If you need to copy a formula into just a few rows, using the fill handle is fine. But if you have several hundred rows to update, you could zoom right past the last row. And if you have thousands of rows, using the fill handle can take quite some time.

One solution is to copy the formula, select the range, and paste the formula into the range. But it can still be a bit tricky to select the entire range you need to paste to.

If you have at least one column with data entered in every row, you can double-click the fill handle and have it quickly fill the formula down the column.

 LET ME TRY IT

Filling a Formula Down a Column

To quickly copy a formula down a column, follow these steps:

1. If the column to the left of your formula column has any blank spaces, hide that column. The column to the left of the formula column must not contain any blank spaces, or else the formula will be copied down to only the first blank row.

2. Place your cursor on the fill handle until it turns to a black plus sign, as shown in Figure 3.6.

3. Double-click and the formula will be copied down the sheet until it runs into a blank row in the column to the left.

Figure 3.6 *Double-click when the cursor becomes a black plus sign to quickly copy the formula down the column.*

Converting Formulas to Values

Formulas take up a lot of memory, and the recalculation time can make working in a large workbook a hassle. At times, you need a formula only temporarily; you just want to calculate the value once and won't ever need to calculate it again. You could manually type the value over the formula cell, but if the result is a long number, or if you have a lot of calculation cells, this isn't convenient. You're probably used to copying the cell and doing a Paste Special, Values, but there's a faster way.

SHOW ME   Media 3.2—Converting Formulas to Values
*You can watch a free video of this task when you log on to
my.safaribooksonline.com/9780132182287/media.*

LET ME TRY IT

Quickly Replacing Formulas with Values

Follow these steps for a quick way to paste values:

1. Select the range of formulas.

2. Place your cursor on the right edge of the black border so that it turns from the white plus sign to four black arrows.

3. While holding your right mouse button down, drag the range to the next column and back to the original column.

4. Let go of the right mouse button.

5. From the context menu that appears, select Copy Here as Values Only.

Using Text to Columns

Text to Columns can be used to separate data in a single column into multiple columns, for example, if you have full names in one column and need a column with first names and a column with last names. The button to call the wizard is found on the Data tab. In step 1 of the wizard, select whether the text is Delimited or Fixed Width. In step 2, you provide more details on how you want the text separated. In step 3, you tell Excel the basic formatting to apply to each column.

> If you have data in the columns to the right of the column you are separating, Excel will overwrite the data. Be sure to insert enough blank columns before beginning Text to Columns.

 TELL ME MORE   Media 3.3—Pasting and Delimited Text

You can listen to a free audio recording about a potentially useful bug that happens when you paste text after using Text to Columns when you log on to my.safaribooksonline.com/9780132182287/media.

Working with Delimited Text

Delimited text is text that has some character, such as a comma, tab, or space, separating each group of words that you want placed into its own column.

 LET ME TRY IT

Separating Delimited Text into Multiple Columns

To separate delimited text into multiple columns, follow these steps:

1. Highlight the range of text to be separated.

2. Go to Data, Text to Columns. The Convert Text to Columns Wizard opens.

3. Select Delimited from step 1 of the wizard, as shown in Figure 3.7, and click Next.

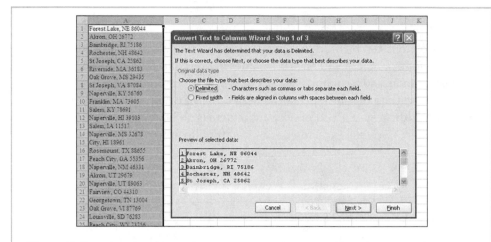

Figure 3.7 *Select the Delimited option to separate text joined by delimiters, such as commas, spaces or tabs.*

4. Select one or more delimiters used by the grouped text, as in Figure 3.8, and click Next.

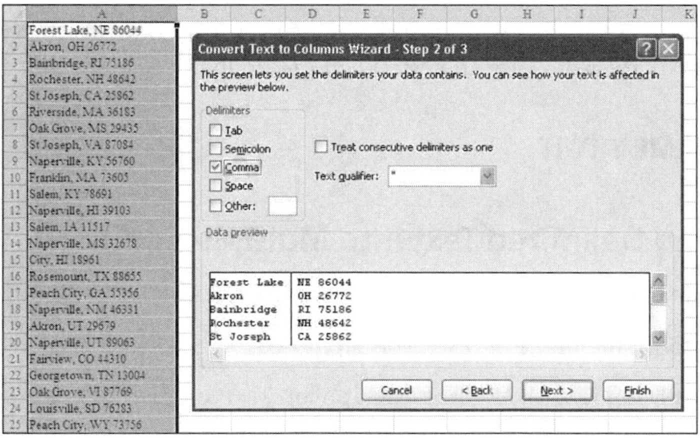

Figure 3.8 *Use a comma delimiter to separate the city from the state and ZIP code.*

> If you need more than one delimiter but one of the delimiters is used normally in the text, such as the space between city names and the space between a state and ZIP Code (Sioux Falls, SD 57057), consider running Text to Columns twice: once to separate the city (Sioux Falls) from the state ZIP (SD 57057) and again to separate the state and ZIP.

5. For each column of data, select the data format. For example, if you have a column of ZIP Codes, you will want to set the format as Text so any leading zeros are not lost. But be warned—setting a column to Text will prevent Excel from properly identifying formulas entered into that column.

6. Click Finish. The text will be separated, as shown in Figure 3.9.

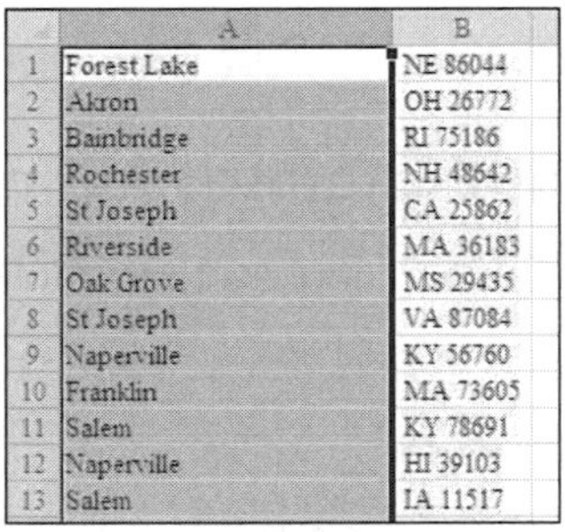

	A	B
1	Forest Lake	NE 86044
2	Akron	OH 26772
3	Bainbridge	RI 75186
4	Rochester	NH 48642
5	St Joseph	CA 25862
6	Riverside	MA 36183
7	Oak Grove	MS 29435
8	St Joseph	VA 87084
9	Naperville	KY 56760
10	Franklin	MA 73605
11	Salem	KY 78691
12	Naperville	HI 39103
13	Salem	IA 11517

Figure 3.9   *Using Text to Columns with a comma delimiter separated the city from the state and ZIP code.*

Working with Fixed Width Text

Fixed width text describes text where each group is a set number of characters. You can draw a line down all the records to separate all the groups, as shown in Figure 3.10. If your text doesn't look like it's fixed width, try changing the font to a fixed width font, such as Courier. It's possible that it's fixed width text in disguise.

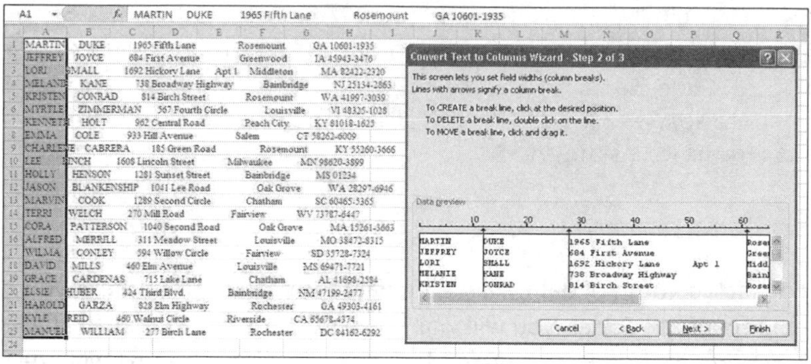

Figure 3.10 *Use the Fixed Width option when each group in the data has a fixed number of characters.*

LET ME TRY IT

Separating Fixed Width Text into Multiple Columns

To separate fixed width text into multiple columns, follow these steps:

1. Highlight the range of cells that include text to be separated.

2. Go to Data, Text to Columns.

3. Select Fixed Width from step 1 of the wizard and click Next.

4. Excel will guess at where the column breaks should go, as shown in Figure 3.10. You can move a break by clicking and dragging it to where you want it, insert a new break by clicking where it should be, or remove a break by double-clicking it. Click Next.

Don't worry about leading spaces—Excel will remove them for you.

5. For each column of data, select the data format. For example, if you have a column of Zip Codes, you will want to set the format as Text so any leading zeros are not lost, as shown in Figure 3.11. But be warned—setting a column to Text will prevent Excel from properly identifying formulas entered into that column.

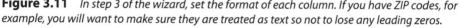

Figure 3.11 *In step 3 of the wizard, set the format of each column. If you have ZIP codes, for example, you will want to make sure they are treated as text so not to lose any leading zeros.*

   6. Click Finish.

Using Text to Columns to Convert Text to Numbers

A previous section, "Fixing Numbers as Text," mentioned that Text to Columns can be used to convert a number stored as text to a real number. This is done in step 3 of the Text to Columns wizard.

 **LET ME TRY IT**

Converting Numbers as Text to Just Numbers

Follow these steps to convert a column of numbers stored as text to just numbers:

   1. Highlight the range of text to be converted.

   2. Go to Data, Text to Columns.

   3. Click Finish. The numbers are no longer considered numbers stored as text.

Controlling the Next Cell Selection

You can use several tricks to control what cell you enter data into next.

Enter Versus Tab

Normally, when you hit the Enter key as you enter data, the active cell moves down the column. If instead you want the selection to move to the right, you must either use the Tab key or the right arrow to move your selection. Then when you get to the end of the row, use Enter to move down to the beginning of the next row. Somehow, Excel will keep track of which column you started your data entry on and return you there, making it easier to start the next row of data.

Moving Cell Pointer Direction

If you don't want to use both Tab and Enter, you can go to File, Options, Advanced, After Pressing Enter Move Selection, and change the Direction from Down to Right. But Excel will no longer move the selection to the next row when you get to the last column—because it doesn't realize you are at the last column.

Preselecting the Data Range

If you have the selection set to move right when you press Enter, you can tell Excel when to go down to the next row by selecting the range into which you are entering data before you begin the data entry. In this way, Excel knows when you've reached the last column and will move down to the next row.

Entering Data in a Circle

If the data you need to fill in isn't in consecutive columns or rows, such as a form, you can configure Excel to jump around to the different cells as you press the Enter key. You do this by setting up the data entry cells in a named range.

 **LET ME TRY IT**

Using a Named Range to Indicate Data Entry Cells

The following steps will show you how to set up a named range to assist in data entry:

1. Ignore the first data entry field, and select the second field.

2. Hold down the Ctrl key and select each data entry field in the order you want to enter the data.

3. After all the other data entry fields have been selected, while still holding down the Ctrl key, select the first field.

4. Type a name for the selected range in the Name Box and press Enter.

5. The next time you need to enter data in the fields, select the named range from the name box and the fields will be highlighted, as shown in Figure 3.12. Begin entering data in the first field and press Tab or Enter to automatically go to the next field, repeating until you are done.

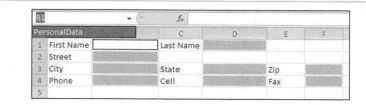

Figure 3.12 *Quickly identify and go to the data entry fields by using a named range.*

Working with Tables

When your data is defined as a Table, additional functionality in Excel is made available. For example, with Excel's intelligent tables

- Autofilter drop-downs are automatically added to the headings.

- You can apply predesigned formats, such as banded rows or borders.

- You can remove duplicates based on the values in one or more columns.

- You can toggle the total row on and off.

- Adding new rows or columns will automatically extend the table.

- You can take advantage of automatically created range names.

Defining a Table

For your data to convert to a table, it must be set up properly. This means that, except for the headings row, each row must be one complete record of the table—for example, a customer or inventory item—as shown in Figure 3.13. Headings are not required, but if they are included, they must be at the top of the data. If your data does not include headers, Excel will insert some for you.

	A	B	C	D	E	F	G
1	Region	Product	Date	Customer	Quantity	Revenue	COGS
2	East	XYZ	1/1/2008	Exclusive Shovel Trader	1000	22810	10220
3	Central	DEF	1/2/2008	Bright Hairpin Company	100	2257	984
4	East	DEF	1/4/2008	Cool Jewelry Corporatic	800	18552	7872
5	East	XYZ	1/4/2008	Tasty Kettle Inc.	400	9152	4088
6	East	ABC	1/7/2008	Remarkable Meter Corp	400	8456	3388
7	East	DEF	1/7/2008	Wonderful Jewelry Inc.	1000	21730	9840
8	Central	ABC	1/9/2008	Remarkable Meter Corp	800	16416	6776
9	Central	XYZ	1/10/2008	Safe Flagpole Supply	900	21438	9198

Figure 3.13 *Set up your data properly to define it as a table to uncover new functionality in Excel.*

After your data is set up properly, you can define the table with one of the following methods. Select a cell in the dataset and

- Go to Insert, Tables, Table.

- Go to Home, Styles, Format as Table, and select a style to apply to the data.

- Press Ctrl+T.

- Press Ctrl+L.

When you use any one of the preceding methods, Excel determines the range of your data by looking for a completely empty row and column. A dialog will appear showing the range Excel has defined. You can accept this range or modify it as needed. If Excel was able to identify headers, the My Table Has Headers box will be selected, so make sure that Excel has correctly identified whether your data has headers and click OK. If there were no headers, make sure the box is unselected and press OK. Your table will be formatted with autofilter drop-downs in the headers, as shown in Figure 3.14.

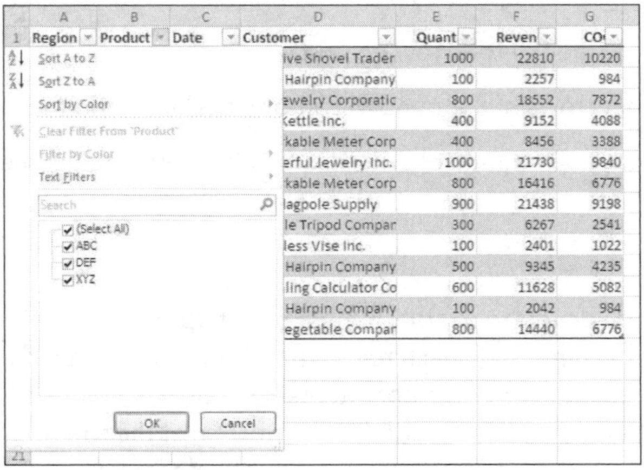

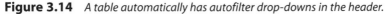

Figure 3.14 *A table automatically has autofilter drop-downs in the header.*

With the Web App, you should select your data range before defining the table because if you need to make a change, you will have to cancel out of the dialog.

 **LET ME TRY IT**

Defining a Table

To define your data as a table, follow these steps:

1. Select a cell in the data.

2. Go to Insert, Table.

3. In the Create Table dialog, verify the range Excel has selected. If it is incorrect, make the required changes.

4. If your data has headers, make sure the My Table Has Headers box is selected; otherwise, make sure it is not selected.

5. Click OK.

Expanding a Table

After your data is defined as a table, the table automatically expands as you add adjacent rows and columns. If you don't want the new entry to be part of the table, you can tell Excel by clicking the lightning bolt icon that appears and then selecting either Undo Table AutoExpansion or Stop Automatically Expanding Tables, as shown in Figure 3.15.

Figure 3.15 *If you don't want a new row to be part of the table, instruct Excel to undo or stop the AutoExpansion.*

When adding new rows to the bottom of a table, make sure the total row is turned off; otherwise, Excel cannot identify the new row as belonging with the existing data. The exception is if you tab from the last data row, Excel will insert a new row and move the total row down.

To manually resize a table, click and drag the angle bracket icon in the lower-right corner of the table. You can also select a cell in the table and go to Table Tools, Design, Properties, Resize Table. Specify the new range in the Resize Table dialog that appears.

Adding a Total Row to a Table

When you select Table Tools, Design, Table Style Options, Total Row, Excel adds a total row to the bottom of the active table. By default, Excel adds the word Total to the first column of the table and sums the data in the rightmost column, as shown in Figure 3.16. If the rightmost column contains text, Excel will return a count instead of a sum.

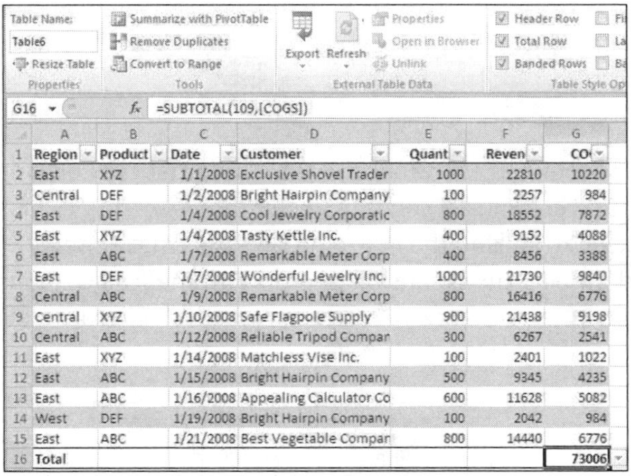

	A	B	C	D	E	F	G
1	Region	Product	Date	Customer	Quant	Reven	CO
2	East	XYZ	1/1/2008	Exclusive Shovel Trader	1000	22810	10220
3	Central	DEF	1/2/2008	Bright Hairpin Company	100	2257	984
4	East	DEF	1/4/2008	Cool Jewelry Corporatic	800	18552	7872
5	East	XYZ	1/4/2008	Tasty Kettle Inc.	400	9152	4088
6	East	ABC	1/7/2008	Remarkable Meter Corp	400	8456	3388
7	East	DEF	1/7/2008	Wonderful Jewelry Inc.	1000	21730	9840
8	Central	ABC	1/9/2008	Remarkable Meter Corp	800	16416	6776
9	Central	XYZ	1/10/2008	Safe Flagpole Supply	900	21438	9198
10	Central	ABC	1/12/2008	Reliable Tripod Compar	300	6267	2541
11	East	XYZ	1/14/2008	Matchless Vise Inc.	100	2401	1022
12	East	ABC	1/15/2008	Bright Hairpin Company	500	9345	4235
13	East	ABC	1/16/2008	Appealing Calculator Co	600	11628	5082
14	West	DEF	1/19/2008	Bright Hairpin Company	100	2042	984
15	East	ABC	1/21/2008	Best Vegetable Compar	800	14440	6776
16	Total						73006

Figure 3.16 *Clicking the Total Row check box adds a default total row to the bottom of the table. Use the drop-downs in each cell in the total to add or change the function.*

Each cell in the total row has a drop-down of functions that can be used to calculate the data above it. For example, instead of the sum, you can calculate the average, max, min, and more. Just make a selection from the drop-down and Excel will insert the formula in the cell.

The functions listed in the drop-down are calculated using variations of the SUBTOTAL function. For more information on this function, see Chapter 9, "Subtotals and Grouping."

 **LET ME TRY IT**

Adding Totals to a Table

To add a total row containing multiple calculations, follow these steps:

1. Select a cell in the table.

2. Go to Table Tools, Design, Table Style Options, and select Total Row. A total row will appear at the bottom of the table, with a formula summing the rightmost column.

3. Select the cell in the total row of the column whose calculation you need to change. A drop-down arrow appears.

4. Click the drop-down arrow and select the desired function.

5. Repeat Step 4 for any other columns that require calculations.

Data Validation

Data validation, found under Data, Data Tools, Data Validation, allows you to limit what a user can type in a cell. For example, you can limit users to whole numbers, dates, a list of selections, or a specific range of values. Custom input and error messages can be configured to guide the user entry.

The available validation criteria are:

- **Any Value**—The default value allowing unrestricted entry.

- **Whole Number**—Requires a whole number be entered. You can select a comparison value (between, not between, equal to, and so on) and set the minimum and maximum value.

- **Decimal**—Requires a decimal value be entered. You can select a comparison value (between, not between, equal to, and so on) and set the minimum and maximum value.

- **List**—Requires user to select from a predefined list, as shown in Figure 3.17. The source can be within the data validation dialog or can be a vertical range on any sheet.

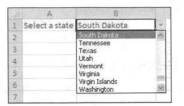

Figure 3.17   *Provide users with a list of entries to choose from.*

- **Date**—Requires a date be entered. You can select a comparison value (between, not between, equal to, and so on) and set the minimum and maximum value.

- **Time**—Requires a time be entered. You can select a comparison value (between, not between, equal to, and so on) and set the minimum and maximum value.

- **Text Length**—Requires a text value be entered. You can select a comparison value (between, not between, equal to, and so on) and set the minimum and maximum number of characters.

- **Custom**—Uses a formula to calculate TRUE for valid entries or FALSE for invalid entries.

 LET ME TRY IT

Limiting User Entry to a Selection from a List

Data validation allows you to create a drop-down in a cell, restricting the user to selecting from a predefined list of values, as shown in Figure 3.17. To set up the source range and configure the data validation cell, follow these steps:

1. Create a vertical list of the values to appear in the drop-down. You can place these values in a sheet different from where the drop-down will actually be placed, then hide the sheet, preventing the user from changing the list.

2. Select the cell you want the drop-down to appear in.

3. Go to Data, Data Tools, Data Validation. The Data Validation dialog will appear.

4. From the Allow field of the Settings tab, select List.

5. Place your cursor in the Source field.

6. Select the list you created in step 1, as shown in Figure 3.18. If your list is short, instead of the separate list you created in step 1, you can enter the values separated by commas directly in the Source field. For example, you could enter Yes, No in the source field (no quotes, no equal sign).

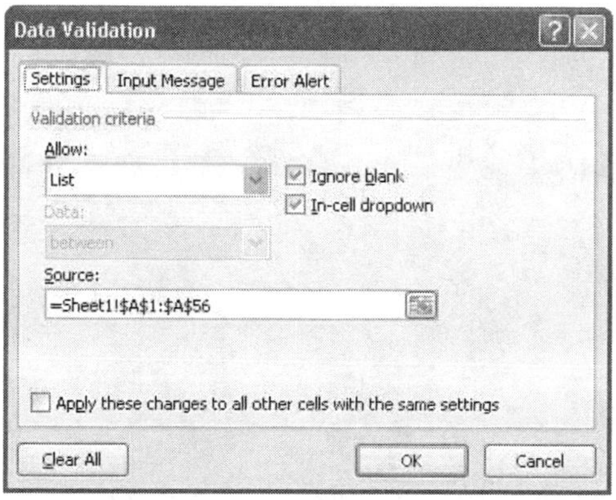

Figure 3.18   *The source for the validation list can be a different sheet. You can then hide the sheet from users.*

7. If you want to provide the user with an input prompt, go to the Input Message tab and fill in the Title and Input Message fields.

8. If you want to provide the user with an error message, go to the Error Alert tab and fill in the Style, Title and Error Message fields.

9. Click OK.

The font and font size of the text in the drop-down is controlled by your Windows settings, not Excel.

Data Formatting

You don't have to format the data in a workbook, but good use of formatting can make a dull presentation pop or even highlight the point you are trying to get across. This chapter reviews formatting from the most basic options, such as bolding text, to the more advanced options, such as data bars.

Cell Formatting

All the formatting options described in this section can be found on the Format Cells dialog in Excel and Excel Starter, which you can open by right-clicking a cell and selecting Format Cells or by pressing Ctrl+1 (the number one). Many formatting options are also available on the minitoolbar in Excel and Excel Starter. Instead of using either of those dialogs, instructions will reference the button or group on the Home tab, if one is available.

Font Group

The Font group on the Home tab consists of several tools you can use to add emphasis to a range.

Font Typeface

The default font in Excel is Calibri, but many others are available. To change the font, select the range, and then select a new font from the drop-down in the Font group, as shown in Figure 4.1. In Excel and Excel Starter, you can preview the selection in the selected range as you move your cursor through the list.

Font Size

To change the font size, select the range, and then select a new size from the drop-down. Excel and Excel Starter have two additional buttons next to the font size drop-down, shown in Figure 4.2. To increase the font size by one point (two after 12 point), click the A with the up arrow (A^); to decrease the font size by one point (two after 12 point), click the slightly smaller A with the down arrow (A˅).

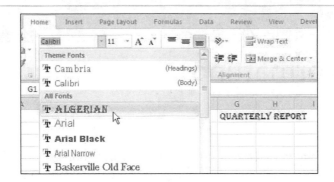

Figure 4.1   *When you select a font from the drop-down, the active cell will update to show you how the font will look with your text.*

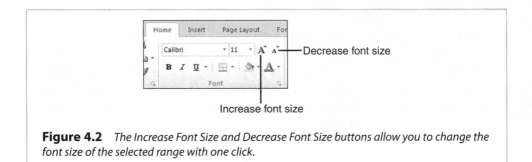

Figure 4.2   *The Increase Font Size and Decrease Font Size buttons allow you to change the font size of the selected range with one click.*

Applying Bold, Italic, and Underline

The three icons for bold, italic, and underline toggle the property on and off. The Bold icon is a bold letter **B**. The italic icon is an italic letter *I*. The Underline icon, which is a drop-down in Excel and Excel Starter, is either an underlined U or a double-underlined D. To apply formatting, select the range and click the desired formatting button. In Excel and Excel Starter, you can select one specific word in a cell and apply the formatting just to it.

Strikethrough, Superscript, Subscript

The strikethrough, superscript, and subscript effects are available only in the Effects group on the Font tab of the Format Cells dialog in Excel and Excel Starter. To apply the formatting, select the cell or specific characters in the cell, right-click over the selection, and select Format Cells to bring up the dialog and select the desired formatting option.

Borders

The borders drop-down includes 13 of the most popular border options (there are seven options on the Web App). These borders are applied to the selected cell or range, either the inside borders or the outside borders, depending on your selection. For more options, go to the Borders tab in the Format Cells dialog.

> The Excel Web App is limited to thin border lines shown in its Borders drop-down.

 LET ME TRY IT

Formatting a Table with a Thick Outer Border and Thin Inner Lines

Follow these steps (Excel and Excel Starter only) to create a table that has a thick outer border and a thin border around each inner cell, as shown in Figure 4.3.

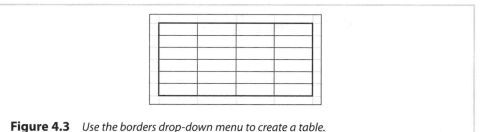

Figure 4.3   *Use the borders drop-down menu to create a table.*

1. Select the range to format.

2. From the border drop-down, select the All Borders option.

3. Return to the border drop-down and select the Thick Box Border option.

Fill

Fill refers to the color applied inside of a cell; it is represented by a paint bucket on its button. When you click the button, a drop-down of available colors opens up. As you move your cursor over the colors, the selected range automatically updates to reflect the color your cursor is currently over. When you've decided on the color you want, click the color and the drop-down will close, and the range is colored as specified.

The Format Cells dialog offers additional fill effects, such as patterns, styles, and gradient fills. Pattern Color and Pattern Style work together to fill a cell with a pattern (various dots, lines) in the selected color. This effect is placed on top of the Background color. A gradient fill is when a color slowly changes from one color to another within a cell.

 **LET ME TRY IT**

Applying a Two-Color Gradient to a Cell

To apply a two-color gradient to a range, follow these steps:

1. Select one or more cells. If you select a range, the gradient will repeat across the range.

2. Press Ctrl+1 to bring up the Format Cells dialog.

3. Go to the Fill tab.

4. Click the Fill Effects button. The Fill Effects dialog, shown in Figure 4.4, will open.

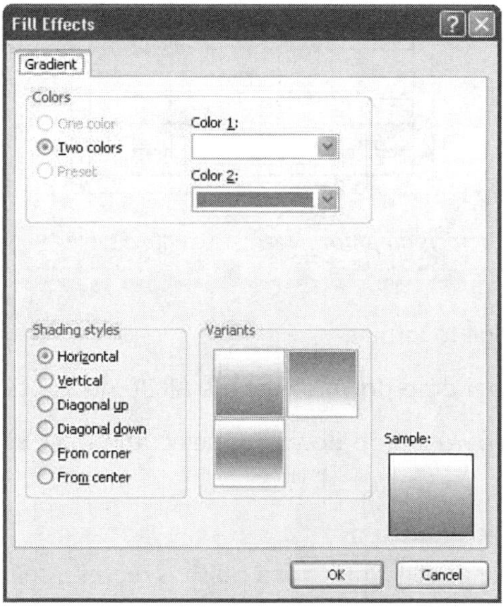

Figure 4.4 *The Fill Effects dialog offers more options for applying color inside of a cell.*

5. Select a color from the Color 1 drop-down.

6. Select a different color from the Color 2 drop-down.

7. Select a shading style from the Shading Styles section.

8. Make a selection from the Variants section. The Sample box will update to reflect your selection.

9. Click OK twice.

Font Color

The Font Color drop-down is the button with the A underscored by a thick red line, which changes when you select a different color from the available colors. Any color in the drop-down can be applied to a cell. Excel and Excel Starter will even allow you to change the color of single selected character within a cell.

Alignment Group

The Alignment group consists of tools that affect how a value is situated in a cell or range.

Alignment

There are six alignment buttons in the Alignment group, representing the most popular settings for how a value is situated in a cell. Top Align, Middle Align, and Bottom Align describe the vertical placement of the value in the cell. Align Text Left, Center, and Align Text Right describe the horizontal placement of the value in the cell. More options are available in the Format Cells dialog on the Alignment tab.

 **LET ME TRY IT**

Centering Text Across a Selection

Follow these steps to center a title across the top of a table without merging the cells, as shown in Figure 4.5.

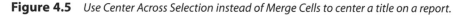

A1	▾	(	ƒx	Quarterly Sport Sales	
	A		B	C	
1		Quarterly Sport Sales			
2	Sport		Qtr	Sales	
3	Baseball		Q1	121	
4	Football		Q1	68	
5	Running		Q1	125	
6	Skiing		Q1	1907	
7	Tennis		Q1	214	
8	Baseball		Q2	2145	
9	Football		Q2	82	
10	Running		Q2	892	
11	Skiing		Q2	12	
12	Tennis		Q2	654	
13	Baseball		Q3	816	
14	Football		Q3	2050	
15	Running		Q3	790	
16	Skiing		Q3	15	
17	Tennis		Q3	121	

Figure 4.5   *Use Center Across Selection instead of Merge Cells to center a title on a report.*

1. Type your title in the leftmost cell to the table.

2. Select the title cell and extend the range to include all cells you want the title centered over.

3. Press Ctrl+1 to bring up the Format Cells dialog.

4. Go to the Alignment tab.

5. From the Horizontal drop-down, select Center Across Selection.

6. Click OK.

Merging Cells

Merge Cells takes two or more adjacent cells and combines them to make one cell. For example, if you are designing a form with many data entry cells, and need space for a large comment area, resizing the column may not be practical as it will also affect the size of the cells above it. Instead, select the range you want the comments to be entered in and merge the cells. Any text other than that found in the top-left cell of the selection is deleted as the newly combined cell takes on the identity of this first cell.

Use caution when merging cells because it can lead to potential issues:

- Unable to sort if there are merged cells within the data.
- Unable to cut and paste unless the same cells are merged in the pasted location.
- Column and row autofit won't work.
- Lookup type formulas return a match only for the first matching row or column.

Wrapping Text

When you type a lot of text in a cell, it continues to extend to the right beyond the right border of the cell. You can widen the column to fit the text, but sometimes that may be impractical. If that's the case, you can set the cell to Wrap Text, moving any text that extends past the edge of the column to a new line in the cell.

Normally, when you wrap a cell, the row height automatically adjusts to fit the text. If it doesn't, make sure you don't have the cell merged with another; Excel will not autofit merged cells. If there are merged cells, unmerge them and manually force an autofit (see the "Setting Row Heights and Column Widths" section). The row height will begin to auto adjust again.

Refer to the "Justifying Text in a Range" if you don't want to wrap text in a single cell and would prefer to have each line on its own row.

Indenting Cell Contents

By default, text entered in a cell is flush with the left side of the cell. To move text away from the left edge, you might be tempted to add spaces before text. If you change your mind about this formatting at a later time, it can be quite tedious to remove the extraneous spaces.

Instead, use the Increase Indent and Decrease Indent buttons to move the value about two character lengths over. Increase Indent will move the value away from edge it is aligned with. Decrease Indent will move the value back toward its edge.

If you use these buttons with a right-aligned number, the number will become left-aligned and adjust from the left margin. This does not occur with right-aligned text.

When adjusting the Indent from the Format Cells dialog, the Alignment tab uses a single Indent field with a number to indicate the number of indentations.

Orienting Text

Vertical text can be difficult to read, but sometimes limited space makes it a requirement. The Orientation button, which looks like ab written at a 45 degree angle, has five variations of vertical text, Angle Counterclockwise, Angle Clockwise, Vertical Text, Rotate Text Up and Rotate Text Down. The Orientation section in Format Cells, Alignment offers more precise control (see Figure 4.6).

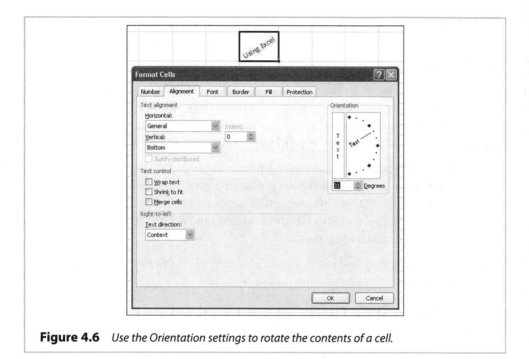

Figure 4.6　*Use the Orientation settings to rotate the contents of a cell.*

Justifying Text in a Range

There's a very handy tool that's not found with the other formatting tools. It didn't even appear on the Excel 2003 toolbars (it was hidden in the Edit menu) and is hidden in the Editing group on the Home tab. The button is the Fill button (a blue down arrow) and the option within it is Justify.

The Justify option reflows the text in a paragraph to fit a certain number of columns. For example, if you paste a paragraph directly into a cell, the height of the cell will increase, but the column width will be unaffected. Use Fill, Justify to reflow the text.

Be careful when selecting the range, because if you do not have enough empty rows available for the text to flow into, Excel will, after warning you, overwrite the rows below the selection.

 **LET ME TRY IT**

Reflowing Text in a Paragraph

To reflow text in a paragraph to fit a certain number of columns, follow these steps:

1. Ensure that the text is composed of one column of cells. The sentences can extend beyond one column, but the left column must contain text and the remaining columns must be blank.

2. Select a range as wide as the finished text should be. Ensure that the upper-left cell of the selection is the first line of text and include several extra rows in the selection rectangle, as shown in Figure 4.7.

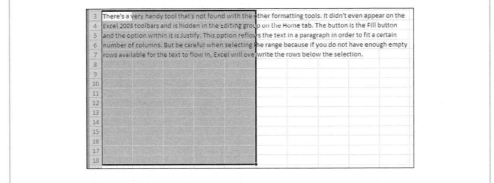

Figure 4.7 *The number of columns selected determines the width of the final result.*

3. From the Home tab, select Editing, Fill, Justify. The text will reflow so that each line is shorter than the selection range, as shown in Figure 4.8.

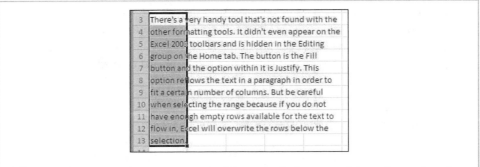

Figure 4.8 *The text flows to the width of the original selection and down the number of rows it needs to.*

Cell Styles

You're probably used to using styles in Word but never realized that styles are also available in Excel. Select a range in Excel and go to Home, Styles, Cell Styles. Move your cursor over the predefined styles and watch your range update to reflect the styles.

You aren't limited to these predefined styles. You can create and save your own style for use throughout the workbook it's saved in.

 SHOW ME   Media 4.1—Creating a Custom Style
Access this video file through your registered Web edition at
my.safaribooksonline.com/9780132182287/media.

LET ME TRY IT

Creating a Custom Style

Follow these steps to quickly create a custom style in the active workbook:

1. Select a cell with all the formatting styles needed.

2. Go to Home, Styles, Cell Styles, New Cell Style.

3. If there is any type of formatting you do not want as part of the style, such as the alignment, unselect the style option.

4. Enter a name for the style in the Style Name field and click OK.

Using Number Formats in Excel and Excel Starter

The way you see number data in Excel is controlled by the format applied to the cell. For example, you may see the date as April 5, 2010, but what's actually in the cell is 40273. Or you may see 10.5%, but the actual value in the cell is 0.105. This is important because when doing calculations, Excel doesn't care what you see. It deals only with the actual values.

There are only a few formatting options on the Home tab in the Numbering group. This section reviews the formatting options available in the Format Cells, Numbering dialog. For a review of the Number Format drop-down and the Increase Decimal and Decrease Decimal buttons, see the "Number Formats in Excel Web Apps" section because the same buttons are used there.

General

General is the default format used by all cells on a sheet when you first open a workbook. Decimal places and the negative symbol are shown if needed. Thousand separators are not.

Number

By default, the Number format uses two decimal places but does not use the thousand separator. You can change the number of decimals, turn on the thousands separator, and choose how to format negative numbers, as shown in Figure 4.9.

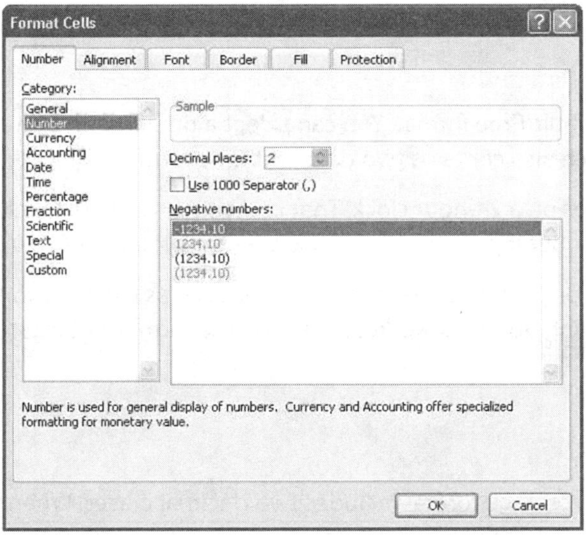

Figure 4.9   *Additional options may be available when you select a format to apply.*

Currency

The default Currency format displays the systems currency symbol, two decimal places and a thousands separator. You can change the number of decimals, the currency symbol, and select a format for negative numbers.

Accounting

Accounting is similar to Currency but automatically lines up the currency symbols on the left side of the column and decimals points to the right side of the cell. The default Accounting format displays the systems currency symbol, two decimal places, and a thousands separator. You can change the number of decimals and the currency symbol.

Date

There is no default Date format. Sometimes Excel will reformat the date you enter, sometimes it keeps it the way you entered it. You can select a date format from the list in the Type box, which also contains date and time formats.

The date formats vary from short dates, such as 4/5, to long dates, such as Monday, April 5, 2010. When selecting a date format, look at the sample above the type list. It will help you differentiate between the format 14-Mar, which is March 14, and the format Mar-01, which is March 2001, not March 1.

Time

There is no default Time format. You can select a time format from the list in the Type box, which also contains two date and time formats.

Excel sees times on a 24-hour clock. That is, if you enter 1:30, Excel assumes you mean 1:30 a.m. But if you enter 13:30, Excel knows you mean 1:30 p.m.

If you need to display times beyond 24 hours, such as if you're working on a timesheet adding up hours worked, use the time format 37:30:55, as shown in Figure 4.10.

Percentage

The default Percentage format includes two decimal places. When you apply this format, Excel takes the value in the cell, multiplies it by 100, and adds a % at the end. When you use the cell in a calculation, the actual (decimal) value is used. For example, if you have a cell showing 90% and multiply it by 1000, the result will be (in General format) 900 (0.9*1000).

If you include the % when you type the value in the cell, in the background Excel converts the value to its decimal equivalent, but the Percentage format is applied to the cell.

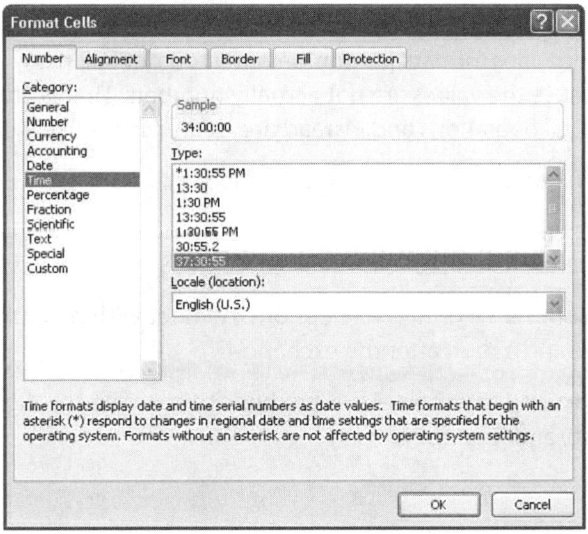

Figure 4.10   *There are various time formats available.*

Fraction

The Fraction category rounds decimal numbers up to the nearest fraction. You can select to round the decimal to one, two, or three digits, or to round to the nearest half, quarter, eighth, sixteenth, tenth, or hundredth.

Scientific

The default Scientific category displays the value in scientific notation accurate to two decimal places. You can change the number of decimals.

Text

There are no controls for the Text category. Setting this format to a cell forces Excel to treat the numbers in the cell as text, and you view exactly what is in the cell. If you set this format before typing in a number, the number becomes a number stored as text and may not work in some calculations.

Special

This category provides formats for numbers that do not fall in any of the preceding categories because the values are not actually numbers. That is, they aren't used for any mathematical operations and instead are treated more like words.

The four special types are specific to U.S. formatting:

- **ZIP Code and ZIP Code + 4**—Ensures that east coast cities do not lose the leading zeros in their ZIP Codes.

- **Phone Number**—Formats a telephone number with parentheses around the area code and a dash after the exchange.

- **Social Security Number**—Uses hyphens to separate the digits into groups of three, two, and four numbers.

Custom Formats

Despite all the options available in the preceding categories, not all the possible situations are covered. That's why there's the option of Custom Formats, allowing you to create a format specific to your situation. Custom formats are saved with the workbook they are created in.

Understanding the Four Sections of a Number Format

A custom number format can contain up to four different formats, each separated by a semicolon.

You should keep several things in mind when creating a custom number format:

- Use semicolons to separate the code sections.

- If there is only one format, it will apply to all numbers.

- If there are two formats, the first section applies to positive and zero values. The second section applies to negative values.

- If all four sections are used, they apply to positive, negative, zero, and text values, respectively.

Figure 4.11 shows a custom number format using all four sections. The table in C9:D13 displays how the formats would be applied to different values. Note the value in D11 is red and a zero, not a blank, must be entered in C12 for "No Sales" to appear.

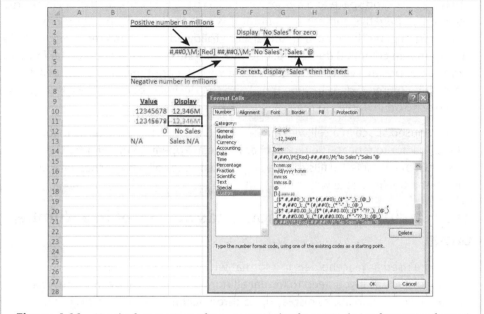

Figure 4.11 *Use the four sections of a custom number format to design formatting for positive, negative, zero, and text values.*

Using Text and Spacing in a Number Format

As shown in Figure 4.12, you can display both text and numbers in a cell. To do this, enclose the text in double quotation marks. If you need only a single character, you can omit the quotation marks and precede the character with a backslash (\). Some characters don't need quotes or a backslash. These special characters are: $ - + / ( ) : ! ^ & ' ~ { } = < > and the space character.

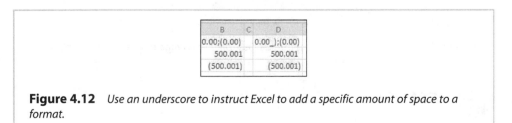

Figure 4.12 *Use an underscore to instruct Excel to add a specific amount of space to a format.*

If using the fourth section of the number format, include the @ sign where you want to display any text in the formatted cell. If the @ is omitted from the format, text entered in the cell will not be displayed.

To have Excel add space to a format, such as to have Excel line up the decimals in a column on negative and positive numbers where the negative numbers are wrapped in parentheses, use an underscore followed by a character. In Figure 4.12, the format in column B doesn't include the _) in the positive section of the format, and so the positive value in the cell is flush with the right margin. In contrast, the format in column C does include the _) and the decimals beneath are lined up. It's like having an invisible) in the cell.

To fill unused space in a cell with a repeating character, use an asterisk followed by the character to repeat. The repeat character can appear before or after the value in the cell. For example *-0 fills the leading space in the cell with dashes, whereas 0*^ fills in the trailing space with carets.

Using Decimals and the Thousands Separator in a Number Format

Zeros are used as placeholders in a format when you need to force the place to be included, such as if you need to format all numbers with exactly three decimal places. If you would like to display up to three decimal places, but it is not necessary, use the pound (#) sign as the place holder. Use a question mark (?) on either side of a decimal to replace insignificant zeros if you will be using a fixed-width font (such as Courier) and want the decimals to line up.

To include a thousands separator, use a comma in the format, such as #,###.0. To scale a number by thousands, as shown in Figure 4.13, include a comma at the end of the numeric format for each multiple of 1000.

	A	B
1	Format	Display
2	#,##0	1,000,000,000
3	#,##0,	1,000,000
4	#,##0,,	1,000
5	#,##0,,,	1

Figure 4.13   *Use a comma as a thousands multiplier to change how a value is displayed.*

LET ME TRY IT

Formatting Significant and Insignificant Digits

To format the positive section to always show three decimals and the negative section to show only what's entered, follow these steps:

1. Right-click over the cell to format and select Format Cells.

2. On the Number tab, select Custom from the Category list.

3. In the Type field enter 0.000;-0.### and click OK.

4. Positive values will display exactly three decimal places and negative values will display up to three decimal places, as shown in Figure 4.14.

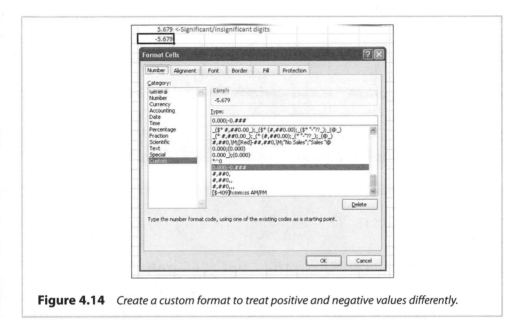

Figure 4.14 *Create a custom format to treat positive and negative values differently.*

Using Color and Conditions in a Number Format

You can use eight text color codes in a format: red, blue, green, yellow, cyan, black, white, and magenta. You place the color in square brackets, such as [cyan]. It should be the first element of a numeric formatting section.

You can use conditions in conjunction with colors to create number formats that apply only when specific conditions are met. The colors and conditions can only be applied to the first two sections of the number format, but the other sections can still be used. For example, to color values greater than or equal to 50 in green, less than 50 in red, a blank for zeros, and have "Sales" joined to any existing text, use this format: [Green][>=50];[Red][<50];"";"Sales "@.

Using Symbols in a Number Format

You can include various currency symbols, percent signs, and scientific notations in the number format.

If formatting with the exponent codes (E-,E+) and the format has a zero or pound sign (#) to the right of the code, Excel will display the number in scientific format and insert an E or e. The number of zeros or pound signs to the right of the code determines the number of digits in the exponent. Code E+ places a minus sign by negative exponents and a plus sign by positive exponents. Code E- places a minus sign by negative exponents. Figure 4.15 shows the results of 0.00E+00 and 0.00E-00 on different numbers.

E	F	G
Value	Result	Format
1563	1.56E+03	0.00E+00
1563	1.56E03	0.00E-00
-1563	-1.56E+03	0.00E+00
-1563	-1.56E03	0.00E-00
0.1563	1.56E-01	0.00E+00
0.1563	1.56E-01	0.00E-00

Figure 4.15   *The use of E+ or E- makes a difference in how the scientific notation will be formatted.*

LET ME TRY IT

Formatting a Cell to Show the Cent (¢) Symbol

Normally, when you apply a currency format, you get the dollar sign ($), but if the value is less than a dollar, you don't get the cent symbol. Follow these steps to format a cell to show the cent symbol when the value is less than 1 and to show the dollar sign for values of 1 or greater:

1. Right-click over the cell to format and select Format Cells.

2. On the Number tab, select Custom from the Category list.

3. In the Type field, enter [<1]0.00¢;$0.00_¢ and click OK. To get the cent symbol, hold down the Alt key and type 0162 on the numeric keypad.

4. Values less than 1 will display with a ¢ at the end, such as 0.23¢. Values 1 or greater will display with the $ at the beginning, such as $12.23. A note of caution—negative values are technically less than zero and so a value such as -12.23 would format with the cent symbol (-12.23¢), but this format would work well on a sales column.

Using Dates and Times in a Number Format

Date and Time formats have the greatest variety of codes available when it comes to creating number formats. Whereas there's no real difference between the codes

and ###, the difference between formatting a date cell mm or mmm are more obvious, as shown in Table 4.1.

Table 4.1 Date and Time Formats

To Display This	Use This Code
Months as 1–12	m
Months as 01–12	mm
Months as Jan–Dec	mmm
Months as January–December	mmmm
Months as the first letter of the month	mmmmm
Days as 1–31	d
Days as 01–31	dd
Days as Sun–Sat	ddd
Days as Sunday–Saturday	dddd
Years as 00–99	yy
Years as 1900–9999	yyyy
Hours as 0–23	H
Hours as 00–23	hh
Minutes as 0–59	m
Minutes as 00–59	mm
Seconds as 0–59	s
Seconds as 00–59	ss
Hours as 4 AM	h AM/PM
Time as 4:36 PM	h:mm AM/PM
Time as 4:36:03 P	h:mm:ss A/P
Elapsed time in hours; for example, 25.02	[h]:mm
Elapsed time in minutes; for example, 63:46	[mm]:ss
Elapsed time in seconds	[ss]
Fractions of a second	h:mm:ss.00

There are a couple of things to keep in mind when creating date and time formats:

- If the time format has an AM or PM in it, Excel will base the time on a 12-hour clock. Otherwise, Excel uses a 24-hour clock. See the previous section on Time for more information.

- When creating a time format, the minutes code (m or mm) must appear immediately after the hour code (h or hh) or immediately before the seconds code (ss) or Excel will display months instead of minutes.

Dealing with Formatting Issues

Most of the time, you can type in a number and then set the formatting, and the cell will reflect the formatting. This works about 99% of the time. But there is that 1% of cases that has caused headaches for many users until they understand what is going on.

You've spent hours designing your sheet, copying ranges from various workbooks, moving data around. You have a column of numbers and add a SUM formula at the bottom. A couple of things may happen:

- After pressing Enter, you see the formula exactly as you typed it in. It doesn't sum the selected range.

- The data sums, but the number doesn't look correct.

Check the format of the cell in question. If you were using the cell for something else earlier, it may still retain that format, such as text. If you're looking at the formula cell, change the format to General. You still see the formula. That's because the format has been applied to the cell, but not the contents of the cell. You need to force the format by entering the cell (F2, or double-click) and then pressing Enter. If the issue is the range being summed, you can either go to *each* cell and force the formatting onto the contents as described previously, or refer to the section "Fixing Numbers as Text" in Chapter 3, "Entering Data in Excel."

Using Number Formats in Excel Web Apps

The Web App offers one format (two for dates) that you can apply to your data.

Using the Number Format Drop-down

The Number Format drop-down in the Number group of the Home tab has 11 formatting options available. Figure 4.16 shows an example of each format.

Using Increase and Decrease Decimal

Use the Increase Decimal and Decrease Decimal buttons on the Home tab in the Number group (see Figure 4.17) to quickly increase and decrease the number of

Figure 4.16 *Even without the Format Dialog, the Excel Web App offers multiple formatting options.*

decimals shown in number formats that use decimals. The Increase Decimal button has an arrow pointing left, whereas the Decrease Decimal button has an arrow pointing right.

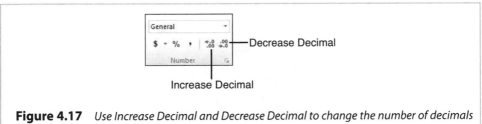

Figure 4.17 *Use Increase Decimal and Decrease Decimal to change the number of decimals shown in the selected range.*

Using Format Painter

The Format Painter is a handy, but tricky, little icon in the Clipboard group on the Home tab. It's handy because it enables you to quickly copy the formatting of one cell to another. It's tricky because whether you single-click or double-click the button affects how it functions. If you click the button once, you can copy the format of the selected range to one other range. If you double-click the button, it remains on, enabling you to copy from the format of the selected range to as many other ranges as needed. Use the Esc key, or click or double-click the button again to turn it off.

 SHOW ME   Media 4.2—Using Format Painter
You can watch a free video of this task when you log on to
my.safaribooksonline.com/9780132182287/media.

 LET ME TRY IT

Copying the Formatting of a Range

To copy a format from a source range to a destination range, follow these steps:

1. Select the source range.

2. Click the Format Painter button once. The cursor changes to a paintbrush with a plus sign, as shown in Figure 4.18.

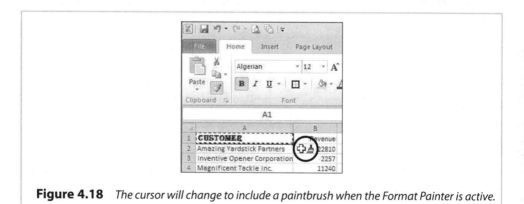

Figure 4.18   *The cursor will change to include a paintbrush when the Format Painter is active.*

3. Select the cell in the upper-left corner of the destination range if the range is the same size. If the destination range is larger, select the entire range.

4. The operation is complete and the cursor changes back to normal, as shown in Figure 4.19.

5. If you accidentally selected the wrong range, undo and start over.

Figure 4.19 *When in single-click mode, the cursor returns to normal immediately after for-matting the selected range.*

Adjusting Row Heights and Column Widths

You can use several ways to adjust the column widths on a sheet. Each method described here will also work on row heights:

- Click and drag the border between the column headings—Place your cursor on the border between two column headings, as shown in Figure 4.20, and you can drag to the right to make the column to the left wider or drag to the left to make the column narrower. The advantage of this method is you have full control of the width of the column. The disadvantage is that it affects only one column. This is the only option that works in the Excel Web App.

Figure 4.20 *The border between columns is the key to quickly adjusting the column width.*

- **Double-click the border between the column headings**—Excel will auto-matically adjust the left column to fit the widest value in that column. The advantage of this method is that the column is now wide enough to display all the contents. The disadvantage is if you have a cell with a very long entry, the new width may be impractical.

- **Select multiple columns and drag the border for one column**—The width of all the columns in the selection will adjust to the same width as the one you just adjusted.

- **Select multiple columns and double-click the border for one column**—Each column in the selection will adjust to accommodate its widest value.

- **Apply one column's width to other columns**—If you have a column with a width you want other columns to have, you can copy that column and paste its width over the other columns.

- **Use the controls on the Ribbon**—Select the column(s) to adjust. Go to Home, Cells, Format, Column Width. Enter a width and click OK.

- **Autofit a column to fit all the data below a title row**—If you have a long title and need to fit the column to all the data below, double-clicking the border between column headings won't work. Instead, select the range and use the AutoFit Column Width option under Home, Cells, Format.

 LET ME TRY IT

Applying One Column's Width to Other Columns

To apply one column's width to other columns, follow these steps:

1. Select the column with the correct width.

2. Press Ctrl+C to copy.

3. Select the columns you want to apply the width to.

4. Go to Home, Clipboard, Paste, Paste Special, Column Widths.

 LET ME TRY IT

AutoFitting the Data in a Column

To size a column based on a selected range, follow these steps:

1. Select the first cell of the data range.

2. Press the End key.

3. Hold down the Shift key and press the down-arrow key to select the range from the first cell downward.

4. Select Home, Cell, Format, AutoFit Column Width.

Using Themes

Themes are collections of fonts, colors and graphic effects that can be applied to a workbook. This can be useful if you have a series of company reports that need to have the same color and fonts. Only one theme can affect a workbook at a time.

Excel includes several built-in themes, and you can download more. You can also create and share themes you design.

A theme has the following components:

- **Fonts**—A theme includes a font for headings and a font for body text.
- **Colors**—There are 12 colors in a theme: 4 for text, 6 for accents and 2 for hyperlinks.
- **Graphic Effects**—Graphic effects include lines, fills, bevels, shadows, and so on.

Applying a New Theme

The Themes group on the Page Layout tab has four buttons:

- **Themes**—Allows you to switch themes or save a new one.
- **Colors**—Allows you to select a new color palette from the available built-in themes.
- **Fonts**—Allows you to select a new font palette from the available built-in themes.
- **Effects**—Allows you to select a new effect from the available built-in themes.

Before applying a theme, arrange the sheet so you can see any themed elements such as charts or SmartArt. Then go to Page Layout, Themes and watch the elements update as you move your cursor over the various themes. When you find the one you like, click it, and it will be applied to the workbook.

If you just want to change a theme component, make a selection from the components drop-down in the same way you would a theme.

Creating a New Theme

To create a new theme, you need to specify the colors and fonts and select an effect from the respective component's drop-down. Then, under the Themes drop-down, choose Save Current Theme to save the theme.

SHOW ME   Media 4.3—Creating a New Theme
Access this video file through your registered Web edition at my.safaribooksonline.com/9780132182287/media.

LET ME TRY IT

Creating a Theme

To create a new theme, follow these steps:

1. Select Page Layout, Themes, Colors, Create New Theme Colors.

2. To change an item's color, choose its drop-down to open the color chooser.

3. When you find the desired color, click it to apply it to your theme.

4. Repeat steps 2 and 3 for each color you want to change.

5. In the Name field at the bottom, type a name for your color theme.

6. Click Save.

7. Select Page Layout, Themes, Fonts, Create New Theme Fonts.

8. To change the heading font, choose its drop-down to open the list of available fonts.

9. When you find the desired font, click it to apply it to your theme. The Sample box on the right will update to reflect your selection.

10. Repeat steps 8 and 9 for the body font.

11. In the Name field at the bottom, type a name for your font theme.

12. Click Save.

13. Select Page Layout, Themes, Effects.

14. Select an effect from the gallery of built-in effects.

15. Go to Page Layout, Themes, Themes, Save Current Theme.

16. Browse to where you want to save the theme, type a name for it, and click Save.

Sharing a Theme

To share a theme with other people, you'll have to send them the *.thmx file you saved when you created the theme.

When they receive the file, they should save it to either their equivalent theme folder or some other location and use the Browse for Themes option under Page Layout, Themes, Browse for Themes.

Using Conditional Formatting

Although you can't set up conditional formatting in the Excel Web App, a workbook with formatting designed in Excel or Excel Starter and then uploaded to SkyDrive will still work.

An unformatted sheet of just numbers isn't going to grab your audience's attention. But you don't have time to create a colorful report—or do you? Conditional Formatting allows you to quickly apply color and icons to data. You're no longer limited to the simple formatting options in legacy versions of Excel. The new formatting options consist of the following:

- **Data Bars**—A data bar is a semitransparent fill of color that starts at the left edge of the cell. The length of the bar represents the value in the cell compared to other values in the range the format is applied to. The smallest numbers have just a tiny amount of color and the largest numbers in the range fill the cell.

- **Color Scales**—A color scale is a color that fills the entire cell. Two or three different colors are used to relay the relative size of each cell to other cells in the range the format is applied to.

- **Icon Sets**—An icon set is a group of three to five images that provide a graphic representation of how the number in a cell compares to the other cells in the range the format is applied to.

The quickest way to apply one of the new conditional formattings is to select the range, go to Home, Conditional Formatting, click the formatting type, and select one of the formatting options from the submenu that appears, as shown in Figure 4.21. As you move your cursor over the options, your range will change to reflect the connection. When you find the formatting you want, click it, and it will be applied to your range.

 SHOW ME   Media 4.4—**Applying Conditional Formatting**
You can watch a free video of this task when you log on to
my.safaribooksonline.com/9780132182287/media.

Figure 4.21 *Quickly apply formatting to your data by selecting one of the prebuilt options in the Conditional Formatting drop-down.*

 **LET ME TRY IT**

Applying a Custom Icon Set

You can mix and match the individual icons. Follow these steps to use a green check for values in the top 67%, a red stoplight for items below 33%, and a yellow exclamation point for everything in between:

1. Select the range to which you want to apply the formatting.

2. On the Home tab, go to Conditional Formatting, Icon Sets, More Rules.

3. Click the first drop-down under the Icon heading and select the green check, as shown in Figure 4.22.

4. To the right of the drop-down, select >= from the drop-down.

5. Enter 67 in the Value field.

6. Select Percent from the Type drop-down.

7. Click the second drop-down under the Icon heading and select the yellow exclamation point.

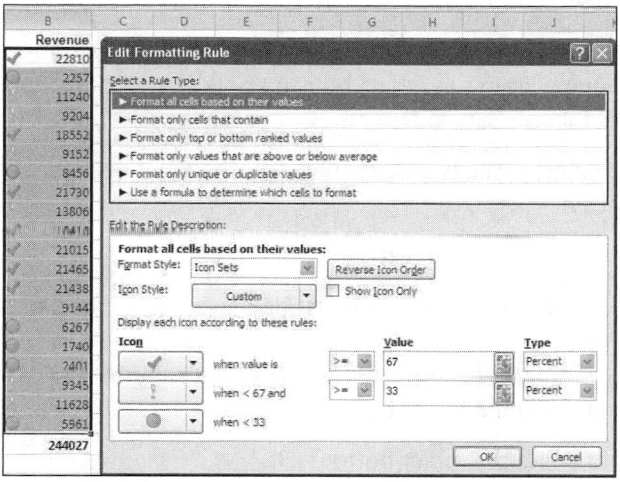

Figure 4.22 *You can mix and match the conditional formatting icons.*

8. To the right of the drop-down, select >= from the drop-down.

9. Enter 33 in the Value field.

10. Select Percent from the Type drop-down.

11. Click the third drop-down under the Icon heading and select the red stop-light.

12. Click OK.

Using Rules

Use the preset conditional formats if all you need is to format all the cells in a range based on how they compare to each other. But if your needs are more advanced, such as formatting only the top 10% or only cells that meet a specific condition, then you'll want to apply formatting using rules.

TELL ME MORE   **Media 4.5—Using Preset Conditional Formatting Rules**

You can listen to a free audio recording about using the built-in conditional formatting rules in Excel 2010 when you log on to my.safaribooksonline.com/9780132182287/media.

Built-in Rules

Under Conditional Formatting, Highlight Cells Rules and Top/Bottom Rules options, you'll find several built-in rules that you can apply to your data. Apply selected formatting to the following:

- Cells containing values greater than, less than, between, or equal to the value you specify.

- Cells containing specific text.

- Cells containing a date from the last day, two days, and so on.

- Cells containing duplicate values.

- Cells containing the top or bottom *n* items.

- Cells containing the top or bottom *n*%.

- Cells containing values above or below the average.

For all of the preceding built-in rules, you can apply one of Excel's preset formats or design your own custom format.

 **LET ME TRY IT**

Using a Custom Format for the Top *n* Items in a Range

To apply a custom format to the Top *n* items in the selected range, follow these steps:

1. Select the range to which you want to apply the formatting.

2. On the Home tab, go to Conditional Formatting, Top/Bottom Rules, Top 10 Items.

3. Enter the number of items you want formatted.

4. From the format drop-down, select Custom Format.

5. From the Format Cells dialog that appears, design the format you want applied (see Figure 4.23). You can go to any of the tabs (Number, Font, Border, and Fill) to make your selections. The only change you cannot make is to the font type and size on the Font tab.

Building Custom Rules

You can customize any of the prebuilt rules, but if what you need is not listed, you'll want to build your own conditional formatting rule based on a formula.

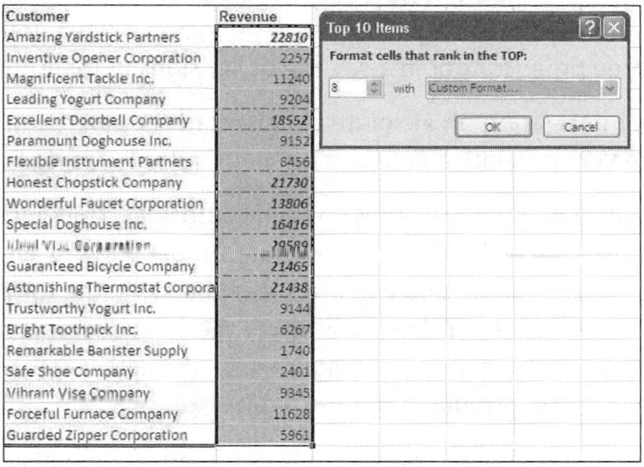

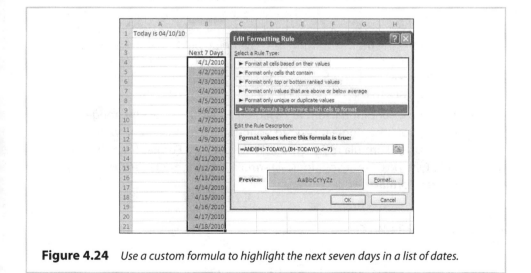

Figure 4.23 *Using Custom Format, the top eight items had bold italic format and borders applied.*

The formula box, shown in Figure 4.24 has a few rules for writing a formula:

Figure 4.24 *Use a custom formula to highlight the next seven days in a list of dates.*

- The formula must start with an equal (=) sign.

- The formula must evaluate to a logical value of True or False or the equivalents of 1 and 0.

- If you use your mouse to select cells on the sheet, Excel will insert the address using absolute referencing. If relative referencing is what you need, press the F4 key three times to toggle away the dollar signs in the formula.

- For more information on absolute versus relative referencing, see the section "Absolute Versus Relative Referencing" in Chapter 5, "Using Formulas."

- The formula you write will apply to the topmost left cell of your selection, so you need to look at the Name Box in the formula bar and see what cell is the active cell. If you are writing a relative formula, write the formula as it would appear for the active cell. Excel will apply the formula appropriately to all the other cells you have selected. In Figure 4.24, the active cell is B4, which is also referenced in the formula.

- By default, the keyboard navigation keys (up arrow, down arrow, left arrow, right arrow, Page Up, Page Down, Home) are tied to the sheet and won't work in the formula field. If you try to use the arrow keys to change your cursor position while typing in the formula field, Excel will instead place the cell address you just selected. To work around this behavior, press F2 before using the navigation keys. You can verify what mode you are in by looking in the lower-left corner of the status bar. There are three modes:
  - **Enter**—The default mode for entering a formula in the formula field. Using the navigation keys will change the selection on the sheet.
  - **Edit**—The mode for using the navigation fields to move through the formula field.
  - **Point**—The mode for selecting cells on the sheet. Excel automatically switches to this mode when selecting cells on the sheet.

- To set up a conditional format based on a formula, select the range it applies to and, from the Home tab, go to Conditional Formatting, New Rule, and select Use a Formula to Determine Which Cells to Format from the Select a Rule Type box. Enter your logical formula in the formula field and set the desired Format.

 **LET ME TRY IT**

Using a Custom Formula to Format Data

To create a conditional formatting based on a custom logical formula, follow these steps:

1. Select the range to which you want to apply the formatting.

2. On the Home tab, go to Conditional Formatting, New Rule and select Use a Formula to Determine Which Cells to Format from the Select a Rule Type box.

3. Type the logical formula in the formula field.

4. Click Format to bring up the Format Cells dialog and apply the desired formatting.

5. Click OK twice to apply the conditional format to the selected range.

Combining Rules

You can have multiple conditions evaluate to True and as each condition is met, the format is applied to the cell. For example, one rule sets the fill color to red and another rule italicizes the contents, as shown in Figure 4.25. If both rules are met, the cell is formatted in italic with a red fill. If a cell meets one condition, only the corresponding format is applied. If the formatting of the rules is conflicting, for example the first rule applies a red font and the second rule applies a blue font, the formatting of the first rule, the red font, is applied.

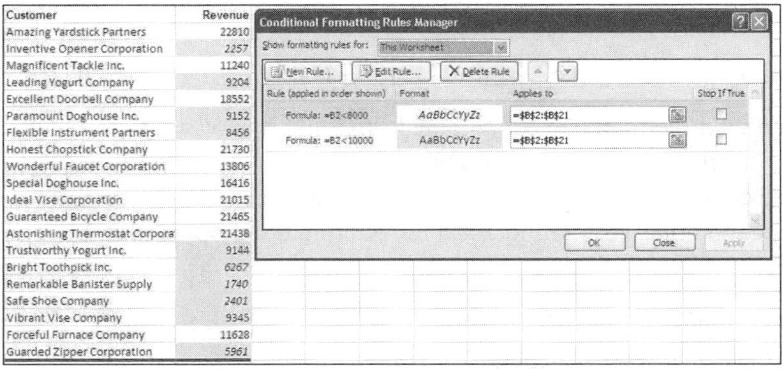

Figure 4.25 *Setting up multiple rules can apply multiple formatting to cells.*

Stopping Further Rules From Being Checked

Because rules are applied starting at the top, you might want to prevent further rules from being applied if a certain condition is met. In that case, check the Stop If True option in the Conditional Formatting Rules Manager for the rule you want to be the last if the condition is True. For example, in Figure 4.25, values below 8000 were italic with a red fill. But if you want to differentiate between items below 8000 and those between 8001 and 10000 (without setting up a rule referencing the specific range), you would check the Stop If True for the first rule, as shown in Figure 4.26.

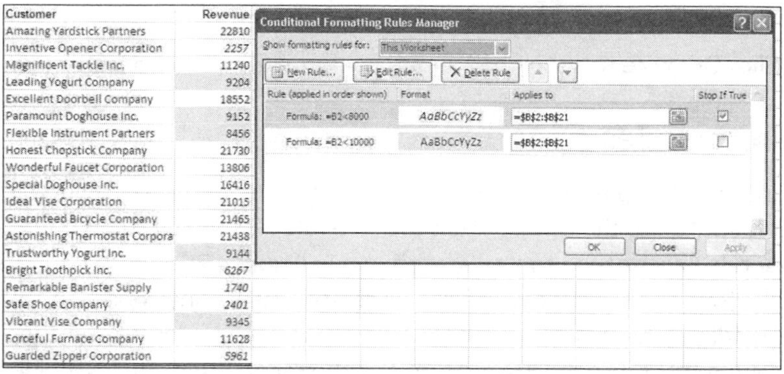

Figure 4.26   *Check the Stop If True checkbox to prevent further rules from being applied to the data.*

Clearing Conditional Formatting

You can set more than one conditional formatting rule on a range, so if you want to replace a format with another, you will need to clear the previous rule. Or, you may want to clear all the formatting on a sheet. To clear conditional formatting, go to Home, Conditional Formatting, Clear Rules. From the drop-down that appears you can:

- Clear Rules from Selected Cell
- Clear Rules from Entire Sheet
- Clear Rules from This Table
- Clear Rules from This PivotTable

This chapter will teach you about entering and troubleshooting formulas.

5

Using Formulas

Excel is great for simple data entry, but its real strength is its capability to perform calculations. After you design a sheet to perform calculations, you can easily change the data and watch Excel instantly recalculate. This chapter introduces you to formula basics that you can later apply to Chapter 6, "Using Functions."

The Importance of Laying Data Out Properly

Except for when using certain functions, such as VLOOKUP, Excel doesn't really care how you lay out your data. For example, you can lay out your data as shown in Figure 5.1, with dates across the top. But if you later decide you want to use a pivot table or certain functions, your options are limited. You'll have fewer limitations if you lay out your data in the optimal fashion, shown in Figure 5.2, with a column assigned to each type of information entered.

		1/1/2010	1/2/2010	1/3/2010	1/4/2010	1/5/2010
Bright Hairpin Company	Quantity			100		
Bright Hairpin Company	Revenue			2257		
Bright Hairpin Company	COGS			984		
Bright Hairpin Company	Profit			1273		
Cool Jewelry Corporation	Quantity				800	
Cool Jewelry Corporation	Revenue				18552	
Cool Jewelry Corporation	COGS				7872	
Cool Jewelry Corporation	Profit				10680	
Exclusive Shovel Traders	Quantity	1000				
Exclusive Shovel Traders	Revenue	22810				
Exclusive Shovel Traders	COGS	10220				
Exclusive Shovel Traders	Profit	12590				
Remarkable Meter Corporation	Quantity					
Remarkable Meter Corporation	Revenue					
Remarkable Meter Corporation	COGS					
Remarkable Meter Corporation	Profit					
Tasty Kettle Inc.	Quantity				400	
Tasty Kettle Inc.	Revenue				9152	

Figure 5.1 *Laying out data with dates across the top may make sense when you want to see the data by date, but it can make it more difficult to apply functions.*

Date	Customer	Quantity	Revenue	COGS	Profit
1/1/2008	Exclusive Shovel Traders	1000	22810	10220	12590
1/2/2008	Bright Hairpin Company	100	2257	984	1273
1/4/2008	Cool Jewelry Corporation	800	18552	7872	10680
1/4/2008	Tasty Kettle Inc.	400	9152	4088	5064
1/7/2008	Remarkable Meter Corporat	400	8456	3388	5068
1/9/2008	Remarkable Meter Corporat	800	16416	6776	9640
1/15/2008	Bright Hairpin Company	500	9345	4235	5110
1/16/2008	Appealing Calculator Corpo	600	11628	5082	6546
1/19/2008	Bright Hairpin Company	100	2042	984	1058
1/21/2008	Best Vegetable Company	800	14440	6776	7664
1/21/2008	Cool Jewelry Corporation	200	3552	1694	1858
1/23/2008	Remarkable Meter Corporat	800	14592	6776	7816
1/24/2008	Reliable Tripod Company	600	12606	5082	7524
1/25/2008	Appealing Calculator Corpo	1000	20770	8470	12300
1/26/2008	Reliable Tripod Company	400	8128	3388	4740

Figure 5.2 *Providing a column field for each data type allows you to take full advantage of many of Excel's functions.*

Adjusting Calculation Settings

By default, Excel calculates and recalculates whenever you open or save a workbook or make a change to a cell used in a formula. At times, this isn't convenient—such as when you're working with a very large workbook with a long recalculation time. In times like this, you will want to control when calculations occur.

The Calculation group on the Formulas tab has the following options:

- **Calculation Options**—Has the options Automatic, Automatic Except for Data Tables, and Manual.
- **Calculate Now**—Calculates the entire workbook.
- **Calculate Sheet**—Calculates only the active sheet.

The calculation options under File, Options, Formulas include the same Calculation Options as the preceding list, but the Manual option allows you to turn on/off the way Excel recalculates a workbook when saving it.

Formulas Versus Values

You can't tell the difference between a cell containing numbers and one with a formula just by looking at it on the sheet. To see whether a cell contains a formula, select the cell and look in the formula bar. If the formula bar contains just a number, the cell is static. But if the formula bar contains a formula, which always starts with an equal sign (=), as shown in Figure 5.3, you know the number you're seeing on the sheet is a result of a calculation.

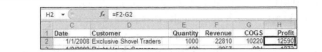

Figure 5.3 *The formula bar reveals whether a cell, in this case H2, contains a number or a formula.*

Entering a Formula

Entering a basic formula is straightforward. Select the cell, enter an equal sign, type in the formula, and press Enter. Typing the formula is very similar to entering an equation on a calculator, with one exception. If one of the terms in your formula is already stored in a cell, you can point to that cell instead of typing in the number stored in the cell. The advantage of this is that if the other cell ever changes, your formula will recalculate.

 SHOW ME Media 5.1—Entering a Basic Formula
You can watch a free video of this task when you log on to my.safaribooksonline.com/9780132182287/media.

 LET ME TRY IT

Enter a Formula

To enter a formula that includes a pointer to another cell, follow these steps:

1. Select the cell you want the formula to be in.

2. Type an equal sign. This tells Excel you are entering a formula.

3. Type the first number and an operator, as you would on a calculator. There's no need to include spaces in the formula.

4. Select the cell you want to include in the formula.

5. Press Enter. Excel calculates the formula in the cell.

Relative Versus Absolute Formulas

When you copy a formula, such as **=B2*C2**, down a column, the formula automatically changes to **=B3*C3**, then **=B4*C4**, and so on. Excel's capability to change B2 to B3 to B4 and so on is called *relative referencing*. This is Excel's default behavior when dealing with formulas, but it might not always be what you want to happen. If the cell address must remain static as the formula is copied, you need to use *absolute referencing*. This is achieved through the strategic placement of dollar signs ($) before the row or column reference, as shown in Table 5.1.

Table 5.1   Relative Versus Absolute Reference Behavior

Format	Copied Down	Copied Across
A1	A2—the row reference updates	B1—the column reference updates
$A$1	$A$1—neither reference updates	$A$1—neither reference updates
$A1	$A2—the row reference updates	$A1—neither reference updates
A$1	A$1—neither reference updates	B$1—the column reference updates

R1C1 Notation

The default setting in Excel is A1 notation. R1C1 notation is another reference style for cells. To turn it on, go to File, Options, Formulas and in the Working with Formulas section, select R1C1 Reference Style. When you do this, your sheet column headers change from letters to numbers, as shown in Figure 5.4.

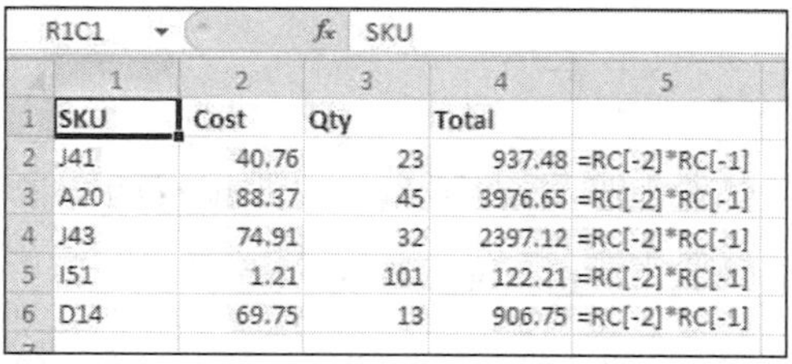

Figure 5.4   *R1C1 notation is very different from the A1 reference style.*

Instead of A1 in the Name Box when you select the top leftmost cell on a sheet, you see R1C1, which stands for Row 1 Column 1. But the change is more than the notation difference, the way you write formulas is deeply affected. In R1C1 notation, the reference RC refers to the current cell. You modify RC by adding or subtracting a particular row or column number. For example, R5C refers to row 5 of the current column. RC5 refers to column 5 of the current row.

If the row or column numbers are enclosed in square brackets, then you are refer-ring to a relative number of cells from the current cell. For example, if you have a formula in G8 and use the reference R[-1]C[3], you are referring to a cell one row above and 3 columns to the right of G8, which would be J7.

In Figure 5.4, all the formulas are the same because the formula is based off the cell the formula is in. Note the formulas shown are actually the formulas in the Total column. The formula multiplies the value in the cell two columns to the left (Cost) by the value one column to the left (Qty) of the formula cell (Total). Both references are to a cell in the same row as the formula, so there is no number by the row refer-ence.

Using F4 to Change the Cell Referencing

When typing in a formula and you select a cell or range, Excel uses the relative ref-erence. If you need the absolute reference, you will probably either type in the address manually or go back and change the address after you are done with the whole formula. Another option is to change the reference to what you need while typing in the formula. You can do this by using the F4 key right after selecting the cell or range. Each time you press the F4 key, it changes the cell address to another reference variation, as shown in Figure 5.5.

When you enter the formula:	
	=B2
Press F4 once:	
	=$B$2
Press F4 again:	
	=B$2
Press F4 again:	
	=$B2

Figure 5.5   *Use F4 to toggle through the variations of relative to absolute referencing.*

If you need to change a reference after you've already entered the formula, you can still place your cursor in the cell address and use the F4 key to toggle through the references.

 **LET ME TRY IT**

Changing a Cell Address to a Column Fixed Reference

To change the cell address in a formula to a column fixed reference as you type it in, follow these steps:

1. Select the cell you want the formula to be in.

2. Type an equal sign.

3. Type the first number and operator, as you would on a calculator.

4. Select the cell you want to include in the formula.

5. Press F4 once and the address changes to absolute referencing. Press F4 again and it becomes a Row Fixed Reference. Press F4 a third time and it becomes a Column Fixed Reference.

> If you miss the reference you need to use the first time, continue pressing F4 until it comes up again.

6. Press Enter. Excel calculates the formula in the cell.

Entering Formulas

After typing the equal sign to start a formula, you have three options for entering the rest of the formula:

- Type the complete formula.

- Type numbers and operator keys, but use the mouse to select cell references.

- Type numbers and operator keys, but use the arrow keys to select cell references.

The method you use depends on what you find most comfortable. Some users consider the first method the quickest because they never have to move their fingers off the main section of the keyboard. For others, using the mouse makes more sense, especially when selecting a large range for use in the formula.

Copying a Formula

You can use four ways to enter the same formula in multiple cells:

- Copy the entire cell and paste it to the new location.

- Enter the formula in the first cell and then use the fill handle to copy the formula.

- Preselect the entire range for the formula. Enter the formula in the first cell and press Ctrl+Enter to simultaneously enter the formula in the entire selection.

- Define the range as a table. Excel automatically copies new formulas entered in a table. See the section "Tables and Table Formulas" for more information.

 LET ME TRY IT

Copying a Formula by Using Ctrl+Enter

To copy a formula using Ctrl+Enter, follow these steps:

1. Select the range you want the formula to be in.

2. Type the formula in the first cell.

3. Press Ctrl+Enter. Excel copies the formula to all cells in the selected range.

 LET ME TRY IT

Copying a Formula by Dragging the Fill Handle

To copy a formula by dragging the fill handle, follow these steps:

1. Select the cell you want the formula to be in.

2. Type the formula in the first cell.

3. Press Ctrl+Enter to accept the formula and keep the cell as your active cell.

4. Click and hold the fill handle, which looks like a little black square in the lower-right corner of the selected cell. When the cursor is positioned correctly, it turns into a black cross, as shown in Figure 5.6.

5. Drag the fill handle to the last cell that needs to hold a copy of the formula.

6. Release the mouse button. The first cell is copied to all the cells in the selected range.

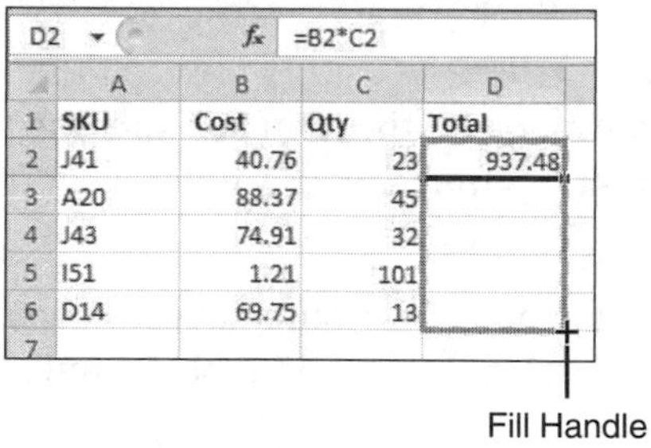

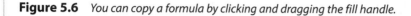

Fill Handle

Figure 5.6 *You can copy a formula by clicking and dragging the fill handle.*

> If you have a large vertical range to copy the formula down, double-clicking the handle may work for you. See the "Copying Formulas Rapidly" section in Chapter 3 for details on how to do this.

Formula Operators

Excel offers the mathematical operators listed in Table 5.2.

Table 5.2 Mathematical Operators

Operator	Description
+	Addition
-	Subtraction
/	Division
*	Multiplication
^	Exponents
()	Override the usual order of operations
-	Unary minus (for negative numbers)
=	Equal to
>	Greater than
<	Less than
>=	Greater than or equal to
<=	Less than or equal to
<>	Not equal to

&	Join two values to produce a single value
,	Union operator
:	Range operator
(space)	Intersection operator

Order of Operations

Excel evaluates a formula in a particular order if it contains many calculations. Instead of calculating from left to right like a calculator, Excel performs certain types of calculations, such as multiplication, before other calculations, such as addition.

You can override this default order of operations using parentheses. If you don't, Excel applies the following order of operations:

1. Unary minus

2. Exponents

3. Multiplication and division, left to right

4. Addition and subtraction, left to right

For example, if you have the formula

=6+3*2

Excel will return 12, because first it does 3*2, then adds the result (6) to 6. But, if you use parentheses, you can change the order:

=(6+3)*2

produces 18 because now Excel will do the addition first (6+3) and multiply the result (9) by 2.

Using Names To Simplify References

It can be difficult to remember what cell you have a specific entry in, such as a tax rate, when you're writing a formula. And if the cell you need to reference is on another sheet, you have to be very careful writing out the reference properly, or you must use the mouse to go to the sheet and select the cell.

It would be much simpler if you could just use the word TaxRate in your formula—and you can, by applying a Name to the cell. After a name is applied to a cell, any references to the cell or range can be done by using the name instead of the cell address. For example, where you once had =B2*$H$1, you could now have =B2*TaxRate, assuming H1 was the cell containing the tax rate.

> The Web App won't allow you to create new names, but you can use existing ones.

There are only a few limitations to remember when creating a name:

- The name must be one word. You can use an underscore (_), backslash (\) or period (.) as spacers.

- The name cannot be a word that might also be a cell address. This was a real problem when people converted workbooks from legacy Excel because some names, such as TAX2009, weren't cell addresses then, but caused problems when you opened a workbook in 2007 or 2010. So name carefully!

- The name cannot include any invalid characters, such as ? ! or -. The only valid special characters are the underscore (_),backslash (\) and period (.).

- Names are not case sensitive. Excel will see "sales" and "Sales" as the same name.

- You should not use any of the reserved words in Excel. These are Print_Area, Print_Titles, Criteria, Database, and Extract.

 **LET ME TRY IT**

Applying and Using a Name in a Formula

To apply a name to a cell and then use the name in a formula, follow these steps:

1. Select the cell or range you want to apply the name to.

2. In the name field, type in the name, as shown in Figure 5.7.

> If the name already exists in the workbook, typing it in will select the cell it refers to.

3. Press Enter for Excel to accept the name.

Name field

	A	B	C	D	E	F	G	H
					TaxRate	▾	f_x	4%
1	Product	Qty Sold	Cost Per	Total	Tax		Tax Rate:	4%
2	Shiny Balls	1203	0.85	1022.55	40.90	=D2*TaxRate		
3	Glowing Bracelets	1398	1.2	1677.6	67.10	=D3*TaxRate		
4	Sparkle Balls	987	1.34	1322.58	52.90	=D4*TaxRate		
5	Blinking Balls	1405	1.76	2472.8	98.91	=D5*TaxRate		

Figure 5.7   *After you select a cell or range, you can type a name for it in the Name field. Column F shows the name used in the formulas in column E.*

4. Go to the cell containing the formula that should reference the name.

5. Replace the cell or range address with the name you just created, or type in a new formula from scratch using the name where you would use the cell or range address.

If you can't remember the name assigned to a range, you can look it up by clicking the drop-down in the name field or by selecting Formulas, Defined Names, Use in Formula, which opens up a drop-down of available names. You can also go to Formulas, Defined Names, Name Manager, which not only lists the defined names, but shows the range they apply to.

Inserting Formulas into Tables

See "Working with Tables" in Chapter 3, for information on defining a table.

When your data has been defined as a Table, Excel will automatically copy new formulas down the rest of the cells in the column.

 **LET ME TRY IT**

Entering a Formula in a Table

To add a new calculated column to a table, follow these steps:

1. Select the first data cell in the column adjacent to the rightmost column of the table. This would be cell I2 in Figure 5.8.

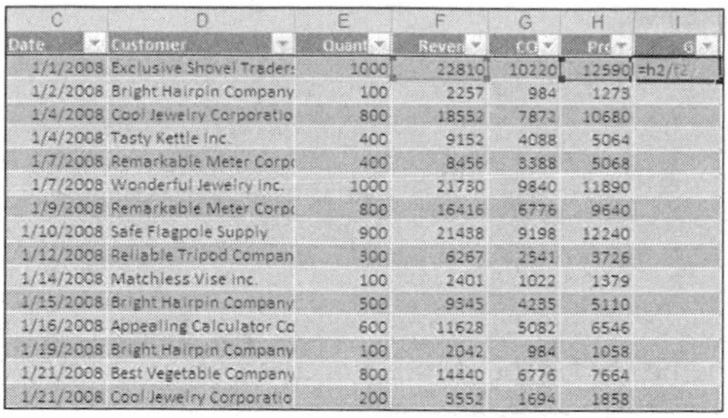

C	D	E	F	G	H	I
Date	Customer	Quant	Rever	CO	Pro	G
1/1/2008	Exclusive Shovel Trader:	1000	22810	10220	12590	=h2/f2
1/2/2008	Bright Hairpin Company	100	2257	984	1273	
1/4/2008	Cool Jewelry Corporatio	800	18552	7872	10680	
1/4/2008	Tasty Kettle Inc.	400	9152	4088	5064	
1/7/2008	Remarkable Meter Corp	400	8456	3388	5068	
1/7/2008	Wonderful Jewelry Inc.	1000	21730	9840	11890	
1/9/2008	Remarkable Meter Corp	800	16416	6776	9640	
1/10/2008	Safe Flagpole Supply	900	21438	9198	12240	
1/12/2008	Reliable Tripod Compan	300	6267	2541	3726	
1/14/2008	Matchless Vise Inc.	100	2401	1022	1379	
1/15/2008	Bright Hairpin Company	500	9345	4235	5110	
1/16/2008	Appealing Calculator Co	600	11628	5082	6546	
1/19/2008	Bright Hairpin Company	100	2042	984	1058	
1/21/2008	Best Vegetable Company	800	14440	6776	7664	
1/21/2008	Cool Jewelry Corporatio	200	3552	1694	1858	

Figure 5.8 *Type a formula in the first cell of a table column and Excel will copy it down the rest of the column.*

2. Enter your formula for the selected cell.
3. Press Enter and Excel copies the formula down the column.

After entering the formula, a lightning bolt drop-down appears by the cell. If you don't want the automated formula copied, select Undo Calculated Column or Stop Automatically Creating Calculated Columns.

Table References in Formulas

Names are automatically created when you define a table. A name for each column and the entire table are created. You can use these names to simplify references to the data in formulas.

To find the name of the table, select a cell in the table and go to Table Tools, Design, Properties. The name of the table will appear in the Table Name field. You can use this name in formulas to reference the entire table. The names for the columns are based on the column headers.

In addition to the table and column specifiers, Excel provides five more. To access these specifiers, you must first type the table name.

- **#All**—Returns all the contents of the table or specified column.
- **#Data**—Returns the data cells of the table or specified column.
- **@ (This Row)**—Returns the current row.
- **#Headers**—Returns all the column headers or that of a specified column.
- **#Totals**—Returns the total rows or that of a specified column.

Writing Formulas That Refer to Tables

The following are rules for writing formulas that refer to tables:

- The reference to the table must start with the table name. If the formula is within the table itself, you can omit the table name.

- Specifiers, such as a column name or the total row, must be enclosed in square brackets, like this: TableName[Specifier]

- If using multiple specifiers, each specifier must be surrounded by square brackets and separated by commas. The entire group of specifiers used must be surrounded by square brackets, like this: TableName[[Specifier1],[Specifier2]]

- If no specifiers are used, the table name refers to the data rows in the table. This does not include the headers or total rows.

- The @ (This Row) specifier must be used with another specifier, like this: TableName[[@Specifier]]

Figure 5.9 shows examples of using specifiers.

Region	Product	Date	Customer	Quant		
East	XYZ	1/1/2008	Exclusive Shovel Traders	1000		
Central	DEF	1/2/2008	Bright Hairpin Company	100	Count all cells in the table	
East	DEF	1/4/2008	Cool Jewelry Corporation	800	2820	=COUNTA(Table1[#All])
East	XYZ	1/4/2008	Tasty Kettle Inc.	400	Count all data cells in the table	
East	ABC	1/7/2008	Remarkable Meter Corporation	400	2815	=COUNTA(Table1[#Data])
East	DEF	1/7/2008	Wonderful Jewelry Inc.	1000	Count the header cells	
Central	ABC	1/9/2008	Remarkable Meter Corporation	800	5	=COUNTA(Table1[#Headers])
Central	XYZ	1/10/2008	Safe Flagpole Supply	800	Count the number of cells in the Product column for this row	
Central	ABC	1/12/2008	Reliable Tripod Company	800	563	=COUNTA(Table1[Product])
East	XYZ	1/14/2008	Matchless Vise Inc.	100	Count the date and header cells in the Date column	
East	ABC	1/15/2008	Bright Hairpin Company	500	564	=COUNTA(Table1[[#Headers],[#Data],[Date]])
East	ABC	1/18/2008	Appealing Calculator Corporation	600		

Figure 5.9   *Column I has examples of using specifiers to return table information.*

Using Array Formulas

> Array formulas cannot be created in the Web App, but they will still calculate in an uploaded file.

An *array* holds multiple values individually in a single cell. An *array formula* allows you to do calculations with those individual values.

It's hard to imagine, but three keys on your keyboard can turn the right formula into a SUPER formula. Three keys can take 10,000 individual formulas and reduce them to a single formula. These three keys are Ctrl+Shift+Enter. Enter the right type of formula in a cell, but instead of just pressing Enter, press Ctrl+Shift+Enter and the formula becomes an array formula, also known as a CSE formula.

For example, with an array formula you can do the following:

- Multiply corresponding cells together and return the sum or average, as shown in Example 2.

- Return a list of the top nth items in a list, while calculating the value by which you are judging their rank, as shown in Example 3.

- Sum (or average) only numbers that meet a certain condition, such as falling between a specified range.

- Count the number or records that match multiple criteria.

Example 1

Look at Figure 5.10. The ROW function returns the row number of what is in the parentheses. In columns A and B, you see the result of a normally entered ROW function looking at rows 1:10—1's all the way down because the formula can only return the first value it holds. In columns C and D, you see the same formula, but entered as an array formula. This time, you can see each value held in the function—the numbers 1 through 10.

	A	B	C	D
1	Normal Formula		Array Formula	
2	1	=ROW($1:$10)	1	{=ROW(1:10)}
3	1	=ROW($1:$10)	2	{=ROW(1:10)}
4	1	=ROW($1:$10)	3	{=ROW(1:10)}
5	1	=ROW($1:$10)	4	{=ROW(1:10)}
6	1	=ROW($1:$10)	5	{=ROW(1:10)}
7	1	=ROW($1:$10)	6	{=ROW(1:10)}
8	1	=ROW($1:$10)	7	{=ROW(1:10)}
9	1	=ROW($1:$10)	8	{=ROW(1:10)}
10	1	=ROW($1:$10)	9	{=ROW(1:10)}
11	1	=ROW($1:$10)	10	{=ROW(1:10)}

Figure 5.10   *Normally, the formula in B2:B11 would return only a single value. But enter the same formula as an array formula and range C2:C11 shows the individual values held in the array formula.*

Example 2

Figure 5.11 goes to the next step, multiplying each value in the array by 2 as shown in columns H and I. In cell H10, you include the SUM array formula, which not only multiplies each value in array by 2, but adds the results. Imagine if you had a sheet with 10,000 quantities and prices. Instead of multiplying each row into a new column and then summing that column, you just have one cell that does the entire calculation. And because you have fewer formulas, the workbook is smaller.

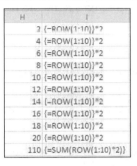

Figure 5.11   *The array formula in H11 multiplies each value in the array and sums the results.*

Example 3

An array formula can also return multiple values. These values are placed within the range selected before entering the formula.

For example, if you wanted to return the region, product, and date of the top three revenue generators for the data in Figure 5.12, you would use a formula like this:

```
=INDEX(A1:A46 & "-" & B1:B46 & " on " &
TEXT(C1:C46,"mm/dd/yy"),MATCH(LARGE(D2:D46*E2:E46,{1;2;3}),(D1:D46*E1:E46)
,0))
```

Figure 5.12   *An array formula can be used to return multiple values, such as the top three revenue makers.*

1. Look for the three largest revenues at the same time they're being calculated, like this:

    ```
    LARGE(D2:D46*E2:E46,{1;2;3})
    ```

LARGE is a function that returns the nth largest value in a range, which we are creating by multiplying corresponding values in columns D and E (D2*E2, D2*E3 and so forth). In this case, we are looking top three items and place 1;2;3 in curly brackets. By placing the numbers manually in curly brackets separated by semi-colons (;), we're identifying them as an array.

2. Now that we have the top three values, we have to locate them within the range, like this:

   `MATCH(LARGE(D2:D46*E2:E46,{1;2;3}),(D1:D46*E1:E46),0)`

   MATCH returns the row numbers of the calculated revenues by matching their location within an array of the calculated revenues. The 0 tells the function we need an exact match to the values.

3. The formula now holds the rows that the three largest values are found in. The INDEX function is then used to look up and return the desired details from those rows.

4. After you select three cells, type the entire formula and enter it by pressing Ctrl+Shift+Enter, Excel copies the formula down to each of the three cells. The first cell returns the first answer in the calculated array, the second cell returns the second value in the calculated array, and the third cell returns the third value.

When an array formula is holding more than one calculated value, you must select a range at least the size of the most values it is returning before entering it and pressing the CSE combination. If the range selected is too small, only some of the values will be returned. If the range selected is too large, an error will appear in the extra cells. Because you have the same formula in multiple cells, the workbook is smaller; Excel has to track only a single formula.

TELL ME MORE   Media 5.2—Typing an Array Within an Array

You can listen to a free audio recording about how to type an array in a formula when you log on to my.safaribooksonline.com/9780132182287/media.

Editing Array Formulas

Following are a few rules to use when editing multicell array formulas:

- You cannot edit just one cell of an array formula. A change made to one cell affects them all.

- You can increase the size of the range, but not decrease it. To decrease it, you must delete the formula and reenter it.

- You cannot move just a part of the range, but you can move the entire range.

- The range must be continuous—you cannot insert blank cells within it.

Deleting Array Formulas

You cannot delete just one cell of an array formula. The entire range containing the array formula must be selected before you can delete it. The message You Cannot Change Part of an Array will appear if you try to delete just a portion of the range containing the formula. You can use Go to Special, Current Array to select the entire array.

If you need to resize an array to be smaller, you will have to delete and reenter it.

LET ME TRY IT

Deleting an Array Formula

Follow these steps to select an entire array formula and delete it:

1. Select a cell in the array formula.

2. Press Ctrl+G to bring up the Go To dialog.

3. Click the Special button in the lower-left corner of the dialog.

4. Select Current Array and click OK.

5. Press Delete on the keyboard to delete the entire array formula range.

Troubleshooting Formulas

It can be frustrating to enter a formula and have it either return an incorrect value or an error. An important part of solving the problem is to understand what the error is trying to tell you. After you have an idea of the problem you're looking for, you can use several tools to look deeper into the error.

For assistance in troubleshooting functions, refer to the section on Using the Wizard to Troubleshoot Formulas in Chapter 6.

Error Messages

After entering a formula, you may run into one of the following errors:

- **#DIV/0!**—Occurs when a number is divided by zero.

- **#N/A**—Occurs when a value isn't available in the formula; for example, if you're doing a lookup function and the lookup value isn't found.

- **#NAME?**—Occurs when a formula includes unrecognizable text.

- **#NULL!**—Occurs when an intersection is specified but the areas do not intersect or if a range operator is incorrect. For example, if you entered =SUM(A1:A10 B1:B10), you would get the error because the error separating the ranges is missing. The correct formula would be =SUM(A1:A10,B1:B10).

- **#NUM!**—Occurs when there is an invalid numeric value in a formula or function.

- **#REF!**—Occurs when a cell reference isn't valid; for example, if the cell has been deleted. This can be difficult to trace because the #REF can occur within the formula itself—for example, =#REF*A2—and there's no direct way to trace back to the original reference.

- **#VALUE!**—Occurs when trying to do math with nonnumeric data; for example, D1+D2 will return the error if D1 is the column header.

- **######**—This isn't really an error. It can occur if the column width is not wide enough for the formula result or if you're trying to subtract a later date from an earlier date.

The initial help provided by Excel and Excel Starter may help trace the problem. When an error cell is selected, an exclamation icon appears from which you can select Trace Error. If Trace Error is selected, blue and red lines will appear on the sheet, as shown in Figure 5.13. A red arrow will connect to the first cell causing a problem. From that cell, blue lines will appear, pointing out the cells used in that cell's formula. In Figure 5.13, the culprits are the 0 quantities being used in the Price Per calculation.

Trace Precedents and Dependents

When you select a cell containing a formula and press F2, Excel highlights any cells on the sheet that are used by the formula, but it doesn't highlight the cells on other sheets. To do that and more, use the trace precedent and trace dependent auditing arrows.

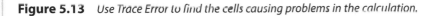

	0	20770	8470	38	#DIV/0!
	900	17505	7623	9882	19.45
	800	14136	6776	7360	17.67
	600	10602	5082	5520	17.67
	400	8016	3388	4628	20.04
	400	7520	3388	4132	18.8
	100	1817	847	970	18.17
	800	15288	6776	8512	19.11
	500	8715	4235	4480	17.43
	0	17136	7623	9513	#DIV/0!
	800	11922	5000	6910	19.87
	300	6309	2541	3768	21.03
	300	5592	2541	3051	18.64
	1000	21120	8470	12650	21.12
					#DIV/0!

Figure 5.13   *Use Trace Error to find the cells causing problems in the calculation.*

Use the formula auditing arrows found on the Formulas tab in the Formula Auditing group if you have a cell you want to trace, whether it's to locate other cells used in that cell's formula or what cells reference the selected cell. Just select the cell in question and click a trace button.

There are two types of auditing arrows:

- **Trace Precedents**—If the selected cell contains a formula, arrows will point to the cells used by the formula.

- **Trace Dependents**—If the selected cell is used in a formula in another cell, arrows will point to the cell containing that formula.

When you click one of the trace buttons, arrows appear, linking the cell to other cells that are directly connected to it, as shown in Figure 5.14. Click the trace button again and you will get the next level of cell connections. You can continue to click the button and Excel will continue adding tracing arrows to the sheet.

If the connecting cell is on another sheet, Excel will display a dashed arrow pointing to a sheet icon, as shown in Figure 5.14. If you double-click the line, a Go To dialog will appear, listing every cell containing a link to the selected cell. You can then double-click one of the listed items and be brought directly to the linked cell.

To clear all the arrows, select Formulas, Formula Auditing, Remove Arrows. There is no way to go back just one level or remove one type of arrow.

Precedent Arrow   Trace to Other Sheet

300	5886	2541	3345	19.62
200	3922	16⊞	2228	19.61
100	1861	847	1014	18.61
0	20770	8470	12300	#DIV/0!
900	17505	7623	9882	19.45
800	14136	6776	7360	17.67
600	10602	5082	5520	17.67
400	8016	3388	4628	20.04
400	7520	3388	4132	18.8
100	1817	847	970	18.17
800	15288	6776	8512	19.11
500	8715	4235	4480	17.43
0	17136	7623	9513	#DIV/0!
600	11922	5082	6840	19.87
300	6309	2541	3768	21.03
300	5592	2541	3051	18.64
1000	21120	8470	12650	21.12
				#DIV/0!

—Dependent Arrow

Figure 5.14   *Use the Trace Precedents and Trace Dependents buttons to locate links to the selected cell, including links to other sheets.*

Watch Window

The Watch Window found in the Formula Auditing group of the Formulas tab allows you to watch a cell update as you make changes that will affect it. This can be useful when you have formulas that span multiple sheets and you need to watch a cell on one sheet while you make changes to another.

Double-click a cell in the Watch Window to jump to that cell.

 **LET ME TRY IT**

Watching a Formula Update on Another Sheet

To watch a formula update on another sheet, follow these steps:

1. Select Formulas, Formula Auditing, Watch Window. The Watch Window dialog appears.

2. Click Add Watch to bring up the Add Watch dialog.

3. Select the cell you want to watch update and click Add.

4. Repeat steps 2 and 3 for any additional cells that you want to monitor.

5. Leave the Watch Window open and make changes to cells that will affect the watched cells.

6. Whether directly linked or not, if the watched cells are in any way affected by the changes you make, the Watch Window will update to reflect the new value of the cell.

Evaluating Formulas

If you want to watch how Excel calculates each part of a formula, you can use Formulas, Formula Auditing, Evaluate Formula.

The Evaluate Formula window has three buttons you can use to investigate a formula. The buttons will work only on the underlined portion of the formula:

- **Evaluate**—Replaces the underlined portion of the formula with the value.

- **Step In**—Displays the actual contents of a cell if the underlined portion is a cell address. This may be a value or a formula. If it's a formula, you have the option to continue stepping in until it is resolved.

- **Step Out**—Returns to the previous level of evaluation.

You can continue to evaluate a formula until it is completely resolved.

SHOW ME   Media 5.3—Evaluating a Formula
You can watch a free video of this task when you log on to my.safaribooksonline.com/9780132182287/media.

LET ME TRY IT

Using Evaluate to Watch a Formula Calculate

To see how Excel is calculating a formula, follow these steps:

1. Select the cell with the formula to evaluate.

2. Select Formulas, Formula Auditing, Evaluate Formula.

3. The formula appears in the evaluation window with some part of it underlined.

4. Click the Step In button if it is activated. If it isn't, skip to step 8.

5. A new section appears in the window, showing the result of the underlined portion.

6. Repeat steps 4 and 5 if the Step In button is still active.

7. When the Step In button is no longer active, click the Step Out button to return to the previous level. Each click of the button returns you to the previous level.

8. Click the Evaluate button and Excel will evaluate the underlined portion, replacing it in the formula with the returned or calculated value.

9. Continue to click Evaluate or Step In to watch the formula calculate.

10. Excel is done with the evaluation when only the calculated value appears in the Evaluation field. You can either click Restart to go through the steps again, or click Close to return to Excel.

Evaluating with F9

With the Evaluate Window, you have to go in the order that Excel calculates the formula. If you want to jump directly to a portion of the formula, you can highlight that portion and press F9 to evaluate to its value.

You should keep two things in mind when using F9 to evaluate a formula:

- When highlighting the portion to evaluate, you must be careful to select the entire portion, including any relevant parentheses.

- You must press Esc to leave the cell. If you don't, Excel will replace your formula with the value you just evaluated to.

This chapter will show you methods for finding the right function. It also reviews some functions you may find useful for everyday use.

6

Using Functions

Excel offers more than 400 functions. These include logical functions, lookup functions, statistical functions, financial functions and more. This chapter shows you how to look up functions and reviews some functions helpful for everyday use.

Breaking Down a Function

A function is like a shortcut for using a long or complex formula. You've probably used the SUM function like this: =SUM(A1:A5). Without the function, you would have to enter =A1+A2+A3+A4+A5.

Normally, the syntax of a function is like this:

```
FunctionName(Argument1, Argument2, ...)
```

A function consists of the name used to call it. It may or may not include arguments, which are variables used in the calculation. In the previous SUM function, the argument was A1:A5.

- Arguments must be entered in the order required by the function.

- Arguments must be separated by commas.

- Arguments can be cell references, numbers, logicals, or text.

- Some arguments are optional. Optional arguments are placed after the required ones.

- If you skip an optional argument to use one after it, you still have to place a comma for the one you skipped.

- Some functions, such as NOW(), do not require arguments, but the parentheses must still be included in the formula.

Finding Functions

You can always use Excel's Help to find a function, but you may get more than just the function information you're looking for. Instead, narrow down the results by using tools provided for specifically searching functions.

The Formulas tab has a Function Library group with drop-downs grouped by function type. Selecting any function listed in a drop-down will open it up in the formula wizard.

If you aren't sure which function you need, or if you need more help in using a function, there are several ways of bringing up the Insert Function dialog, which will help you find the required function:

- Select the More Functions link at the bottom of the AutoSum drop-down on the Home or Formulas tab.

- Select the Insert Function link at the bottom of one of the other function library drop-downs on the Formulas tab.

- Click the Insert Function button in the Function Library group on the Formulas tab.

- Click the fx button by the formula bar.

Entering Functions

After you know which function you want to use, you can enter it using two ways: through the formula wizard or directly in the cell.

> The only help available in the Web App is a drop-down list of available functions. There is no assistance with figuring out which function you need or its arguments.

The Formula Wizard

In the first step of the formula wizard, you select a function from the Insert Function dialog, as described in the previous section, "Finding Functions." The second step is the Function Arguments dialog, shown in Figure 6.1. It assists in entering the arguments for the selected function.

A field exists for each argument. If the function has a variable number of arguments, like the SUM function, a new field will be automatically added when needed. The following list identifies the parts of the Function Arguments dialog shown in Figure 6.1.

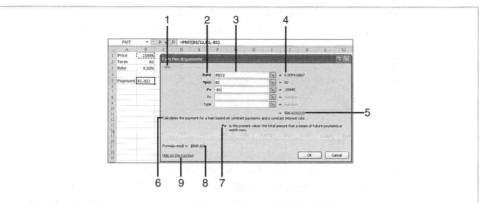

Figure 6.1 *The Function Arguments dialog helps with the arguments of the selected function.*

1. The function name.

2. The argument name. Required arguments are bold; optional arguments are not.

3. The field holding cell addresses, values or formulas (even other functions) for the argument.

4. The resolved value of the argument. If a problem exists with the field entry, an error message will appear.

5. The calculated value.

6. Description of the function.

7. Clarification of the current argument.

8. The result that will be placed in the function's cell.

9. A link to Excel's detailed help on the function.

 LET ME TRY IT

Entering a Function Using the Wizard

To insert a function into a cell using the wizard, follow these steps:

1. Select the cell that will hold the formula.

2. Go to Formulas, Function Library, and select a function from one of the drop-downs.

3. Enter the argument in the first field. The argument can be a cell address (you can type it in or select it on the sheet), a value, or a formula.

4. Enter any other additional arguments.

5. If you do not see any error messages, click OK to have the cell accept the formula.

Using In-Cell Tips

If you are already familiar with the function you need, you can begin typing it in the cell directly. After you enter an equal sign and select the first letter of the function, Excel drops down a list of possible functions, narrowing down the list with each letter entered. You can also select from the list using the arrow and Tab keys.

After the function is selected, an in-cell tip appears, as shown in Figure 6.2. The current argument will be in bold. Optional arguments appear in square brackets. If you want to use the Function Arguments dialog, press Ctrl+A after typing the function name in the cell. For more help with the function, click the function name in the tip, and Excel's detailed help file for the function will appear.

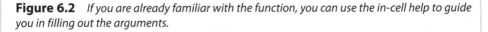

Figure 6.2   *If you are already familiar with the function, you can use the in-cell help to guide you in filling out the arguments.*

If the in-cell help is in the way, you can select the box and drag it out of your way.

 **LET ME TRY IT**

Typing a Function Directly into a Cell

To type a function directly into a cell, follow these steps:

1. Select the cell that will hold the formula.

2. Type an equal sign.

3. Begin typing the name of the function. When the drop-down list appears, you can continue typing or scroll the list to highlight the function and press Tab.

4. Enter the first argument. The argument can be a cell address (you can type it in or select it on the sheet), a value, or a formula.

5. If there is another argument, type a comma and then enter the next argument. Repeat this step for each argument.

6. When you're finished entering all the arguments, type the closing parentheses and press Enter or Tab for the cell to accept the formula.

You don't always have to enter the closing parentheses; sometimes Excel will do it for you. But because the location and need is a guess by Excel, it's best to be in the habit of doing it yourself.

AutoSum

Excel provides one-click access to the SUM function through the AutoSum button found under Home, Editing and Formulas, Function Library.

You can use several ways to apply the AutoSum function to a range of cells:

- Select a cell adjacent to the range and click the AutoSum button.

- Highlight the range including the adjacent cell where you want the formula placed, and then select the AutoSum button.

- If you need to sum multiple ranges, select the entire table, including the adjacent row or column where you want results to appear, and then click the AutoSum button.

 SHOW ME   Media 6.1—Using the AutoSum Functionality
You can watch a free video of this task when you log on to my.safaribooksonline.com/9780132182287/media.

Unless you select the range you want to calculate, Excel will guess which cells you are trying to sum and highlight them. If the selection is correct, press Enter to accept the solution. If the selection is incorrect, make the required changes and then press Enter to accept the solution.

You should keep an eye out for a couple of things when using the AutoSum function:

- Be careful of numeric headings (like years) when letting Excel select the range for you. Excel cannot tell that the heading isn't part of the calculation range, and you will need to correct the selection before accepting the formula.

- Excel will look for a column to sum before a row. In Figure 6.3, the default selection by Excel is the numbers above the selected cell, instead of the adjacent row of numbers.

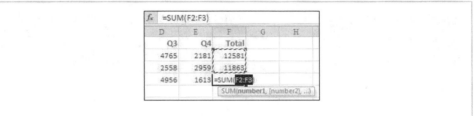

Figure 6.3 *Excel defaults to calculating columns before rows.*

Other Auto Functions

The default action of the AutoSum button is the SUM function, but several other functions are available. To access these other functions, click the drop-down arrow:

- **Sum**—The default action that adds the values in the selected range
- **Average**—Averages the values in the selected range
- **Count Numbers**—Returns the number of cells containing numbers
- **Max**—Returns the largest value in the selected range
- **Min**—Returns the smallest value in the selected range

 **LET ME TRY IT**

Averaging a Range Quickly

To quickly average all the columns of a table, follow these steps:

1. Select all the data in the table. Include a blank row below the table.

2. Go to Home, Editing, and click the drop-down arrow of the AutoSum button.

3. Select Average from the list. Excel calculates the averages for each column of data and places the value at the bottom of the table.

Lookup Functions

This section reviews some of the methods available for looking up a value. In the function's syntax, an argument in square brackets is an optional argument.

CHOOSE

The syntax of the CHOOSE function is

```
CHOOSE(index_num, value1, [value2],...)
```

The CHOOSE function returns a value from the list based on an index number. For example, if the values in the list are 10 through 20 and the index number is 5, the fifth value in the list, 14, is returned.

- If the index_num is a decimal, it will be rounded to the next lowest integer. For example, if it is 4.8, the formula will use 4.

- If the index_num is less than 1 or greater than the number of available values, the function will return a #VALUE! error.

- You can enter 1 to 254 argument values.

- Arguments can be numbers, cell references, names, formulas, functions, or text.

VLOOKUP

The syntax of the VLOOKUP function is

```
VLOOKUP(lookup_value, table_array, col_index_num, [range_lookup])
```

The VLOOKUP function returns a value from the specified column in a table:

- **lookup_value**—The value to match in the leftmost column of the table_array.

- **table_array**—The entire range from which you want to look up and return a value.

- **col_index_num**—The column from the table_array from which to return the value. This is not equivalent to the column heading, but instead is the location of the column in the table. For example, if the table begins in column G and the col_index_num is 2, a value from column H will be returned.

- **range_lookup**—If TRUE or omitted, the table must be in ascending order by the first column for the function to match correctly. The function will attempt to do an exact match. If this isn't possible, it will find the first closest match from the top of the table. If FALSE, the function will only look for an exact match. If not found, a #N/A error will be returned.

Figure 6.4 shows how VLOOKUP can be used to return customer information to an invoice. The customer's name is entered in cell B3. Functions in cells B4:B5 match the customer's name in the table on Sheet2 and return address and phone information. Note the use of IFERROR with VLOOKUP. If an exact match is not found, "Not Available" is entered in the cells, instead of the #N/A error.

	A	B	C	D	E	F	G	H	I
1	Invoice								
2									
3	Customer Name:	Bill Jelen							
4	Street Address:	P.O. Box 56		=IFERROR(VLOOKUP($B$3,Sheet3!$C$2:$E$50,2,FALSE),"Not Available")					
5	Phone:	(555)123-9834		=IFERROR(VLOOKUP($B$3,Sheet3!$C$2:$E$50,3,FALSE),"Not Available")					

Sheet1 Sheet2 Sheet3

	A	B	C	D	E	F	G	H	I
1		Invoice #	Customer Name	Street Address		Phone			
2		Q12378	Thomas Stewart	123 Walnut Street		(555)123-2345			
3		Q12376	Paul Mccartney	789 Elm Avenue		(555)398-2346			
4		Q12356	Bill Jelen	P.O. Box 56		(555)123-9834			
5		Q12348	Jon Tessmer	23 Sands Ave, Suite #1		(555)123-1946			

Sheet1 Sheet2 Sheet3

Figure 6.4   *Use VLOOKUP formulas to return customer information from a table on another sheet.*

VLOOKUP Troubleshooting

If VLOOKUP returns an error or incorrect value but you can manually verify that the lookup value is present in the table, the exact issue may be one of the following:

- The entire cell contents must match 100%. If you're looking up "Bracelet" and the term in the table is "Bracelets," Excel will not return a match.

- Be careful of extra spaces before and after a word. "Bracelet " and "Bracelet" are not matches—the first occurrence has a space at the end.

- If matching numbers, make sure both the lookup value and the matching value are formatted the same type—for example, both as General or one as General and the other as Currency, allowing Excel to still see them as numbers. Sometimes when importing data, numbers get formatted as Text. If you have a lookup value formatted General and the matching value is formatted as Text, Excel will not see this as a match. See the section "Dealing with Formatting Issues" in Chapter 4, "Data Formatting" for instructions on how to force the numbers stored as text to become true numbers.

- Make sure the table_array encompasses the entire table.

MATCH and INDEX

The syntax of the MATCH function is

```
MATCH(lookup_value, lookup_array, [match_type])
```

The syntax of the INDEX function is

```
INDEX(array, row_num, [column_num])
```

There are two syntaxes for the INDEX function, array or reference, but this section will only use the array version.

VLOOKUP works only when returning data from columns to the right of the lookup column. If your data is also to the left of the lookup column, use MATCH and INDEX together.

The MATCH function looks up a value and returns its position (row or column) in an array:

- **lookup_value**—The value to match and return the location of
- **lookup_array**—The range from which to return the location
- **match_type**—A 1, 0, or -1 telling the function how to match the lookup_value
  - If 1, the function returns the largest value that is less than or equal to the lookup_value. The lookup_array must be sorted in ascending order.
  - If 0, the function returns the first value that is an exact match to the lookup_value.
  - If -1, the function returns the smallest value that is greater than or equal to the lookup_value. The lookup_array must be sorted in descending order.

The INDEX function returns a value based on a row and column number:

- **array**—A range of cells from which to return a value.
- **row_num**—The number of the row within the range to return a value from.

- **column_num**—The number of the column within the range to return a value from.

Figure 6.5 shows how the two functions are used to return information to the left of the customer name column. First the MATCH function is used to locate which row in the customer list matches the name. That information is used in the INDEX function to tell it from which row to return the value.

	A	B	C	D	E	F	G
1	Invoice:	Q12356		=INDEX(Sheet3!B1:B5,MATCH(B3,Sheet3!C:C,0),1)			
2							
3	Customer Name:	Bill Jelen					
4	Street Address:	P.O. Box 56					
5	Phone:	(555)123-9834					

Lookup Invoice.xlsm:1

	A	B	C	D	E	F	G
1		Invoice #	Customer Name	Street Address	Phone		
2		Q12378	Thomas Stewart	123 Walnut Street	(555)123-2345		
3		Q12376	Paul Mccartney	789 Elm Avenue	(555)398-2346		
4		Q12356	Bill Jelen	P.O. Box 56	(555)123-9834		
5		Q12348	Jon Tessmer	23 Sands Ave, Suite #1	(555)123-1946		
6							
7							

Sheet1 | Sheet2 | Sheet3

Figure 6.5 *Use MATCH and INDEX to return information located to the left of the customer name.*

TELL ME MORE Media 6.2—Using the INDEX Function

You can listen to a free audio recording about using INDEX and MATCH in a formula when you log on to my.safaribooksonline.com/9780132182287/media.

INDIRECT

The syntax of the INDIRECT function is

```
INDIRECT(ref_text, [a1])
```

The INDIRECT function returns a reference specified by a string, allowing for dynamic cell references. For example, if you have sheet names that are also sales-people names, you can use INDIRECT to build a sheet name reference in a formula based on the salesperson's name, as shown in Figure 6.6. You can change the name in the cell referenced by the function and instantly refer to another sheet.

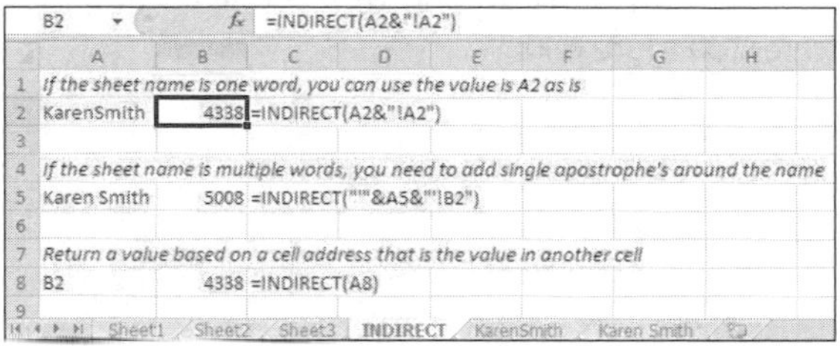

Figure 6.6   *INDIRECT provides flexibility in creating dynamic cell references.*

- **ref_text**—A cell or string reference.
- **a1**—Specifies the type of reference in the cell ref-text. If TRUE or omitted, ref_text is treated as an A1-style reference. If FALSE, the ref-text is treated as an R1C1-style reference.

SUMIFS

The SUMIFS function works only in Excel 2007 and 2010. If sharing the workbook with legacy Excel users, check out the SUMPRODUCT function for summing cells based on multiple criteria.

The syntax of the function is (optional arguments are in square brackets):

```
SUMIFS(sum_range, criteria_range1, criteria1, [criteria_range2, crite-
ria2],...)
```

The SUMIFS function adds up the values in a specified column based on one or more criteria:

- **sum_range**—The range containing the cells to sum
- **criteria_range1**—The range of cells to evaluate for the first criteria
- **criteria1**—A number, expression or text to match in criteria_range1

If you have only a single criteria, you can also use SUMIF, which has similar syntax to SUMIFS.

Key items to keep in mind when entering the criteria arguments in the function (cell references refer to Figure 6.7):

	H5	▼	fx	=SUMIFS($E$2:$E$21,$A$2:$A$21,$G5,$B$2:$B$21,H$4)									
	A	B	C	D	E	F	G	H	I	J	K	L	M
1	Region	Product	Date	Quantity	Revenue								
2	East	XYZ	1/1/2001	1000	22810								
3	Central	DEF	1/2/2001	100	2257		Fill in the table below based on the row and column headers						
4	East	ABC	1/2/2001	500	10245			ABC	DEF	XYZ			
5	Central	XYZ	1/3/2001	500	11240		East	18701	40282	76843			
6	Central	XYZ	1/4/2001	400	9204		Central	31283	2257	41882			
7	East	DEF	1/4/2001	800	18552		West	19110	0	22950			
8	East	XYZ	1/4/2001	400	9152		H5=SUMIFS($E$2:$E$21,$A$2:$A$21,$G5,$B$2:$B$21,H$4)						
9	Central	ABC	1/5/2001	400	6860		I5=SUMIFS($E$2:$E$21,$A$2:$A$21,"East",$B$2:$B$21,"DEF")						
10	East	ABC	1/7/2001	400	8456								
11	East	DEF	1/7/2001	1000	21730		Sum the Revenue between the date range and Quantity less than 600						
12	West	XYZ	1/7/2001	600	13806		1/3/2001	1/5/2001					
13	Central	ABC	1/9/2001	800	16416		25216						
14	East	XYZ	1/9/2001	900	21015		=SUMIFS(E2:E21,C2:C21,">" & H11,C2:C21,"<=" & I11,D2:D21,"<600")						

Figure 6.7   *SUMIFS sums a column based on one or more criteria.*

- Can be a direct cell reference, for example $G5 in the formula shown in H8.

- Words must be entered in quotation marks, for example "East" in the formula shown in H9.

- Equality and inequality symbols (<, >, >=, <=,=, <>) must be placed in quotation marks with the value in the comparison, as shown in H14.

- If using equality and inequality symbols with a cell reference, the cell reference should be outside the quotation marks around the symbol. Also, build the statement using the ampersand (&), as shown in H14.

SUMPRODUCT

The syntax of the function is (optional arguments are in square brackets):

```
SUMPRODUCT(array1, [array2], [array3], ...)
```

The SUMPRODUCT function multiplies corresponding components in the argument arrays and returns the sum of the products. For example, if array1 is A1:A10 and array2 is B1:B10, the function is actually doing this:
```
((A1*B1)+(A2*B2)+(A3*B3)...(A10*B10)).
```

Although the arrays do not have to be the same rows, as in the preceding example, they must be the same size. So if array1 has 10 rows, array2 must also have 10 rows.

The SUMPRODUCT function can also be used as a multiple criteria lookup, returning the sum of the values matching the criteria. This was a common use for the function before SUMIFS was introduced in Excel 2007 and is still useful if you're sending a workbook to legacy Excel users.

The function can deal only with numbers. If the lookup values are strings, Excel has to be tricked into treating them like numbers. You can do this by placing a "—" (two unary minuses) in front of the comparison argument, like this: —(C1:C5="Karen").

When the function does the comparison (C1=Karen), it returns TRUE or FALSE. The first unary minus changes a TRUE to a -1 and a FALSE to -0 (there is no such thing as -0, so you would see 0 only if you looked into it). The second unary minus negates the first, changing TRUE to 1 and FALSE to 0. Now we have 1s and 0s, numbers that can be multiplied together with the value to sum. Figure 6.8 shows a detailed breakdown of how the function works.

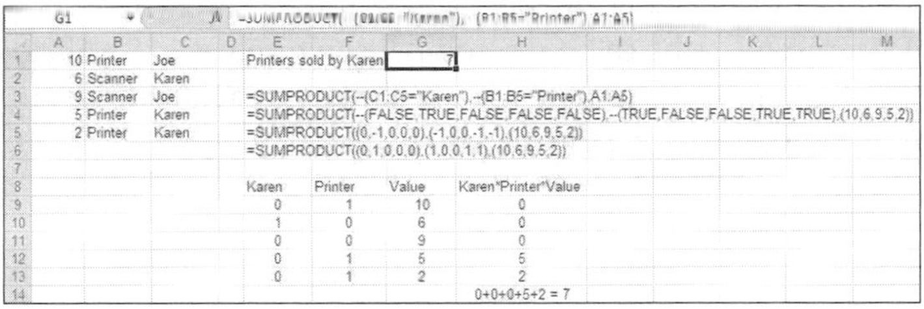

Figure 6.8 *SUMPRODUCT can be used to do a multiple criteria lookup of text values.*

Logical Functions

The logical functions are (optional arguments are in square brackets) as follows:

- **IF**—Specifies a logical text to perform, returning one value if the formula evaluates to TRUE and another if it evaluates to FALSE. The function syntax is

  ```
  IF(logical_test, [value_if_true], [value_if_false])
  ```

- **IFERROR**—Returns the value specified if the formula evaluates to an error; otherwise, returns the result of the formula. The function syntax is

  ```
  IFERROR(value, value_if_error)
  ```

- **AND**—Returns TRUE if *all* its arguments are TRUE. Returns FALSE if any of the arguments evaluate to FALSE. The function syntax is

  ```
  AND(logical1, [logical2], ...)
  ```

- **OR**—Returns TRUE if **any** of its arguments are TRUE. Returns FALSE if all the arguments evaluate to FALSE. The function syntax is

  ```
  OR(logical1, [logical2, ...])
  ```

- **NOT**—Reverses the logic of its arguments. The function syntax is

  ```
  NOT(logical)
  ```

- **TRUE**—Returns TRUE. TRUE can be entered directly into cells and formulas; it is provided as a function for compatibility with other spreadsheet applications.

- **FALSE**—Returns FALSE. FALSE can be entered directly into cells and formulas; it is provided as a function for compatibility with other spreadsheet applications.

IF/AND/OR/NOT

The first argument of an IF statement is a logic test usually using at least one of the comparison operators in Table 6.1. If the comparison resolves to TRUE, the second argument is returned to the cell. If the comparison resolves to FALSE, the third argument is returned. If you were to read an IF statement aloud, it would sound like this: "If this is true, then do this, else do this."

Table 6.1   Comparison Operators

Comparison Operator	Definition	Example
>	Greater than	A1>B1
<	Less than	A1<B1
=	Equal to	A1=100
>=	Greater than or equal to	A1>=0
<=	Less than or equal to	A1<=B1
<>	Not equal to	A1<>"Karen"

The second and third arguments can be numbers, text, formulas, or functions. If text, the words must be enclosed in quotations marks, unless returning TRUE or FALSE, because these are functions in their own right.

AND, OR, and NOT can be used to expand the first argument, allowing multiple comparisons or reversing a comparison. Figure 6.9 shows multiple examples of combining these functions to compare data in multiple ways.

Figure 6.9   *Use AND, OR, or NOT with IF statements to expand on the type of comparisons the function can do.*

Nested IF Statements

A nested IF statement is when an IF statement is used as an argument within an IF statement, like this:

```
=IF(A1>B1, IF(B1>C1,0,IF(D1=C1,D1*B1,A1)))
```

Excel 2007 and 2010 allow 64 nested IF statements, but if you're sharing the workbook with legacy Excel users, you're limited to seven nested IF statements. Also, too many nested IF statements can be difficult to read, though you can use Alt+Enter to force linebreaks in a formula. An alternative is to create a User-Defined Function using Select Case statements. For more information on this, refer to Chapter 13, "Macros and UDFs."

IFERROR

The IFERROR function works only in Excel 2007 and 2010. If you're sharing the workbook with legacy Excel users, you will not be able to use this function.

If there's a chance a formula may return an error, use the IFERROR function to prevent the error from appearing in the cell. Instead of an error, a text message or other value may appear.

In Figure 6.10, the top table uses a straightforward division formula to calculate the unit price. In F9, the column is summed, but returns an error because of the error in F5.

The bottom table in Figure 6.10 uses IFERROR to return the text "No Sales" if an error occurs in the calculation, as shown in F12. In F17, the SUM formula is used again, but this time there isn't an error in the range to throw Excel off, and so the sum is calculated.

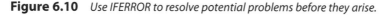

	A	B	C	D	E	F	G	H	I
1	Region	Product	Date	Quantity	Revenue	Unit Price			
2	East	XYZ	1/1/2001	1000	22810	22.81			
3	Central	DEF	1/2/2001	100	2257	22.57			
4	East	ABC	1/2/2001	500	10245	20.49			
5	Central	XYZ	1/3/2001	0	0	#DIV/0!	=E5/D5		
6	Central	XYZ	1/4/2001	400	9204	23.01			
7	East	DEF	1/4/2001	800	18552	23.19			
8	East	XYZ	1/4/2001	500	11240	22.48			
9						#DIV/0!	=SUM(F2:F8)		
10									
11	Central	ABC	1/5/2001	400	8456	21.14			
12	East	ABC	1/7/2001	0	0	No Sales	=IFERROR(E12/D12,"No Sales")		
13	East	DEF	1/7/2001	1000	21730	21.73			
14	West	XYZ	1/7/2001	600	13806	23.01			
15	Central	ABC	1/9/2001	800	16416	20.52			
16	East	XYZ	1/9/2001	900	21015	23.35			
17						109.75	=SUM(F11:F16)		

Figure 6.10   *Use IFERROR to resolve potential problems before they arise.*

Date and Time Functions

Dates and times in Excel are not stored the same way we're used to seeing them. For example, you may type 4/19/10 into a cell, but Excel actually sees 40287. That number, 40287, is called a date serial number. The formatted value, 4/19/10, is called a date value. Storing dates and times as serial numbers allows Excel to do date and time calculations.

Time serial numbers are stored as decimals, starting at 0.0 for 12:00 a.m. and ending at 0.999305556 for 11:59 p.m. The rest of the day's decimal values are equivalent to their calculated percentage, based on the number of hours in a day, 24. For example, 1:00 a.m. is 1/24 or .04166. 6:00 p.m. would be the 18th hour of the day, 18/24 = 0.75.

Understanding how Excel stores dates and times is important so that you can successfully use formulas and functions when calculating with dates and times.

You might already be familiar with the functions that return the system date and time. DATE() returns the system date. NOW() returns the system date and time. The next few sections review additional functions in Excel for dealing with dates and times.

Convert and Breakdown Dates

Table 6.2 lists the functions that can convert a date value to its serial value, or vice versa. It also lists the functions that can return part of a date, such as the month. The date used in the examples is April 19, 2010.

Table 6.2   Date Conversion Functions

Function	Description	Example
DATE (year, month, day)	Returns the serial number of a date. Note: since Excel automatically reformats date cells, you may have to format the cell to General yourself.	=DATE(2010,4,19) returns 40287
DATEVALUE (date_text)	Converts a text date to a serial number. Note: if you try to use a date value, the function will return an error.	=DATEVALUE("4/19/10") returns 40287
DAY (serial_number)	Returns the day from a serial number.	=DAY(40287) returns 19
MONTH (serial_number)	Returns the month from a serial number.	=MONTH(DATEVALUE("4/19/10")) returns 4
YEAR (serial_number)	Returns the year from a serial number.	=YEAR(40287) returns 2010
EDATE[1] (start_date, months)	Returns the serial number of the date indicated by the months before or after the start date. Note that the start_date must be the serial number of the date.	=EDATE(DATEVALUE("4/19/10"),3.5) returns 40378, which is 7/19/2010
EOMONTH[1] (start_date, months)	Returns the serial number of the last day of the month indicated by the months before or after the start date. Note that the start_date must be the serial number of the date.	=EOMONTH(40287, -3.5) returns 40209, which is 1/30/2010
WEEKDAY (serial_number, [return_type])	Converts a serial number to a day of the week. Return_type is a value expressing what Excel should consider the first and last day of the week. The default is 1, meaning 1 is Sunday and 7 is Saturday.	=WEEKDAY(40287) returns 2, which is Monday. =WEEKDAY(40287,3) returns 0 because the value 3 code tells the function to count Monday as the beginning of the week starting with 0 and ending with 6 for Sunday.
WEEKNUM[1] (serial_number, [return_type])	Converts a serial number to a week number representing what week of the year the date falls on. Return_type is a value expressing what day of the week is the beginning of the week.	=WEEKNUM(40287) returns 17, with the week starting on Sunday. =WEEKNUM(40287,12) returns 16 because the week doesn't begin until Tuesday.

[1]*Function was originally part of the Analysis Toolpak. If you send the workbook to a legacy Excel user who does not have the toolpak installed or active, the function will return an error.*

Convert and Breakdown Times

Table 6.3 lists the functions that can convert a time value to its serial value or vice versa. It also lists the functions that can return a part of a time, such as the hour. The time used in the examples is 4:53 p.m.

Table 6.3   Time Conversion Functions

Function	Description	Example
TIME (hour, minute, second)	Returns the serial number of the specified time based on a 24-hour clock	=TIME(16,53,0) returns 4:53 PM
TIMEVALUE (time_text)	Converts a time in the form of text to a serial number	=TIMEVALUE("4:53 PM") returns 0.70347
HOUR (serial_number)	Returns the hour in a serial number, based on a 24-hour clock	=HOUR(0.70347) returns 16, which is 4 PM
MINUTE (serial_number)	Returns the minutes in a serial number	=MINUTE(TIMEVALUE("4:53 PM")) returns 53
SECOND (serial_number)	Returns the seconds in a serial number	=SECOND(0.70347) returns 0

Date Calculation Functions

The following functions were originally part of the Analysis Toolpak add-in. If you send the workbook to a legacy Excel user who does not have the add-in installed or active, the function will return an error.

Table 6.4 lists functions that return calculated information, such as the end date based on a starting date, or the number of days between two dates. The date used in the examples is April 19, 2010.

Table 6.4   Date Calculation Functions

Function	Description	Example
WORKDAY (start_date, days, [holidays])	Returns the serial number of the date before or after a specified number of workdays. Holidays can be a range of dates, or an array constant list of serial dates.	=WORKDAY(DATEVALUE("4/19/2010"),3) returns 40290, which is 4/22/2010 =WORKDAY(DATEVALUE("4/19/2010"),60,{40329, 40363}) 40329 is the serial value of May 31, 2010. 40363 Is the serial value of July 4, 2010. Note that DATEVALUE could not be used within the array constant. Also the curly brackets were entered manually; this is not an array formula.
WORKDAY.INTL (start_date, days, [weekend], [holidays])	Returns the serial number of the date before or after a specified number of workdays, taking into account which days during the week are considered weekends and what dates are holidays. Weekend is a code value. Holidays can be a range of dates, or an array constant list of serial dates.	=WORKDAY.INTL(4287,10,3) returns 40300, which is 5/2/2010. The code value of 3 told Excel Monday, Tuesday were to be considered weekends.
NETWORKDAYS (start_date, end_date, [holidays])	Returns the number of workdays between two dates. Holidays can be a range of dates, or an array constant list of serial dates.	=NETWORKDAYS(40287,DATEVALUE("4/30/10")) returns 10.
NETWORKDAYS.INTL (start_date, end_date, [weekend], [holidays])	Returns the number of workdays between two days, taking into account which days during the week are considered weekends and what dates are holidays. Weekend is a code value. Holidays can be a range of dates, or an array constant list of serial dates.	=NETWORKDAYS.INTL(40287,DATEVALUE("4/30/10"),3) returns 8. The code value of 3 told Excel Monday, Tuesday were to be considered weekends.
YEARFRAC (start_date, end_date, [basis])	Returns a decimal year value of the number of whole days between dates. Basis is a code value of the type of date count basis to use.	=YEARFRAC(DATE(2008,1,1),DATE(2009,1,1)) returns 1. The basic count of 0, the default, instructs Excel to count the days based on 30/360 American plan. =YEARFRAC(DATE(2008,1,1),DATE(2009,1,1),3) returns 1.002739. The basis code of 3 instructs Excel to count the actual days between the dates divided by 365.

Troubleshooting: Calculating with Dates

As long as the dates on a sheet are serial dates, you can perform a variety of calculations with them.

Calculate Days Between Dates

If you need to find the number of days between two dates on a sheet, you can enter a direct formula, such as =F21-F20. After pressing Enter, you may get an odd answer, such as 1/25/1900. You didn't have the cell formatted as date, but because the variables were dates, Excel feels the answer should be formatted as one. There's nothing you can do about this—you will have to manually format the cell as general to get the actual number of days between the dates.

If you get a ###### error, the formula is trying to subtract a new date from an older date.

Dates Stored as Strings

If you receive a sheet where the dates are stored as strings (you may see '4/19/10 in a cell), there are two ways to convert the dates: either using Paste Special to add a blank cell onto the range or using text to columns to convert the column.

 **LET ME TRY IT**

Using Paste Special to Convert Text to Dates

To convert text dates to real dates using paste special, follow these steps:

1. Copy a blank cell.

2. Select the range of text dates to convert.

3. Go to Home, Clipboard, Paste, Paste Special, and select Add.

4. Click OK and the text dates will convert to dates that can be formatted and that Excel can do calculations with.

LET ME TRY IT

Using Text to Columns to Convert Text to Dates

To convert a column of text dates to real dates using text to columns, follow these steps:

1. Select the range of text dates.

2. Go to Data, Data Tools, Text to Columns.

3. From the wizard dialog that appears, click Next twice to reach step 3 of the wizard. You can go with the default settings of the first two steps.

4. In step 3, select the Date option and select the desired format.

5. Click Finish and the text dates will convert to dates that can be formatted and that Excel can do calculations with.

Calculating Overtime

You have a sheet similar to the one in Figure 6.11 where start and end times are entered; then the number of hours worked each day are calculated by subtracting the start time from the end time. At the end of the week, all the times are added together—and you get a number that is most definitely not correct, as shown in D7.

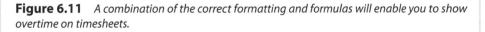

Figure 6.11 *A combination of the correct formatting and formulas will enable you to show overtime on timesheets.*

The problem isn't the method of summing the column, but instead, the format applied to the cell. The standard format of h:mm can't handle more than 24 hours. To get Excel to show more than 24 hours, change the format of the calculated cell to [h]:mm.

See the section on date and time formatting in Chapter 4, "Data Formatting," for more details on time formats.

SHOW ME   Media 6.3—Calculating Times Over 24 Hours
You can watch a free video of this task when you log on to
my.safaribooksonline.com/9780132182287/media.

LET ME TRY IT

Calculating Overtime

If you have a sheet with daily work times, and you need to calculate the total number of hours worked and also the overtime, follow these steps:

1. For each workday, calculate the time elapsed, as shown in cell E2 of Figure 6.11.

2. Select the range of elapsed time.

3. Go to Home, Editing, and click the AutoSum button.

4. Right-click the cell containing the totaled time and select Format Cells.

5. On the Number tab, select the Custom Category.

6. In the Type field, enter [h]:mm. Click OK to return to the sheet.

7. In the overtime cell, enter a MAX function that returns the greater of 0 or the calculated overtime. To calculate the overtime, divide the number at which overtime begins (example 40) by 24. Take that calculation and subtract it from the calculated time, as shown in D9.

8. Right-click the cell containing the overtime and select Format Cells.

9. On the Number tab, select the Custom Category.

10. In the Type field, enter [h]:mm. Click OK to return to the sheet. This is a precaution in case the amount of overtime exceeds 24 hours.

Data Analysis Tools

The Analysis Toolpak is an add-in that adds the Data Analysis button to the Data tab. The tool contains a variety of functions to assist in statistical and engineering analysis, as shown in Table 6.5.

Table 6.5   Data Analysis Tools

Tool	Description
Anova: Single Factor	Measures variance for two or more samples with a single variable.
Anova: Two-Factor with Replication	Measures variance for two or more samples with two variances.
Anova: Two-Factor without Replication	Measures variance for two or more samples with two variances, allowing for only a single observation per pair.
Correlation	Measures the extent to which two measurement variables vary together, independent of the units involved. Coefficients are scaled to lie between -1 and +1, inclusive.
Covariance	Measures the extent to which two measurement variables vary together. Coefficients are not scaled.
Descriptive Statistics	Generates a report of univariate statistics for data in the input range, providing information about the central tendency and variability of the data.
Exponential Smoothing	Predicts a value that is based on the forecast for the prior period, adjusted for the error in that prior forecast.
F-Test Two-Sample for Variances	Performs a two-sample F-test to compare two population variances.
Fourier Analysis	Uses the Fast Fourier Transform method to solve problems in linear systems and analyze periodic data.
Histogram	Calculates individual and cumulative frequencies for a cell range of data and data bins.
Moving Average	Projects values in the forecast period, based on the average value of the variable over a specific number of preceding periods.
Random Number Generator	Fills a range with independent random numbers drawn from one of several distributions.
Rank and Percentile	Produces a table containing the ordinal and percentage rank of each value in a data set.
Regression	Performs linear regression analysis using the least squares method to fit a line through a set of observations.
Sampling	Creates a sample from a population by treating the input range as a population.
t-Test: Paired Two Sample for Means	Tests for equality of the population means underlying the sample by assuming the two samples represent before-treatment and after-treatment observations on the same subjects.
t-Test: Two-Sample Assuming Equal Variances	Tests for equality of the population means underlying the sample by assuming the population variances are equal.
t-Test: Two-Sample Assuming Unequal Variances	Tests for equality of the population means underlying the sample by assuming the population variances are not equal.

Table 6.5   Data Analysis Tools

Tool	Description
z-Test: Two Sample for Means	Performs a two sample z-Test for means with known variances.

To enable the Analysis Toolpak:

1. Go to File, Options, Add-Ins.

2. From the Manage drop-down at the bottom of the Excel Options dialog, select Excel Add-ins and click Go.

3. Select Analysis ToolPak from the Add-ins dialog.

   If Analysis ToolPak is not listed, click Browse to locate it.

   If prompted that the Analysis ToolPak is not currently installed on the computer, click Yes to install it.

4. Click OK and Excel will load the add-in. It will be available whenever Excel is opened.

For detailed help on using the data analysis tools, see *Microsoft Excel 2010 In Depth*, by Bill Jelen (ISBN 0-7897-4308-6).

Goal Seek

Goal Seek, found under Data, Data Tools, What-If Analysis, adjusts the value of a cell to get a specific result from another cell. For example, if you have the price, term, and rate of a loan, you can use the PMT function to calculate the payment. But what if the calculated payment wasn't satisfactory and you wanted to recalculate with additional prices? You could take the time to enter a variety of prices, recalculating the payment. Or use Goal Seek to tell Excel what you want the payment to be and let it calculate the price for you.

SHOW ME   Media 6.4—Using Goal Seek to Return a Value
You can watch a free video of this task when you log on to my.safaribooksonline.com/9780132182287/media.

 **LET ME TRY IT**

Using Goal Seek

To use Goal Seek to return a value, follow these steps:

1. Select the cell whose value you want to be a specific value.

2. Go to Data, Data Tools, What-If Analysis, Goal Seek.

3. In the Set Cell field should be the address of the cell selected in step 1. If not, select the cell whose value you want sought.

4. In the To Value field, enter the value you want the Set Cell to be.

5. In the By Changing Cell field, select the cell whose value you want Excel to change so the Set Cell field calculates to the desired value.

6. Click OK. Excel will attempt to return a solution as close to the desired value as possible.

Using the Wizard to Troubleshoot Formulas

If you have one function using other functions as arguments and the formula returns an error, you can use the function wizard to track down which function is generating the error. To do this, place your cursor in the function name in the formula bar and click the fx button. The function wizard will open, with the selected function filled in. You can review the arguments to make sure they are correct and falling into the correct fields. To check the next function, click the function name in the formula bar—you do not need to close the wizard and start from the beginning.

 LET ME TRY IT

Troubleshooting a Formula

To troubleshoot a formula through the function wizard, follow these steps:

1. Select the cell with the formula to troubleshoot.

2. Click one of the functions in the formula bar.

3. Click the fx button to the left of the formula bar. The Function Arguments dialog (also known as the function wizard) appears for the selected function, with its arguments filled in.

4. If you see the error in the selected function, you can fix it and click OK to recalculate the formula. Otherwise, continue to the next step.

5. If you do not see what is causing the error, click another function in the formula bar. Repeat this step until you have inspected all the functions or resolved the issue.

This chapter will show you the various ways you can sort your data, even by color.

7

Sorting

Sorting data is a significant capability in Excel, allowing you to view data from least to greatest, greatest to least, by color, or even by your own customized sort listing. This chapter shows you the variety of ways you can sort your data in Excel.

Preparing Data

Your data should adhere to a few basic formatting guidelines to make the most of Excel's sorting capabilities:

- There should be no blank rows or columns. The occasional blank cell is acceptable.

- Every column should have a header.

- Headers should be in only one row; otherwise, Excel gets confused and is unable to find the header row on its own.

Sorting in the Web App

The sorting capabilities in the Web App are not nearly as extensive as the ones in Excel and Excel Starter, reviewed in the rest of this chapter. To sort in the Web App, select a cell in the data and click Home, Tables, Sort & Filter as Table. Excel will verify the data range before turning it into a table. After the range is a table, you can select to sort a column ascending or descending by clicking the filter arrow in the column header and selecting Sort Ascending or Sort Descending.

The Sort Dialog

The Sort dialog has four entry points:

- On the Home tab, select Editing, Sort & Filter, Custom Sort.

- On the Data tab, select Sort & Filter, Sort (this works only for Excel, not Excel

Starter or the Web App).

- Right-click any cell and select Sort, Custom Sort.

- From a filter drop-down, select Sort by Color, Custom Sort.

The Sort dialog allows up to 64 sort levels. Through the dialog, you can sort multiple columns by values, cell color, font color, or by conditional formatting icons. The sort order can be ascending, descending, or by a custom list (see the section on Sorting Non-Alphabetically for more information on custom lists). If your data has headers, they will be listed in the Sort by drop-down; otherwise, the column headings will be used.

Sorting by Values

When you use the Sort dialog, Excel applies each sort in the order it appears in the list. In Figure 7.1, the Region column will be sorted first. The second column to be sorted will be the Customer column. When you look at the data after it is sorted, you'll notice the regions are grouped together; for example, Central will be at the top of the list. Within Central, the customer names will be alphabetized. If you scroll down to the next region, East, the customer names will be alphabetized within that region. If the data should have listed the customers and then the regions, the two sort fields need to be switched so that Excel sorts the Customer field first and the Region field second.

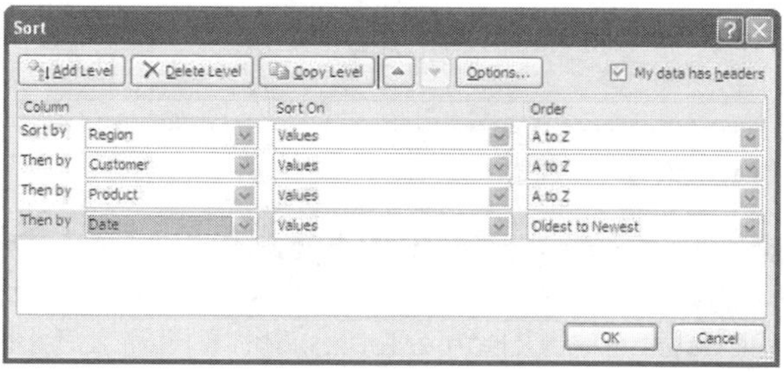

Figure 7.1   *Use the Sort dialog to sort data by multiple levels.*

SHOW ME   **Media 7.1—Sorting Values with the Sort Dialog**
Access this video file through your registered web edition at
my.safaribooksonline.com/9780132182287/media.

 **LET ME TRY IT**

Sorting Values

To sort data by values, follow these steps:

1. Ensure that the data has no blank rows or columns and that each column has a one-row header.

2. Select a cell in the data. Excel will use this cell to determine the location and size of the data.

3. Go to Home, Editing, Sort & Filter, Custom Sort to open the Sort dialog.

4. Make sure the My Data Has Headers check box is selected. Excel will not select the headers themselves.

5. Make sure all the data's columns are selected. If they are not all selected, a blank column exists, confusing Excel as to the size of your data.

6. From the Sort By drop-down, select the first column header to sort by.

7. From the Sort On drop-down, select Values.

8. From the Order drop-down, select the order by which the column's data should be sorted.

9. If you need to sort by another column, click Add Level and repeat steps 6 to 8. Repeat these steps until all the columns to sort by are configured, as shown in Figure 7.1.

10. If you realize that a field is in the wrong order, use the up or down arrows to move it to the correct location.

11. Click OK to sort the data.

Sorting by Color or Icon

Although sorting by values is the most typical use of sorting, Excel can also sort data by fill color, font color, or icon set from conditional formatting. You can apply fill and font colors through conditional formatting or the cell format icons.

In addition to sorting colors and icons through the sort dialog, the following options are also available when you right-click a cell and select Sort from the context menu:

- Put Selected Cell Color on Top

- Put Selected Font Color on Top
- Put Selected Cell Icon on Top

If you use one of the preceding options to sort more than one color or icon, the latest selection will be placed above the previous selection. So, if yellow rows should be placed before the red rows, sort the red rows first, and then the yellow rows.

 **LET ME TRY IT**

Sorting by Color Using the Sort Dialog

To sort data by the color fill in the cells using the sort dialog, follow these steps:

1. Ensure that the data has no blank rows or columns and that each column has a one row header.

2. Select a cell in the data. Excel will use this cell to determine the location and size of the data.

3. Right-click the cell and select Sort, Custom Sort.

4. Make sure the My Data Has Headers check box in the upper-right corner is selected. Excel will not select the headers themselves.

5. Make sure all the data's columns are selected. If they are not all selected, a blank column exists, confusing Excel as to the size of your data.

6. From the Sort By drop-down, select the first column header to sort by.

7. From the Sort On drop-down, select Cell Color.

8. From the first Order drop-down, select the color by which the column's data should be sorted.

9. From the second Order drop-down, select whether the color should be sorted to the top or bottom of the data. If you select multiple colors to sort at the top of the data, the colors will still appear in the order chosen.

10. If you need to sort by another column, click Add Level and repeat steps 6 to 9. Repeat these steps until all the columns to sort by are configured.

11. If you realize a field is in the wrong order, use the up or down arrows to move it to the correct location.

12. Click OK to sort the data.

Doing a Case-Sensitive Sort

Normally, Excel doesn't pay attention to case when sorting text: ABC is the same as abc. If case is important in the sort, you need to direct Excel to include case as a parameter. This is done from the Options in the Sort dialog. If Case Sensitive is selected, Excel will sort lowercase values before uppercase values in an ascending sort.

Using the Quick Sort Buttons

The quick sort buttons offer one-click access to sorting cell values. They do not work with colors or icons. There are four entry points to the quick sort buttons:

- On the Home tab, select Editing, Sort & Filter, Sort A to Z[1] or Sort Z to A[1].

- On the Data tab, select Sort & Filter, AZ or ZA (available only in Excel, not Excel Starter or the Web App).

- Right-click any cell and select Sort, Sort A to Z[1] or Sort Z to A[1].

- From a filter drop-down, select Sort A to Z[1] or Sort Z to A[1].

The quick sort buttons are very useful when sorting a single column. When sorting just one column, make sure you select just one cell in the column. If you select more than one cell, Excel will sort the selection, not the column. Also ensure there are no adjacent columns or Excel will want to include them in the sort. If there are adjacent columns, then select the entire column before sorting.

If you use the quick sort buttons to sort a table of more than one column, Excel will sort the entire table automatically. Because there is no dialog, it's very important that every column have a header. If just one header is missing, Excel will not treat the header row as such and will include it in the sorted data.

Quick Sorting Multiple Columns

If you keep in mind that Excel keeps previously sorted columns sorted as new columns are sorted, you can use this to sort multiple columns. For example, if column A is sorted, Excel doesn't randomize the data in column A when column B is

---

[1]*The actual button text may change depending on the type of data in the cell. For example, if the column contains values, the text will be Sort Smallest to Largest. If the column contains text, it will be Sort Z to A.*

sorted. Instead, column A retains its sort to the degree it falls within the column B sort. The trick is to apply the sorts in reverse to how they would be set up in the sort dialog.

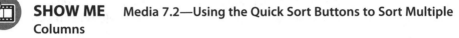 **SHOW ME**   Media 7.2—Using the Quick Sort Buttons to Sort Multiple Columns
Access this video file through your registered web edition at my.safaribooksonline.com/9780132182287/media.

 **LET ME TRY IT**

Using the Quick Sort Buttons to Sort Multiple Columns

To sort multiple columns in a table using the quick sort buttons, follow these steps:

1. Make sure all columns have headers. If even one column header is missing, Excel will not sort the data properly.

2. Select a cell in the column that should be sorted last.

3. Click the desired quick sort button on Home, Editing, Sort & Filter.

4. Select a cell in the next column to be sorted.

5. Click the desired quick sort button on Home, Editing, Sort & Filter.

6. Repeat steps 4 and 5 until all desired columns are sorted.

Random Sort

Excel doesn't have a built-in tool to do a random sort, but by using the RAND function in a column by the data and then sorting, you can create your own randomizer.

 **LET ME TRY IT**

Randomizing Data

To randomize data in a column, follow these steps:

1. Add a new column to the right of the data. Give the column a header.

2. In the first cell of the new column, type **=RAND()** and press Ctrl+Enter (this will keep the formula cell as the active cell). The formula will calculate a value between 0 and 1.

3. Double-click the fill handle in the lower-right corner of the cell to copy the formula to the rest of the rows in the column.

4. Select one cell in the new column.

5. Go to Home, Editing, Sort & Filter, AZ. The list will be sorted in a random sequence, as shown in Figure 7.2.

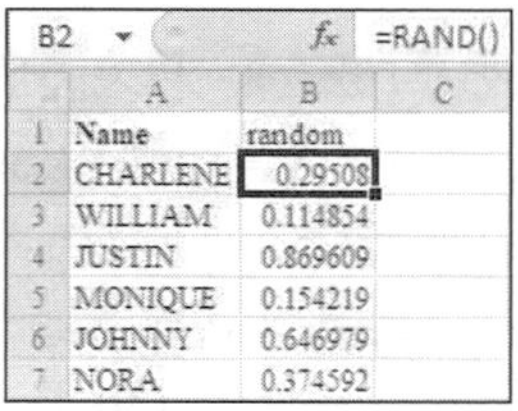

Figure 7.2   *Use the RAND function with a sort to randomize data.*

6. Delete the data in the temporary column that you added in step 1.

Right after Excel performs the sort, it recalculates the formula in the temporary column, so it may appear that the numbers are out of sequence.

Sorting with a Custom Sequence

At times, data may need to be sorted in a custom sequence that is neither alphabetical nor numerical. For example, you may want to sort by month, by weekday, or by some custom sequence of your own. You can do this by sorting by a custom list.

Using a Custom List

Within the Sort dialog, you can select Custom List from the Order field for each level of sort configured. When this option is selected, the Custom Lists dialog appears from which you can select the custom list to sort the selected column by.

LET ME TRY IT

Sorting by a Custom List

To sort one or more columns based on a custom list, follow these steps:

1. Ensure that the data has no blank rows or columns and that each column has a one row header.

2. Select a cell in the data. Excel will use this cell to determine the location and size of the data.

3. Go to Home, Editing, Sort & Filter, Custom Sort to open the Sort dialog.

4. Make sure the My Data Has Headers check box in the upper-right corner is selected. Excel will not select the headers themselves.

5. Make sure all the data's columns are selected. If they are not all selected, a blank column exists, confusing Excel as to the size of your data.

6. From the Sort By drop-down, select the first column header to sort by.

7. From the Sort On drop-down, select Values.

8. From the Order drop-down, select Custom List. The Custom Lists dialog, shown in Figure 7.3, appears.

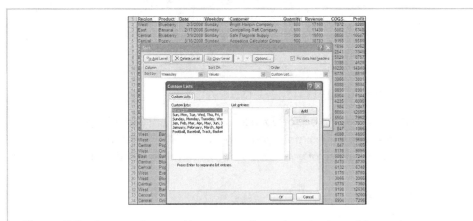

Figure 7.3   *Data can be sorted by a custom list, such as the days of the week.*

9. The list box on the left provides a list of available custom lists. Selecting one will display all the entries in the right list box. Select the desired list and click OK.

10. If you need to sort by other columns, click Add Level. Otherwise, skip to step 13.

11. Repeat steps 6 to 9. If you don't need to use another custom list, select the desired order from the drop-down instead of Custom List.

12. If you realize that a field is in the wrong order, use the up or down arrows to move it to the correct location.

13. Click OK to sort the data.

 TELL ME MORE   Media 7.3—Creating Custom Lists

To listen to a free audio recording about creating custom lists, log on to my.safaribooksonline.com/9780132182287/media.

Rearranging Columns

If you receive a report where you're always having to rearrange the columns to suit yourself, the following methods may prove to be very useful.

Using the Sort Dialog

Using the option of sorting left to right instead of top to bottom, you can rearrange the columns on your sheet.

 SHOW ME   Media 7.4—Rearranging Columns Using the Sort Dialog

Access this video file through your registered web edition at my.safaribooksonline.com/9780132182287/media.

 LET ME TRY IT

Rearranging Columns

To rearrange the columns on a sheet, follow these steps:

1. Insert a new blank row above the headers.

2. In the new row, type numbers corresponding to the new sequence of the columns.

3. Select a cell in the data range.

4. Press Ctrl+* (or Ctrl+Shift+8) to select the current region, including the two header rows.

5. Go to Home, Editing, Sort & Filter, Custom Sort to open the Sort dialog.

6. Click the Options button to open the Sort Options dialog.

7. Select Sort Left to Right.

8. Click OK to return to the Sort dialog.

9. In the Sort By drop-down, select the row in which the numbers you added in step 2 are located.

10. In the Order drop-down, make sure Smallest to Largest is selected.

11. Click OK and Excel will rearrange the columns.

12. Delete the temporary row added in step 1.

Using the Mouse

If you have just a few columns to rearrange, you can use a combination of keyboard shortcuts and the mouse to rearrange them quickly.

 LET ME TRY IT

Rearranging a Few Columns

If you have only a few columns to rearrange, follow these steps to rearrange them using the keyboard and mouse:

1. Select a cell in the column to move.

2. Press Ctrl+spacebar to select the entire column.

3. Place the cursor on the black border surrounding the selection, hold down the right mouse button, and drag the column to the new location.

4. When you release the mouse button, a context menu appears, as shown in Figure 7.4. Select Shift Right and Move.

5. The data will rearrange itself, inserting the column in the new location and moving other columns over to the right to make room.

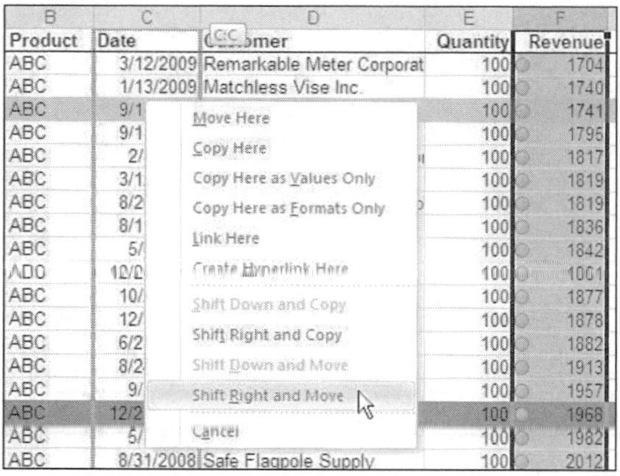

Figure 7.4   *Use Shift Right and Move to quickly move a column to a new location.*

Fixing Sort Problems

If it looks like the data did not sort properly, refer to the following list of possibilities:

- Make sure no hidden rows or columns exist.

- Use a single row for headers. If you need a multiline header, either wrap the text in the cell or use Alt+Enter to force line breaks in the cell.

- If the headers were sorted into the data, there was probably at least one column without a header.

- Column data should be of the same type. This may not be obvious in a column of ZIP Codes where some, such as 57057 are numbers, but others that start with 0s are actually text. To solve this problem, convert the entire column to text.

- If sorting by a column containing a formula, Excel will recalculate the column after the sort. If the values change after the recalculation, it may appear that the sort did not work properly, but it did.

This chapter shows you how to use Excel's filtering functionality to look at just the desired records. It will also show you how to create a list of unique items and consolidate data.

8

Filtering and Consolidating Data

Filtering and consolidating data are important tools in Excel, especially when you are dealing with large amounts of data. The filtering tools can quickly reduce the data to the specific records you need to concentrate on. The consolidation tool can bring together information spread between multiple sheets or workbooks.

Preparing Data

To make the most out of Excel's filtering capabilities, your data should adhere to a few basic formatting guidelines:

- There should be no blank rows or columns. The occasional blank cell is acceptable.

- There should be a header above every column.

- Headers should be in only one row; otherwise Excel will get confused and be unable to find the header row on its own.

Applying a Filter to a Dataset

To activate the filtering option, select a single cell in the dataset and use one of the following:

- On the Home tab, select Editing, Sort & Filter, Filter.

- On the Data tab, select Sort & Filter, Filter (works only in Excel, not Excel Starter or the Web App).

- When a dataset is turned into a table (Insert, Tables, Table), the headers automatically become filter headers. This is the only method for turning on filters in the Web App.

It is very important to select only a single cell because it is possible to turn on filtering in the middle of a dataset if you have more than one cell selected.

In Excel and Excel Starter, the Filter button is a toggle button. Click it once to turn filtering on and click it again to turn filtering off.

When a filter is applied to a dataset, drop-down arrows appear in the column headers. One or more selections can be made from each drop-down, filtering the data below the headers. Filters are additive, which means that each time a filter selection is made, it works with the previous selection to further filter the data.

When filters are in use in Excel and Excel Starter, the numbered row headings turn blue. In all Excel applications, an icon will replace the arrow on the column headers that have a filter applied. Although it may look as if the filtered rows are deleted, they are only hidden. After filtering is cleared, all rows reappear.

Clearing a Filter

A filter can be cleared from a specific column or for the entire dataset. To clear all the filters applied to a dataset, use one of the following methods:

- On the Home tab, select Editing, Sort & Filter, Clear.

- On the Data tab, select Sort & Filter, Clear.

- Turn off the Filter entirely using one of the following methods:
  - On the Home tab, select Editing, Sort & Filter, Filter.
  - On the Data tab, select Sort & Filter, Filter (works only in Excel, not Excel Starter or the Web App).

To clear all the filters applied to a specific column, use one of the following methods:

- Click the filter drop-down arrow and select Clear Filter From *column header*.

- Click the filter drop-down arrow and select Select All from the filtering list.

- Right-click a cell in the column to clear and select Filter, Clear Filter From *column header*.

Reapplying a Filter

If data is added to a filtered range, Excel does not automatically update the view to hide any new rows that don't fit the filter settings. You can refresh the filters settings so they include the new rows through one of the following methods:

- On the Home tab, select Editing, Sort & Filter, Reapply.

- On the Data tab, select Sort & Filter, Reapply.

- Right-click a cell in the filtered dataset and select Filter, Reapply.

Filtering in the Web App

A workbook with normal or table filtering can be uploaded, and users in View or Edit mode can interact with the filters. The only way to turn on filtering in an uploaded workbook is to be in Edit mode and to turn the dataset into a table by selecting a cell in the dataset and going to Home, Tables, Sort & Filter as Table or Insert, Tables, Table. After a dataset has been turned into a table in the Web App, it cannot be turned back unless it is opened in Excel or Excel Starter.

The filtering options in the Web App work a bit differently from Excel and Excel Starter, but offer many of the same options. To get to the filtering list, click the columns drop-down and select Filter. A separate dialog window appears, from which you can select one or more items. See the section "Filter Listing for Listed Items" for more details. Most of the Text, Number, and Date Filters options are also available—see the section "Using Text, Number, and Date Special Filters" for more information.

Sometimes you may upload a workbook where the filters are already set and rows are hidden, but when you look at the drop-down, you don't see the option to clear the filter. To force the filters to reset, select Filters from the drop-down to bring up the filter listing. Select one item from the list and click OK. The Clear Filter from *column header* option should now be available.

Turn Filtering on for One Column

Filtering can be turned on for a single column or for two or more adjacent columns. This can be useful if you want to limit the filtering users can apply. If the sheet is then protected, users cannot turn on filtering for the other columns (see the Allow Filtering on a Protected Sheet section for more information). A workbook uploaded to the Web App will retain this setting.

To control what column has filtering, select the header and first cell directly beneath the header. Then do one of the following:

- On the Home tab, select Editing, Sort & Filter, Filter.

- On the Data tab, select Sort & Filter, Filter.

Filtering Options

You can use several methods for filtering from the filter drop-down after the filter is turned on, as shown in Figure 8.1. The next several sections review these methods.

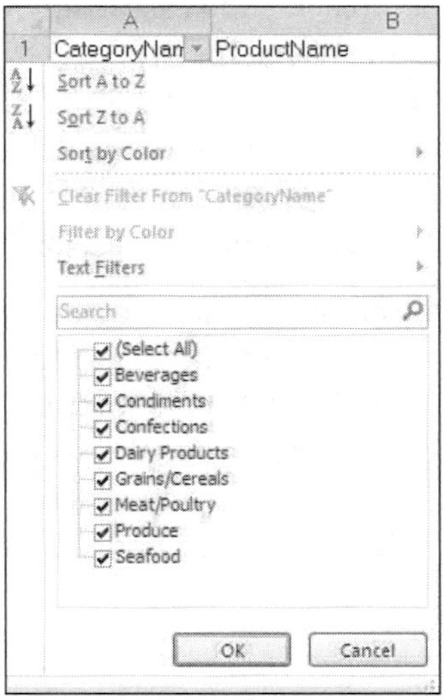

Figure 8.1   *The filter drop-down provides several filtering methods.*

Filter Listing for Listed Items

The filter listing is probably the most obvious filter tool when you open the drop-down. For text, numbers, and ungrouped dates, a listing of all unique items in the column appears (see the "Grouped Dates Filter Listing" section if dates appear grouped by year and month). All items will be checked, because they are all visible the first time you open the drop-down, but you can select just the items that should appear in the data. Any item that no longer bears a check mark will be hidden.

LET ME TRY IT

Filtering a Column for Specific Items

To filter a column for specific items, follow these steps:

If filtering an existing table, skip to step 3.

1. Select a single cell in the dataset to apply filtering to.

2. In Excel or Excel Starter, go to Home, Sort & Filter, Filter. In the Web App, go to Home, Sort & Filter as Table. The Web App will verify the range to be converted to a table. Click OK to continue.

3. Open the drop-down of the column to filter.

4. If in Excel or Excel Starter, skip to step 5. Otherwise, in the Excel Web App, click Filter in the drop-down to open the filter listing dialog.

5. Unselect the Select All item to clear all the check marks in the list.

6. Select the item(s) to be viewed in the dataset.

7. Click OK. The sheet will update, showing only the item(s) selected.

Grouped Dates Filter Listing

This section applies to dates that are grouped, as shown in Figure 8.2. In Excel and Excel Starter, the grouping is controlled by a setting found under File, Options, Advanced, Display Options for This Workbook, Group Dates in the AutoFilter Menu. By default, this option is selected. If unselected, the dates will appear in a list like the filter for number and text items. You can refer to the section on "Filter Listing for Listed Items" for more information on that filter listing.

Dates in the filter listing are grouped by year, month, and day. All items will be checked, because they are all visible the first time you open the drop-down, but you can select just the items that should appear in the data. Any item that no longer bears a check mark will be hidden.

If you click the + icon by a year, it opens up, showing the months. Click the + icon by a month and it opens up to show the days of the month. An entire year or month can be selected or unselected by clicking the desired year or month. For example, to deselect 2009 and January 2010 in Figure 8.2, deselect the 2009 group, then deselect the January group under 2010. The data will filter to show only February and March 2010.

Figure 8.2   *With the group dates option selected, dates appear grouped by year, month, and day in the filter listing.*

LET ME TRY IT

Filtering a Column for Specific Dates

To filter a column for specific dates, follow these steps:

If filtering an existing table, skip to step 3.

1. Select a single cell in the dataset to apply filtering to.

2. In Excel or Excel Starter, go to Home, Sort & Filter, Filter. In the Web App, go to Home, Sort & Filter as Table. The Web App will verify the range to be converted to a table. Click OK to continue.

3. Open the drop-down of the column to filter.

4. If in Excel or Excel Starter, skip to step 5. Otherwise, in the Excel Web App, click Filter in the drop-down to open the filter listing dialog.

5. Deselect the Select All item to clear all the check marks in the list.

6. Click the + icon to the left of the desired year.

7. Click the + icon to the left of the desired month.

8. Select the desired days.

9. Repeat steps 6 to 8 as needed.

10. Click OK. The sheet updates, showing only the dates selected.

Searching Functions for Listed Items

If you have a long list of items in the filter listing, you can search for items to include or exclude from the filter. Searches are done on the entire data list, not just the items currently filtered on. Use an asterisk (*) as a wildcard for one or more characters before, after, or in between any of the search terms.

 SHOW ME   Media 8.1—Using the Search Function to Include and Exclude Items in the Filtering Listing
Access this video file through your registered web edition at my.safaribooksonline.com/9780132182287/media.

Searching for Items to Include in Filter

When a search term is entered in the search field, the filter listing updates with all matches selected. You can deselect the items you want to filter out, check Add Current Selection to Filter if you do *not* want to lose any items you previously filtered for, and click OK.

You should keep two things in mind when using the search function:

*   The search looks through the entire column, including items you may have already filtered out.

*   The search function is additive when the Add Current Selection to Filter is selected. If not selected, each search's results are treated as a new filter.

 LET ME TRY IT

Using the Search Function to Filter Items

To perform multiple searches to filter items, follow these steps:

1. Open the drop-down of the column to filter.

2. Enter the first term, or partial term, to filter by.

3. If you want to filter by all the resulting terms, skip to step 6. Otherwise, continue to step 4.

4. Deselect Select All Search Results.

5. Select the desired items from the search results.

6. Click OK.

7. Open the drop-down of the column to filter again.

8. Enter the second term, or partial term, to filter by.

9. If you want to filter by all the resulting terms, click OK and skip to step 12. Otherwise, continue to step 10.

10. Deselect Select All Search Results.

11. Select the desired items from the search results.

12. Select Add Current Selection to Filter.

13. Click OK.

Searching for Items to Exclude from Filter

The search function can also be used to exclude items from the filter. You do this by entering a search term, deselecting the items to exclude from the results, and then selecting the Add Current Selection to Filter.

You should keep three things in mind when using the search function to exclude items:

- The search looks through the entire column, including items you may have already filtered out.

- To exclude items from the listing, deselect them from the result.

- The search function is additive when the Add Current Selection to Filter is selected. If not selected, each search's results are treated as a new filter.

 **LET ME TRY IT**

Using the Search Function to Exclude Items from Results

To exclude items from a list of filtered results, as shown in Figure 8.3, follow these steps:

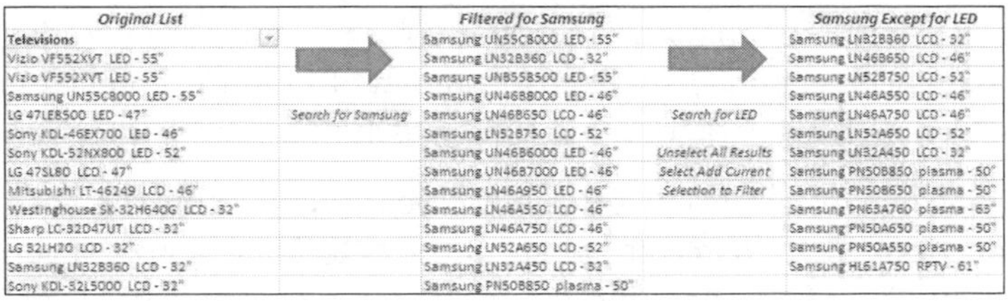

Original List		Filtered for Samsung		Samsung Except for LED
Televisions		Samsung UN55C8000 LED - 55"		Samsung LN32B360 LCD - 32"
Vizio VF552XVT LED - 55"		Samsung LN32B360 LCD - 32"		Samsung LN46B650 LCD - 46"
Vizio VF552XVT LED - 55"		Samsung UN55B8500 LED - 55"		Samsung LN52B750 LCD - 52"
Samsung UN55C8000 LED - 55"		Samsung UN46B8000 LED - 46"		Samsung LN46A550 LCD - 46"
LG 47LE8500 LED - 47"	Search for Samsung	Samsung LN46B650 LCD - 46"	Search for LED	Samsung LN46A750 LCD - 46"
Sony KDL-46EX700 LED - 46"		Samsung LN52B750 LCD - 52"		Samsung LN52A650 LCD - 52"
Sony KDL-52NX800 LED - 52"		Samsung UN46B6000 LED - 46"	Unselect All Results	Samsung LN32A450 LCD - 32"
LG 47SL80 LCD - 47"		Samsung UN46B7000 LED - 46"	Select Add Current	Samsung PN50B850 plasma - 50"
Mitsubishi LT-46249 LCD - 46"		Samsung LN46A950 LED - 46"	Selection to Filter	Samsung PN50B650 plasma - 50"
Westinghouse SK-32H640G LCD - 32"		Samsung LN46A550 LCD - 46"		Samsung PN63A760 plasma - 63"
Sharp LC-32D47UT LCD - 32"		Samsung LN46A750 LCD - 46"		Samsung PN50A650 plasma - 50"
LG 32LH20 LCD - 32"		Samsung LN52A650 LCD - 52"		Samsung PN50A550 plasma - 50"
Samsung LN32B360 LCD - 32"		Samsung LN32A450 LCD - 32"		Samsung HL61A750 RPTV - 61"
Sony KDL-32L5000 LCD - 32"		Samsung PN50B850 plasma - 50"		

Figure 8.3 *Use the search function to exclude items from a filtered list.*

1. Open the drop-down of the column to filter.
2. Enter the first term, or partial term, to filter by.
3. If you want to filter by all the resulting terms, skip to step 6. Otherwise, continue to step 4.
4. Deselect Select All Search Results.
5. Select the desired items from the search results.
6. Click OK.
7. Open the drop-down of the column to filter again.
8. Enter the exclusion term.
9. If you want to filter out all the resulting terms, skip to step 12. Otherwise, continue to step 10.
10. Deselect Select All Search Results.
11. Select the desired items from the search results.
12. Select Add Current Selection to Filter.
13. Click OK.

Using the Search Function for Grouped Dates

If you have a lot of dates in the filter listing, you can search for specific years, months, or dates to include or exclude from the filter. Searches are done on the entire data list, not just the items currently filtered on.

The search function for grouped dates includes a drop-down, allowing you to search by year, month, or date. It does not allow you to search for an entire date, such as 04/19/2010.

- **Year**—Search results will be grouped by year.
- **Month**—Search results will be grouped by year and then month. The search term must be the long version of the month, such as January.

- **Date**—Search results will be grouped by year, then month, then day. Because the search will return partial matches, you should use the two-digit variation for dates. For example, to search for the 1st of a month, enter 01 instead of 1. If you enter 1, every date with a 1, such as 10, 11, 12, will be returned.

- **All**—Search results will be grouped by year, then month, then day. This option looks for a match anywhere in the date. For example, if your dataset includes dates from 2009 and the search term is 09, all dates from 2009 will be returned. If you want only the 9th day returned, use the Date option.

Because searches are additive, proper application of the Add Current Selection to Filter in the search results allows you to include or exclude the results from the filter. For more information, see the sections "Searching for Items to Include in Filter" and "Searching for Items to Exclude from Filter."

 SHOW ME   Media 8.2—Using the Search Function to Filter for Specific Dates
Access this video file through your registered web edition at my.safaribooksonline.com/9780132182287/media.

 LET ME TRY IT

Filtering for Specific Days from All Months in a Specific Year.

To filter for specific days from each month of a specific year, follow these steps:

1. Open the drop-down of the date column to filter.

2. Select Date from the Search drop-down.

3. Type in the two-digit date.

4. Deselect Select All Search Results.

5. Scroll down the filter listing and select the year of the data to include in the filter. Selecting the year will automatically select all the months and dates in the year's group.

6. Click OK.

7. Open the drop-down of the date column to filter again.

8. Select Date from the Search drop-down.

9. Type in the two-digit date.

10. Deselect Select All Search Results.

11. Select Add Current Selection to Filter.

12. Scroll down the filter listing and select the year of the data to include in the filter.

13. Click OK.

14. Repeat steps 7 to 13 if you want to include more dates in the filter.

Using Text, Number and Date Special Filters

Special filters are available in the filter drop-down depending on which data type (text, numbers, or dates) appears most often in a column. All the special filters, except for ones that take action immediately, open the Custom AutoFilter dialog, allowing two conditions to be combined using AND or OR.

If the column contains mostly text, Text Filters will be available with the options Equals, Does Not Equal, Begins With, Ends With, Contains, and Does Not Contain. Selecting one of these opens a Custom AutoFilter dialog in which text can be entered. Wildcards can also be used in the text fields. Use an asterisk (*) to replace multiple characters or a question mark (?) to replace a single character.

If the column contains mostly numbers, Number Filters will be available with the options Equals, Does Not Equal, Greater Than, Greater Than Or Equal To, Less Than, Less Than or Equal To, Between Top 10, Above Average, and Below Average. Selecting Top 10, Above Average, or Below Average will automatically update the filter to reflect the selection.

If Top 10 is selected, you can specify the top or bottom items or percent to view. For example, you could choose to view the bottom 15% or the top 7 items.

For columns with dates, the special filter offers a wide selection of options, including additional options under All Dates in the Period, as shown in Figure 8.4. The Custom AutoFilter dialog for dates includes calendars to aid in data entry. The options dealing with quarters refer to the traditional quarter of a year, January through March being the first quarter, April through June being the second quarter, and so on.

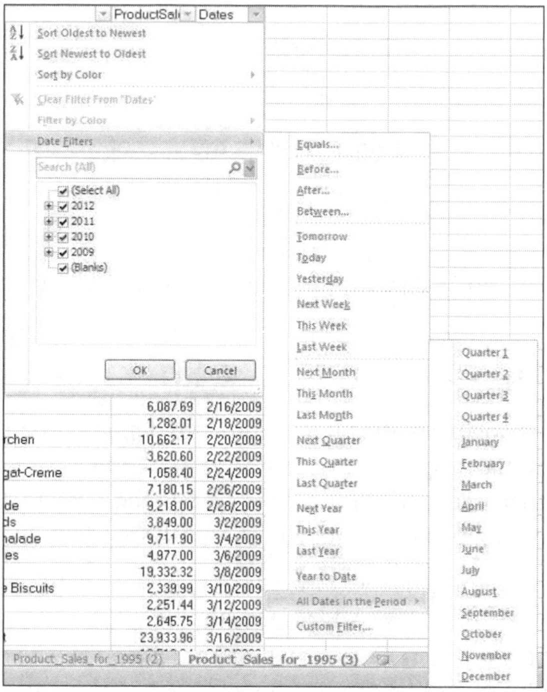

Figure 8.4   *There are numerous options for filtering dates.*

LET ME TRY IT

Filtering a Numeric Column for a Value Range

To filter a numeric column for a value range as shown in Figure 8.5, follow these steps:

1. Open the drop-down of the numeric column to filter.

2. Select Number Filters, Greater Than. The Custom AutoFilter appears.

3. The top-left drop-down should already have Is Greater Than selected, but if not, select it from the drop-down.

4. The top-right drop-down lists all the values in the column. You may select one of those or enter your own value.

5. Between the top and bottom drop-down, make sure AND is selected.

6. In the bottom-left drop-down, select Is Less than.

7. In the bottom-right drop-down, select a value from the list or enter your own value.

8. Click OK. The sheet will update, showing only the values that fell within the selected range.

Custom AutoFilter

Show rows where:
ProductSales

| is greater than | ▼ | 5000 | ▼ |

⦿ And ○ Or

| is less than | ▼ | 26000| | ▼ |

Use ? to represent any single character
Use * to represent any series of characters

OK   Cancel

Figure 8.5   *Use the special filters to filter a list for a range of values.*

Filtering by Color or Icon

Data can be filtered by font color, color (set by cell fill or conditional formatting) or icon by going to the Filter by Color option in the filter listing, as shown in Figure 8.6. There, colors and/or icons used in the column are shown. Filter selections are additive, so if you first select to filter all green rows and then red circles, the filter range will reflect rows that have a green fill and red circle.

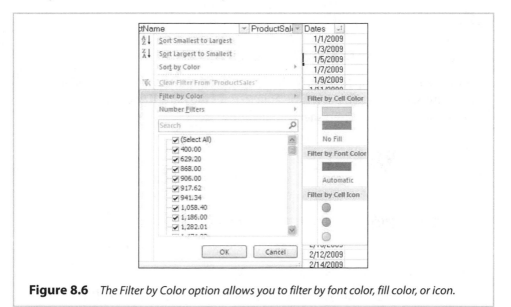

Figure 8.6   *The Filter by Color option allows you to filter by font color, fill color, or icon.*

Filtering By Selection

Even without the filter turned on, you can right-click any cell in a column, go to Filter, and choose to filter by the cell's value, color, font color, or icon. Doing so will turn on the filter and configure the filter for the selected cell's property.

The filtering is additive. If you filter a cell by one value and then go to a cell in another column and filter by its value, the result will be those rows that satisfy both filter criteria. You cannot filter by a property more than once within the same column, but you can filter a column by multiple properties—for example, filter by icon and then value.

 **LET ME TRY IT**

Using Filter Selection

To use filter selection to view records meeting a specific value and font color, follow these steps:

1. Right-click a cell containing the value to filter by.

2. Go to Filter, Filter by Selected Cell's Value.

3. Right-click a cell containing the font color to filter by.

4. Go to Filter, Filter by Selected Cell's Font Color.

Allow Filtering on a Protected Sheet

Normally, if you set up filters on a sheet, protect the sheet, and then send it out to other users, the recipients won't be able to filter the data. If you want others to be able to filter your protected sheet, follow these steps:

If filtering an existing table, skip to step 3.

1. Select a single cell in the dataset to apply filtering to.

2. Go to Home, Sort & Filter, Filter. The filter will be turned on for the dataset.

3. Go to Review, Changes, Protect Sheet.

4. In the listing for All Users of This Worksheet To, scroll down and select Use AutoFilter.

5. If applying a password to the sheet, enter it in the Password to Unprotect Sheet field. Otherwise, skip to step 6.

6. Click OK.

7. If you entered a password in step 5, Excel will prompt you to reenter the password. Do so and click OK.

Using the Advanced Filter

Despite the visual simplicity of the Advanced Filter dialog, it can perform a variety of functions. Depending on the options selected and the setup on the sheet, the Advanced Filter can do the following:

- Filter records in place

- Filter records to a new location on the same or different sheet

- Reorganize columns

- Use formulas as criteria

- Filter for unique records

Select either Filter the List, In-Place or Copy to Another Location to tell the function where to put the resulting dataset. If copying the results to a new location, specify the location in the Copy To field. When specifying the range

- If the results include all columns of the dataset in the original order, only the location of the first header needs to be specified.

- If the results consist of any change to the headers, whether it's a new order or fewer headers, copy the headers to use in the desired order to a new location. The Copy To range must include the entire new range of headers.

- If results need to be on another sheet, the Advanced Filter must be called from the sheet where the results will be placed.

List Range is the dataset, including required headers. Most Advanced Filter functions require each column to have a header.

The Criteria Range is where rules are configured for the filter. See "Using the Criteria Range" section for details.

Select Unique Records Only if duplicates should not be included in the results. See the "Filtering for Unique Items" section for an example of how the option is useful for removing duplicates from a single column.

Using the Criteria Range

Criteria can consist of exact values, values with operators, wildcards, or formulas. You should keep the following things in mind when setting up the criteria range:

- Except for when the criterion is a formula, the first row must consist of the column header used by the filter.

- Starting in the second row, enter the criterion to filter for in the column.

- Criteria entered on the same row are read as joined by AND. In the top table of Figure 8.7, the criteria in the first row is read West AND ABC.

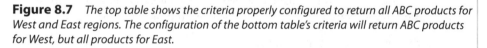

	J	K	L	M	N	O	P	Q
	Region	Product		Date	Customer	Profit	Region	Product
	West	ABC		1/7/2008	Remarkabl	5068	East	ABC
	East	ABC		1/15/2008	Bright Hair	5110	East	ABC
				1/16/2008	Appealing	6546	East	ABC
				1/21/2008	Cool Jewel	1858	West	ABC
				1/21/2008	Best Vege	7664	East	ABC
				1/23/2008	Remarkabl	7816	West	ABC
				1/24/2008	Reliable Tr	7524	East	ABC
				1/26/2008	Reliable Tr	4740	East	ABC
				1/29/2008	Tasty Kett	3748	East	ABC

	J	K	L	M	N	O	P	Q
	Region	Product		Date	Customer	Profit	Region	Product
	West	ABC		1/1/2008	Exclusive !	12590	East	XYZ
	East			1/4/2008	Cool Jewel	10680	East	DEF
				1/4/2008	Tasty Kett	5064	East	XYZ
				1/7/2008	Wonderful	11890	East	DEF
				1/7/2008	Remarkabl	5068	East	ABC

Figure 8.7   *The top table shows the criteria properly configured to return all ABC products for West and East regions. The configuration of the bottom table's criteria will return ABC products for West, but all products for East.*

- Criteria entered on different rows are read as joined by OR. In the top table of Figure 8.7, the criteria is read West AND ABC OR East AND ABC.

- If a cell in the criteria range is blank and has a column header, this is read as returning all records that match the column header. In the bottom table in Figure 8.7, the data returned will be West and ABC or all data in East.

- Operators (<, >, <=, >=, <>) can be combined with numeric values for a more general filter.

- Wildcards can be used with text values. An asterisk (*) replaces any number of characters. A question mark (?) replaces a single character. The tilde (~) allows the use of wildcard characters in case the text being filtered uses such a character as part of its value.

- If the criterion is a formula, do not use a column header as it is applied to the entire dataset. The formula should be one that returns a TRUE or FALSE.

SHOW ME   Media 8.3—Using the Advanced Filter with Various Criteria
*Access this video file through your registered web edition at
my.safaribooksonline.com/9780132182287/media.*

LET ME TRY IT

Filtering a Dataset Using the Advanced Filter

To filter a dataset using the Advanced Filter, combining various criteria, and placing
the results on a new sheet, follow these steps:

1. Copy and paste the desired headers from the dataset to a new sheet.

2. If filtering by a formula, skip to step 4. Otherwise, in row 1 of a blank section of the datasheet, type the column headers to filter by.

3. Below the column headers entered in step 2 fill in the criteria, as shown in Figure 8.8. Note that the criteria is not case sensitive.

Figure 8.8   *The Advanced Filter can use a combination of criteria to filter a dataset. Note:
Results in G6:K25 are a representation of the actual results on the Report sheet.*

4. To filter by a formula, enter the formula in a column on the datasheet that does not have a header, as shown in column J of Figure 8.8. Because the formula in J2 is on the same row as other criteria, Excel will treat it as part of that criteria. But the formula in J3 is alone in its row. It will apply to the entire dataset.

5. After all the criteria are entered, return to the results sheet.

6. Select a blank cell.

7. Go to Data, Sort & Filter, Advanced.

8. Select Copy to Another Location.

9. Place the cursor in the List Range field.

10. Go to the dataset's sheet and select the dataset.

11. Place the cursor in the Criteria Range field.

12. Go to the dataset's sheet and select the criteria range. If the criteria range is just a formula, be sure to include a blank cell above the formula. Do not include any blank rows (except for above formulas).

13. Place the cursor in the Copy To field.

14. Select the column headers for the results.

15. Click OK.

Filtering for Unique Items

When the Unique Records Only option is selected, the Advanced Filter can be used to remove duplicates. Unlike the Remove Duplicates command on the Data tab, the original dataset will remain intact if you choose to copy the results to a new location. But also unlike the Remove Duplicates command, you cannot specify multiple columns to filter by.

If Filter the List, In-Place is selected, the duplicate rows will be hidden. Go to Data, Sort & Filter, Clear to clear the filter and unhide the rows.

 **LET ME TRY IT**

Removing Duplicates from a Single Column

To quickly filter out duplicates in a single column and copy the results to a new location, follow these steps:

1. Select a cell in the column to filter.

2. Go to Data, Sort & Filter, Advanced Filter.

3. Verify the range in the List Range field is the desired range. Correct it if it's wrong.

4. Select Copy to Another Location.

5. Place your cursor in the Copy to Range field.

6. Select a cell on the sheet where you want the first cell of the filtered range copied to.

7. Select Unique Records Only.

8. Click OK.

Removing Duplicates

After a cell is selected in the dataset, Remove Duplicates can be found under Data, Data Tools, Remove Duplicates, or If the dataset is a table, under Table Tools, Design, Tools, Remove Duplicates.

The tool permanently deletes data from a table based on the selected columns in the Remove Duplicates dialog. Unlike other filters, it does not just hide the rows. Because of this, you may want to copy the data before deleting the duplicates.

 LET ME TRY IT

Removing Duplicates from a Dataset

To remove duplicates from a dataset, follow these steps:

1. Select a cell in the dataset.

2. Go to Data, Data Tools, Remove Duplicates.

3. Excel will highlight the dataset. If columns are missing in the selection, go back and make sure there are no blank separating columns.

4. From the Remove Duplicates dialog, make sure My Data Has Headers is selected if the dataset has headers.

5. By default, all the columns are selected. A selected column means the tool will use the columns when looking for duplicates. Duplicates in an unselected column will be ignored. Select the columns to search for duplicates.

6. Click OK. The dataset will update, deleting any duplicate rows. A message box will appear informing you of the number of rows deleted and the number remaining in the dataset.

TELL ME MORE   Media 8.4—Finding Duplicates

To listen to a free audio recording about finding duplicates using conditional formatting, log on to my.safaribooksonline.com/9780132182287/media.

Consolidating Data

You can use the Consolidate tool, found under Data, Data Tools, to combine data in three ways:

- **By Position**—Sum[1] data found on different sheets or in different workbooks based on their positions in the datasets. For example, if the ranges are A1:A10 and C220:C230, the results will be A1+C220, A2+C221, A3+C222, and so on. Do not select either of the options under Use Labels In.

- **By Category**—Sum[1] data found on different sheets or in different workbooks based on matching row and column labels, similar to a pivot table report. The references must include the labels in the leftmost column of the ranges. Select either or both of the options under Use Labels In to have the labels appear in the final data.

- **By Column**—Combine the data to a new sheet, with each dataset in its own column. Select the Top Row option under Use Labels In.

The Reference field is where the datasets are entered. Click Add to add the selection to the All References list. If the dataset is in a closed workbook, you can reference it only by using a range name. Click the Browse button to find and select the workbook. After the exclamation point (!) at the end of the path, enter the range name assigned to the dataset.

> See "Using Names to Simplify References" in Chapter 5, "Using Formulas" for details on how to create a range name.

Create Links to Source Data applies only to external workbooks. If this option is selected, the consolidated data will update automatically when the source is changed. Also, the consolidated data will be grouped, as shown in Figure 8.9. Click the + icon to the left of the data to open the group and see the data used in the summary.

---

[1]*The function applied to the data can be any available from the drop-down list in the Consolidate dialog. These include Sum, Count, Average, and more.*

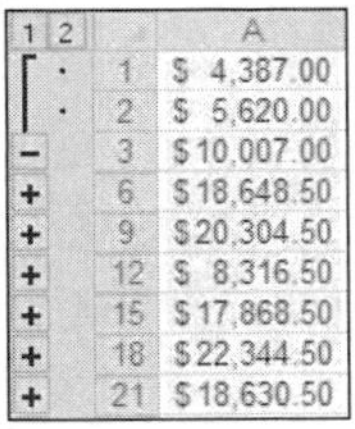

Figure 8.9 *When linking to an external workbook, the consolidation will include the individual values of the selected references.*

  LET ME TRY IT

Consolidating Duplicate Data by Category

To combine duplicate data from within the same workbook, follow these steps:

1. Select the top leftmost cell where the consolidated report should be placed. If other data is on the sheet, make sure there is enough room for the new data.

2. Go to Data, Data Tools, Consolidate.

3. Select the desired function from the Function drop-down.

4. Place the cursor in the Reference field.

5. Go to the sheet with the desired dataset.

6. Select the dataset, making sure the duplicated labels are in the leftmost column and that the column headers are included in the selection.

7. Click the Add button.

8. Repeat steps 4 to 7 for each additional dataset.

9. To include the top and/or left column labels, select the corresponding option.

10. Click OK.

This chapter shows you how data can be summarized and grouped together using Excel's subtotal and grouping tools.

9

Subtotals and Grouping

The ability to group and subtotal data allows you to summarize a long sheet of data to fewer rows. The individual records are still there, so that you can unhide them if you need to investigate a subtotal in detail.

> Although the capability to create groups and outlines is not available in Excel Starter or Web App, workbooks with preexisting groups will still work as designed.

SUBTOTAL Function

The SUBTOTAL function calculates a column of numbers based on the code used in the function. With the correct code, SUBTOTAL can calculate averages, counts, sums, and eight other functions listed in Table 9.1. It can also ignore hidden rows when the 100 version of the code is used.

See Figure 9.1 for examples of the SUBTOTAL function in action. The function will ignore any cells in the range that include SUBTOTAL functions themselves, as shown in column E of the worksheet in the figure. Column G uses the SUM function instead of SUBTOTAL and does not ignore the hidden rows or previous SUM formulas in the Grand Total.

TELL ME MORE   Media 9.1—Adding Grand Totals When the Subtotals Were Manually Entered

You can listen to a free audio recording about an old accounting trick for adding a total to data that has been manually subtotaled when you log on to my.safaribooksonline.com/9780132182287/media.

Table 9.1 SUBTOTAL Function Numbers

Function_num (includes hidden values)	Function_num (ignores hidden values)	Function
1	101	AVERAGE
2	102	COUNT
3	103	COUNTA
4	104	MAX
5	105	MIN
6	106	PRODUCT
7	107	STDEV
8	108	STDEVP
9	109	SUM
10	110	VAR
11	111	VARP

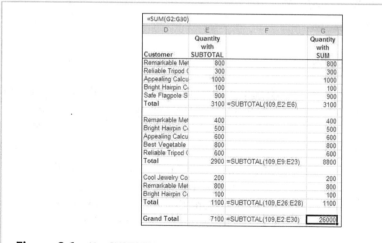

Figure 9.1 *Use SUBTOTAL to ignore hidden rows and prevent counting other SUBTOTAL calculations twice in the Grand Total.*

Subtotal Tool

The SUBTOTAL function is very useful, but if you have a large dataset it can be time consuming to insert all the Total rows. When your dataset is large, use the Subtotal tool from the Data tab in the Outline group. This tool will group the sorted data, applying the selected function.

From the Subtotal dialog, you can select the column to group the data by, the function to subtotal by, and which columns to apply the subtotal to.

SHOW ME   Media 9.2—Using the Subtotal Tool

Access this video file through your registered web edition at my.safaribooksonline.com/9780132182287/media.

LET ME TRY IT

Summarizing Data Using the Subtotal Command

To quickly group and apply subtotals to a dataset, follow these steps:

1. Sort the data by the column the summary should be based on. For example, if summarizing by region, sort the Region column.

> See Chapter 7, "Sorting," for more information about sorting by columns.

2. Select a cell in the dataset.

3. Go to Data, Outline, Subtotal. The Subtotal dialog, shown in Figure 9.2, will open.

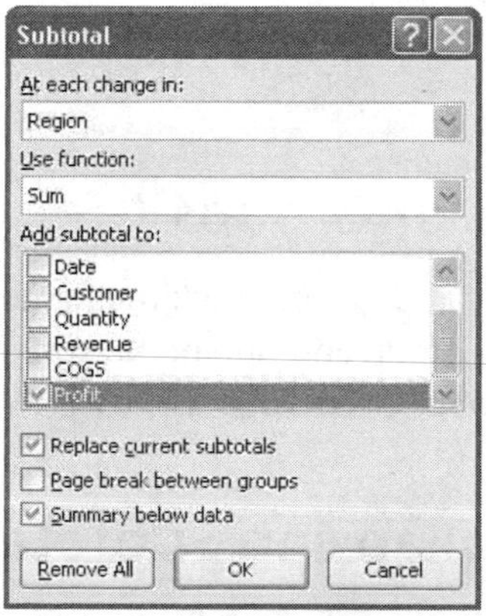

Figure 9.2   *Use the Subtotal dialog to set your subtotaling options.*

4. From the At Each Change In field, select the column by which to summarize the data.

5. From the Use Function field, select the function to calculate the totals by.

6. From the Add Subtotal To field, select the columns the totals should be added to. Notice that, by default, the last column is already selected.

7. Click OK. The data will be grouped and subtotaled, with a grand total at the very bottom, as shown in Figure 9.3.

	A	B	C	D	E	F	G	H
1	Region	Product	Date	Customer	Quantity	Revenue	COGS	Profit
2	West	DEF	1/19/2008	Bright Hairpin Company	100	2042	984	1058
3	West	ABC	1/21/2008	Cool Jewelry Corporation	200	3552	1694	1858
4	West	ABC	1/23/2008	Remarkable Meter Corporation	800	14592	6776	7816
5	West Total							10732
6	East	XYZ	1/14/2008	Matchless Vise Inc.	100	2401	1022	1379
7	East	ABC	1/15/2008	Bright Hairpin Company	500	9345	4235	5110
8	East	ABC	1/29/2008	Tasty Kettle Inc.	400	7136	3388	3748
9	East	DEF	1/4/2008	Cool Jewelry Corporation	800	18552	7872	10680
10	East	XYZ	1/1/2008	Exclusive Shovel Traders	1000	22810	10220	12590
11	East	ABC	1/24/2008	Reliable Tripod Company	600	12606	5082	7524
12	East	ABC	1/26/2008	Reliable Tripod Company	400	8128	3388	4740
13	East	DEF	1/30/2008	Safe Flagpole Supply	300	6714	2952	3762
14	East	ABC	1/16/2008	Appealing Calculator Corporation	600	11628	5082	6546
15	East	ABC	1/7/2008	Remarkable Meter Corporation	400	8456	3388	5068
16	East	ABC	1/31/2008	Remarkable Meter Corporation	800	15640	6776	8864
17	East	DEF	1/29/2008	Remarkable Meter Corporation	700	17150	6888	10262
18	East Total							80273
19	Central	DEF	1/2/2008	Bright Hairpin Company	100	2257	984	1273
20	Central	ABC	1/12/2008	Reliable Tripod Company	300	6267	2541	3726
21	Central	XYZ	1/10/2008	Safe Flagpole Supply	900	21438	9198	12240
22	Central	ABC	1/25/2008	Appealing Calculator Corporation	1000	20770	8470	12300
23	Central	ABC	1/9/2008	Remarkable Meter Corporation	800	16416	6776	9640
24	Central Total							39179
25	Grand Total							130184

Figure 9.3 *Profit is summarized for each region.*

Placing Subtotals Above Data

By default, subtotals appear below the data being summarized. If the subtotals need to appear above the data instead, deselect Summary Below Data in the Subtotal dialog.

Remove Subtotals or Groups

To remove all the subtotals and groups, click the Remove All button in the Subtotal dialog. To remove only the group and outline buttons, leaving the subtotal intact, select Data, Outline, Ungroup, Clear Outline.

Expanding and Collapsing Subtotals

When data is grouped and subtotaled, outline symbols appear to the left of the row headings, as shown in Figure 9.4. Clicking the numbered icons at the top (1,2,3 in Figure 9.4) will hide and unhide the data in the sheet. For example, clicking the 2 will hide the data rows, showing only the Total and Grand Total rows. Clicking the 1 will hide the Total rows, showing only the Grand Total. Clicking the 3 will unhide all the rows.

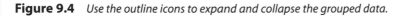

1 2 3		A	B	C	D	E	F
	1	Region	Product	Date	Customer	Quantity	Revenue
+	7	Central Total					67148
	8	East	ABC	1/7/2008	Remarkable Meter Corporat	400	8456
	9	East	ABC	1/15/2008	Bright Hairpin Company	500	9345
	10	East	ABC	1/16/2008	Appealing Calculator Corpor	600	11020
	11	East	ABC	1/21/2008	Best Vegetable Company	800	14440
	12	East	ABC	1/24/2008	Reliable Tripod Company	600	12606
	13	East	ABC	1/26/2008	Reliable Tripod Company	400	8128
	14	East	ABC	1/29/2008	Tasty Kettle Inc.	400	7136
	15	East	ABC	1/31/2008	Remarkable Meter Corporat	800	15640
	16	East	DEF	1/4/2008	Cool Jewelry Corporation	800	18552
	17	East	DEF	1/7/2008	Wonderful Jewelry Inc.	1000	21730
	18	East	DEF	1/29/2008	Remarkable Meter Corporat	700	17150
	19	East	DEF	1/30/2008	Safe Flagpole Supply	300	6714
	20	East	XYZ	1/1/2008	Exclusive Shovel Traders	1000	22810
	21	East	XYZ	1/4/2008	Tasty Kettle Inc.	400	9152
	22	East	XYZ	1/14/2008	Matchless Vise Inc.	100	2401
−	23	East Total					185888
+	27	West Total					20186
−	28	Grand Total					273222

Figure 9.4 *Use the outline icons to expand and collapse the grouped data.*

Below the numbered icons, next to each Total and Grand Total, are the expand (+) and collapse (-) icons. These will expand or collapse the selected group.

Copying Subtotals

If you hide the data rows, copy the subtotals, and paste them to another sheet, all the data, including the hidden data rows, will appear in the new sheet. To copy and paste only the subtotals, select only the visible cells.

 LET ME TRY IT

Copying Only the Totals to a New Location

To copy only the totals to a new location, follow these steps:

1. Click the outline icon so that only the rows to copy are visible.

2. Select the entire dataset.

3. Go to Home, Editing, Find & Select, Go to Special, and select Visible Cells Only, as shown in Figure 9.5. Note: the dashed lines in the figure are shown for emphasis only. They will appear in the next step.

4. Select Home, Clipboard, Copy.

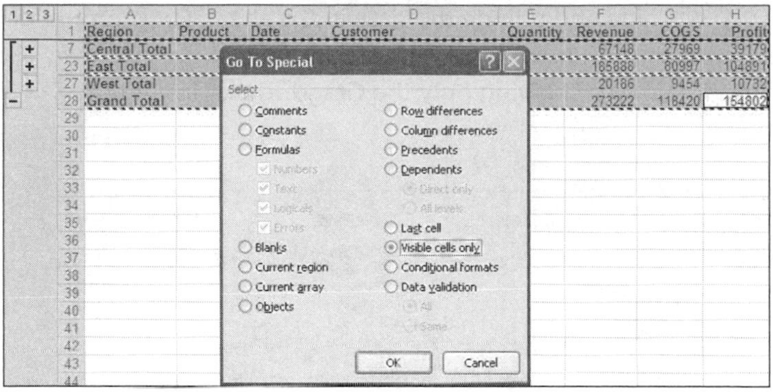

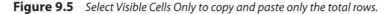

Figure 9.5   *Select Visible Cells Only to copy and paste only the total rows.*

5. Select the cell where the data is to be pasted.

6. Select Home, Clipboard, Paste. The formulas will be converted to values automatically.

A shortcut for step 3 is to press ALT+; (semicolon).

Formatting Subtotals

If you hide the data rows, select the subtotals, and apply formatting to them, all the data, including the hidden data rows, will reflect the new formatting. To format just the subtotals, select only the visible cells.

LET ME TRY IT

Applying Formatting to Only the Totals

To copy just the totals to a new location, follow these steps:

1. Click the outline icon so that only the rows to format are visible.

2. Select the entire dataset. If you don't want to apply the formatting to the header row, do not include it in the selection.

3. Go to Home, Editing, Find & Select, Go to Special, and select Visible Cells Only.

4. Apply the desired formatting.

A shortcut for step 3 is to press ALT+; (semicolon).

Applying Multiple Subtotal Function Types

A dataset can have more than one type of subtotal applied to it—for example, a sum subtotal of one column and a count subtotal of another. Make sure the Replace Current Subtotals option in the Subtotal dialog is deselected so that each subtotal will be applied separately. Each subtotal will be calculated and placed on its own row, pushing any existing subtotal row down, as shown in Figure 9.6.

	A	B	C	D	E	F	G	H
1	Region	Product	Date	Customer	Quantity	Revenue	COGS	Profit
7	Central Count				5			
8	Central Total					67148	27969	39179
24	East Count				15			
25	East Total					185888	80997	104891
26	West	ABC	1/21/2008	Cool Jewelry Corporation	200	3552	1694	1858
27	West	ABC	1/23/2008	Remarkable Meter Corporat	800	14592	6776	7816
28	West	DEF	1/19/2008	Bright Hairpin Company	100	2042	984	1058
29	West Count				3			
30	West Total					20186	9454	10732
31	Grand Count				23			
32	Grand Total					273222	118420	154802

Figure 9.6   *Multiple subtotals can be applied to a dataset. The Total was added first, followed by the Count.*

 **LET ME TRY IT**

Applying Multiple Subtotal Function Types

To apply multiple subtotals to a dataset, follow these steps:

1. Sort the data by the column the summary should be based on. For example, if summarizing by region, sort the Region column.

See Chapter 7 for more information about sorting by column.

2. Select a cell in the dataset.

3. Go to Data, Outline, Subtotal.

4. From the At Each Change In field, select the column by which to summarize the data.

5. From the Use Function field, select the function to calculate the totals by.

6. From the Add Subtotal To field, select the columns the totals should be added to. Notice that, by default, the last column is already selected.

7. Click OK.

8. Go to Data, Outline, Subtotal.

9. Deselect Replace Current Subtotals.

10. Repeat steps 4 to 6, selecting a new function from the Use Function field.

11. Click OK. The dataset will reflect two subtotals.

Combining Multiple Subtotals to One Row

When applying multiple function types, Excel places each subtotal on its own row. There is no built-in option to have the subtotals appear on the same row. But you can manipulate Excel to make this happen by applying a subtotal to a column where you don't want it, and then manually changing the formula.

 **LET ME TRY IT**

Portraying Multiple Function Types on a Single Row

To have multiple function types appear on a single row, as shown in Figure 9.7, follow these steps:

Figure 9.7   *Columns F:H are sums of the grouped data, but column D is a count of the data, as shown in the formula bar (3 is the function code for COUNTA).*

1. Sort the data by the column the summary should be based off of. For example, if summarizing by region, sort the Region column.

   See Chapter 7 for more information about sorting by columns.

2. Select a cell in the dataset.

3. Go to Data, Outline, Subtotal.

4. From the At Each Change In field, select the column by which to summarize the data.

5. From the Use Function field, select the function to calculate the totals by.

6. From the Add Subtotal To field, select the columns the totals should be added to. Also select the column where you want to apply the second function type, like the Customer column selected in Figure 9.8.

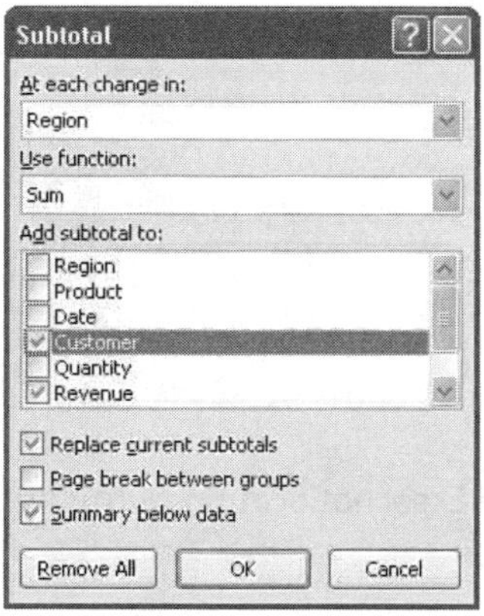

Figure 9.8   *The Customer column is selected as a temporary holder for the actual subtotal formula that will be used.*

7. Click OK.

8. Collapse the dataset by clicking the "2" outline symbol so only the total rows are visible.

9. Select the data in the column where the second function type should be.

10. Go to Home, Editing, Find & Select, Go to Special, and select Visible Cells Only.

11. Go to Home, Editing, Find & Select, Replace.

12. In the Find What field, type "SUBTOTAL(9,".

13. In the Replace With field, type the subtotal function using the desired function number. For example, in Figure 9.9, "SUBTOTAL(2," will replace the SUM function with the COUNTA function.

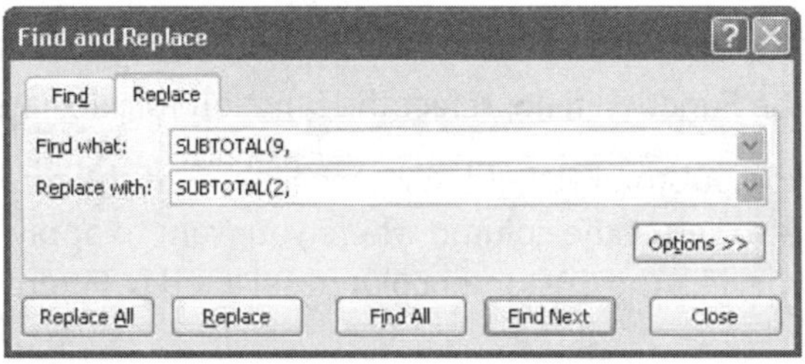

Figure 9.9   *Use Find and Replace to replace the automated subtotals with the desired function argument.*

See the "SUBTOTAL Function" section earlier in this chapter for the available codes.

14. Click Replace All.

15. Click OK to close the Excel notification of the number of replacements made.

16. Click Close. If needed, apply any required formatting to the selected cells.

Subtotaling by Multiple Columns

To add subtotals based on multiple columns, as shown in Figure 9.10, sort the dataset by the desired columns and then apply the subtotals, making sure Replace Current Subtotals is not selected. The subtotals should be applied in order of greatest to least. For example, if the data is sorted by Region, with the products within each region sorted, apply the subtotal to the Region column and then the Product column.

Figure 9.10 *Apply subtotals to Region (the major column) and then Product (the secondary column) to get subtotals of both.*

SHOW ME   Media 9.3—Subtotaling by Multiple Columns

Access this video file through your registered web edition at my.safaribooksonline.com/9780132182287/media.

LET ME TRY IT

Subtotaling by Multiple Columns

To subtotal by multiple columns, as shown in Figure 9.10, follow these steps:

1. Sort the data by the columns the summary should be based on.

> See Chapter 7, "Sorting" for more information about sorting by columns.

2. Select a cell in the dataset.

3. Go to Data, Outline, Subtotal.

4. From the At Each Change In field, select the major column by which to summarize the data.

5. From the Use Function field, select the function to calculate the totals by.

6. From the Add Subtotal To field, select the columns the totals should be added to.

7. Click OK.

8. Repeat steps 3 to 7 for the secondary column.

Sorting Subtotals

If you try to sort a subtotaled dataset while viewing all the data, Excel informs you that to do so would remove all the subtotals. Although the data itself cannot be sorted, the subtotal rows can be, and the data within will remain intact. To do this, collapse the data so that only the subtotals are being viewed, and then apply the desired sort.

 LET ME TRY IT

Sorting a Subtotaled Column

To sort the dataset by a subtotaled column, follow these steps:

1. Collapse the dataset so only the subtotals are in view.

2. Select a cell in the column to be sorted.

3. Go to Data, Sort & Filter, and select the quick sort button for the desired sort order.

Inserting Blank Rows

When subtotals are inserted into a dataset, only one row is added between the groups. The report may appear crunched together for some reviewers (see Figure 9.11), and they may request that rows be inserted, separating the subtotaled groups from each other. You can insert blank rows into a subtotaled report in two ways.

	A	B	C	D	E	F	G	H
1	Region	Product	Date	Customer	Quantity	Revenue	COGS	Profit
2	East	XYZ	1/14/2008	Matchless Vise Inc.	100	2401	1022	1379
3				Matchless Vise Inc. Total		2401	1022	1379
4	East	ABC	1/15/2008	Bright Hairpin Company	500	9345	4235	5110
5	Central	DEF	1/2/2008	Bright Hairpin Company	100	2257	984	1273
6	West	DEF	1/19/2008	Bright Hairpin Company	100	2042	984	1058
7				Bright Hairpin Company Total		13644	6203	7441
8	West	ABC	1/4/2008	Tasty Kettle Inc.	400	9152	3388	3748
9	East	ABC	1/29/2008	Tasty Kettle Inc.	400	7136	3388	3748
10				Tasty Kettle Inc. Total		16288	6776	7496
11	East	DEF	1/4/2008	Cool Jewelry Corporation	800	18552	7872	10680
12	West	ABC	1/21/2008	Cool Jewelry Corporation	200	3552	1694	1858
13				Cool Jewelry Corporation Total		22104	9566	12538
14	East	XYZ	1/17/2008	Exclusive Shovel Traders	1000	22810	10220	12590
15				Exclusive Shovel Traders Total		22810	10220	12590
16	East	ABC	1/24/2008	Reliable Tripod Company	600	12606	5082	7524
17	East	ABC	1/26/2008	Reliable Tripod Company	400	8128	3388	4740
18	Central	ABC	1/12/2008	Reliable Tripod Company	300	6267	2541	3726
19				Reliable Tripod Company Total		27001	11011	15990
20	Central	XYZ	1/10/2008	Safe Flagpole Supply	900	21438	9198	12240
21	East	DEF	1/30/2008	Safe Flagpole Supply	300	6714	2952	3762
22				Safe Flagpole Supply Total		28152	12150	16002
23	Central	ABC	1/25/2008	Appealing Calculator Corporation	1000	20770	8470	12300
24	East	ABC	1/16/2008	Appealing Calculator Corporation	600	11628	5082	6546
25				Appealing Calculator Corporation Total		32398	13552	18846
26	East	DEF	1/29/2008	Remarkable Meter Corporation	700	17150	6888	10262
27	Central	ABC	1/9/2008	Remarkable Meter Corporation	800	16416	6776	9640
28	East	ABC	1/31/2008	Remarkable Meter Corporation	800	15640	6776	8864
29	West	ABC	1/23/2008	Remarkable Meter Corporation	800	14592	6776	7816
30	East	ABC	1/7/2008	Remarkable Meter Corporation	400	8456	3388	5068
31				Remarkable Meter Corporation Total		72254	30604	41650
32				Grand Total		237052	101104	133932

Figure 9.11   *The close rows in this report can make it difficult to see the different groups.*

Separating Subtotaled Rows for Print

If the report is going to be printed, blank rows probably don't need to be inserted. Just the illusion needs to be created because the actual need is for more space between the subtotal and the next group. This can be done by adjusting the row height of the subtotal rows.

 LET ME TRY IT

Increasing the Amount of Space After a Subtotal

To increase the amount of space after a subtotal placed below the data, follow these steps:

1. Collapse the dataset so that only the subtotals are in view.

2. Select the entire dataset, except for the header row.

3. Press Alt+; (semicolon) to select the visible cells only.

4. Go to Home, Cells, Format, and select Row Height.

5. Enter a new value in the Row Height dialog, as shown in Figure 9.12.

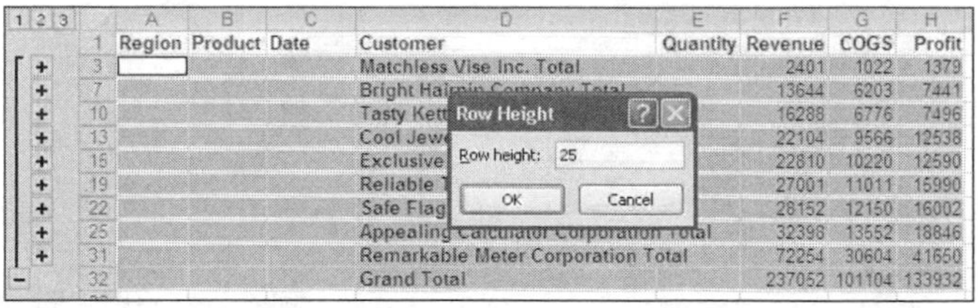

Figure 9.12 *Adjust the row height of the subtotal rows to give the appearance of an extra row between the groups.*

6. Click OK.

7. Go to Home, Alignment, and select the Top Align button.

8. Spacing now appears between each group, as shown in Figure 9.13.

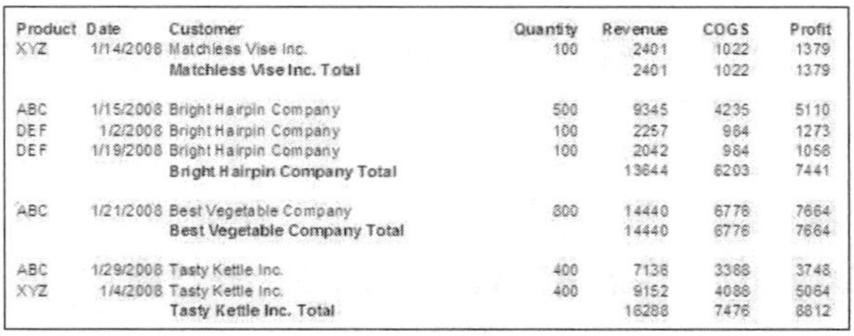

Figure 9.13 *Adjust the row height and text alignment of the subtotal rows to separate the groups.*

Separating Subtotaled Rows for Distributed Files

It's a bit involved, but a blank row can be inserted between groups in a file that you're going to distribute. The method involves using a temporary column to hold the space below where a blank row is needed.

This method will disable Excel's capability to manipulate the subtotals in the dataset. The total rows will remain, but the outline icons no longer work properly, and future subtotal changes will require the groupings and subtotals to be manually removed first.

SHOW ME Media 9.4—Inserting Blank Rows Between Subtotal Groups

Access this video file through your registered web edition at my.safaribooksonline.com/9780132182287/media.

 LET ME TRY IT

Inserting Blank Rows After Subtotals

To insert blank rows after subtotals placed below the data (see Figure 9.14), follow these steps:

1. Collapse the dataset so only the subtotals are in view.

2. In a blank column to the right of the dataset, select a range as long as the dataset.

3. Press Alt+; (semicolon) to select the visible cells only.

4. Type a 1 and press Ctrl+Enter to enter the value in all visible cells.

5. Expand the dataset.

6. Select the cell above the first cell with a 1 in it.

7. Go to Home, Cells, Insert, Insert Cells.

8. From the Insert dialog, select Shift Cells Down, and click OK, as shown in Figure 9.14.

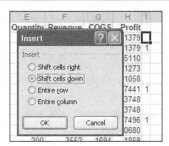

Figure 9.14 *Select the cell above the first cell with a 1 in it then insert a new cell to shift all the values down one row.*

9. Highlight the column with the 1s in it.

10. Go to Home, Editing, Find & Select, Go to Special.

11. From the Go to Special dialog, select Constants and click OK, as shown in Figure 9.15

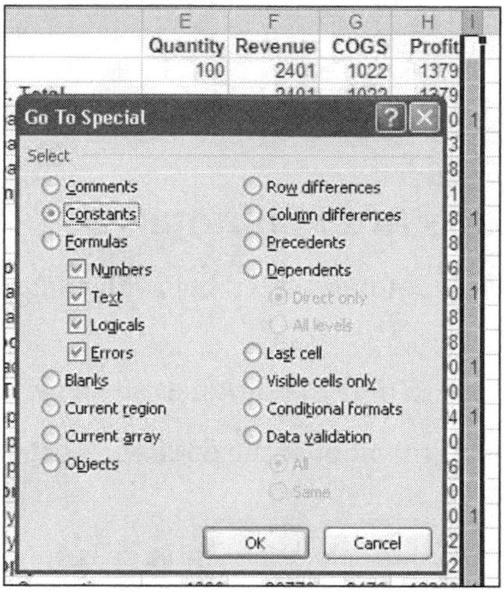

Figure 9.15   *Use Go To Special, Constants to select just the 1s in the temporary column.*

12. Go to Home, Cells, Insert, Insert Sheet Rows. A blank row is inserted above the row containing a 1, as shown in Figure 9.16.

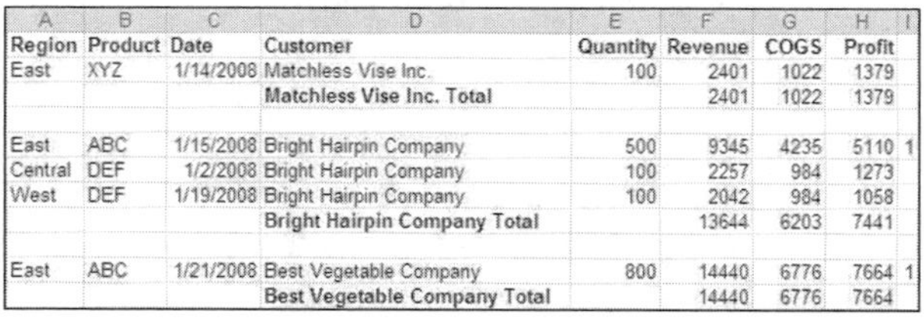

A	B	C	D	E	F	G	H	I
Region	Product	Date	Customer	Quantity	Revenue	COGS	Profit	
East	XYZ	1/14/2008	Matchless Vise Inc.	100	2401	1022	1379	
			Matchless Vise Inc. Total		2401	1022	1379	
East	ABC	1/15/2008	Bright Hairpin Company	500	9345	4235	5110	1
Central	DEF	1/2/2008	Bright Hairpin Company	100	2257	984	1273	
West	DEF	1/19/2008	Bright Hairpin Company	100	2042	984	1058	
			Bright Hairpin Company Total		13644	6203	7441	
East	ABC	1/21/2008	Best Vegetable Company	800	14440	6776	7664	1
			Best Vegetable Company Total		14440	6776	7664	

Figure 9.16   *Use a temporary column to insert blank rows between groups.*

13. Delete the temporary column.

Grouping and Outlining

Selected rows and groups can be grouped together manually using the options in Data, Outline, Group. The Expand/Collapse button will be placed below the last row in the selection or to the right of the last column in the selection.

If the data to be grouped includes a calculated total row or column between the groups, you can use the Auto Outline option. This option creates groups based on the location of the rows or columns containing formulas. If the dataset contains formulas in both rows and columns, though, the option will create groups for both rows and columns. This tool works best if there are no formulas within the dataset itself, unless you do want the groups to be created based off those calculations.

Use the Group option for absolute control of how the rows or columns are grouped. For example, if you have a catalog with products grouped together, users can expand or collapse each group to view the products, as shown in Figure 9.17. By default, the Expand/Collapse buttons will appear below the data. To get them to appear above the grouped data, first apply a subtotal to the dataset with Summary Below Data unselected. Then undo the change and apply the desired groupings.

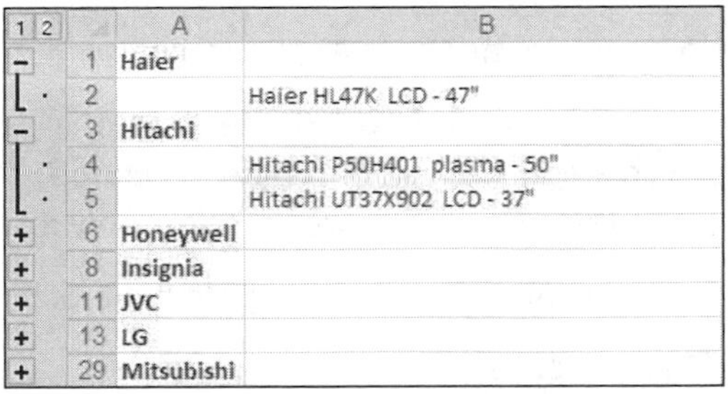

Figure 9.17 *Group items together to make it easier for users to view only the desired items.*

Groups can be cleared one of two ways from the Data, Outline, Ungroup dropdown:

- **Ungroup**—Ungroups the selected data. Will ungroup a single row from a larger group if that is all that is selected.

- **Clear Outline**—Clears all groups on a sheet unless more than one cell is selected, in which case the selected item will be ungrouped. If used on data that was subtotaled using the Subtotal button, the subtotals will remain; only the groups will be removed.

LET ME TRY IT

Manually Grouping Rows

To manually group rows with the Expand/Collapse button above the grouped dataset, follow these steps:

1. Select a cell in the dataset.

2. Go to Data, Outline, Subtotal.

3. A message may appear that Excel cannot determine which row has column labels. Click OK.

4. In the Subtotal dialog, deselect Summary Below Data and click OK.

5. Click the Undo button in the Quick Access toolbar.

6. Select the first set of rows to group together. Do not include the header. For example, to create the Hitachi grouping in Figure 9.17, select rows 4 and 5 to group. To create the Haier group, select only row 2.

7. Go to Data, Outline, Group, Group, or just select the Group button itself.

8. Repeat steps 6 and 7 for each group of rows.

10

Pivot Tables

Pivot tables can summarize one million rows with five clicks of the mouse button. They're so powerful with so many options that this chapter cannot cover it all. This chapter is meant to provide you with the tools to create straightforward, but useful, pivot tables. If you find your needs not covered by the sections in this chapter, refer to *Pivot Table Data Crunching: Microsoft Excel 2010* (ISBN 0-7897-4313-2) by Bill Jelen and Michael Alexander.

Excel is required to create pivot tables, but the functionality in an existing pivot table will carry over to Excel Starter and Web App.

Data Preparation

Your dataset should adhere to a few basic formatting guidelines for working with pivot tables:

- There should be no blank rows or columns.

- If a column contains numeric data, don't allow blank cells in the column. Use zeros instead of blanks.

- Each row should be a complete record.

- There shouldn't be any total rows.

- There should be a unique header above every column.

- Headers should be in only one row; otherwise, Excel will get confused, unable to find the header row on its own.

Figure 10.1 shows a dataset properly formatted for working with pivot tables. Figure 10.2 shows a dataset not suitable for pivot tables. The dates should be in a column of their own. And although a person may understand that all the data shown is relevant to the West region, Excel does not. If your dataset looks like Figure 10.2, refer to the "Making Data Suitable for Pivot Tables" section for steps to help make the dataset more suitable.

	A	B	C	D	E	F	G	H
1	Region	Product	Date	Customer	Quantity	Revenue	COGS	Profit
2	East	XYZ	1/1/2008	Exclusive Shovel Traders	1000	22810	10220	12590
3	Central	DEF	1/2/2008	Bright Hairpin Company	100	2257	984	1273
4	East	DEF	1/4/2008	Cool Jewelry Corporation	800	18552	7872	10680
5	East	XYZ	1/4/2008	Tasty Kettle Inc.	400	9152	4088	5064
6	East	ABC	1/7/2008	Remarkable Meter Corporat	400	8456	3388	5068
7	East	DEF	1/7/2008	Wonderful Jewelry Inc.	1000	21730	9840	11890
8	Central	ABC	1/9/2008	Remarkable Meter Corporat	800	16416	6776	9640
9	Central	XYZ	1/10/2008	Safe Flagpole Supply	900	21438	9198	12240
10	Central	ABC	1/12/2008	Reliable Tripod Company	300	6267	2541	3726
11	East	XYZ	1/14/2008	Matchless Vise Inc.	100	2401	1022	1379
12	East	ABC	1/15/2008	Bright Hairpin Company	500	9345	4235	5110
13	East	ABC	1/16/2008	Appealing Calculator Corpoi	600	11628	5082	6546

Figure 10.1 *This dataset is great for pivot tables.*

	A	B	C	D	E	F
1	Region	Customer	Product	Jan	Feb	Mar
2	Central	Alluring Shoe Company	ABC	10445		
3			DEF		22784	4472
4			XYZ	20444		
5		Alluring Shoe Company Total		30889	22784	4472
6		Appealing Calculator Corporation	ABC	38275	1817	
7			DEF			
8			XYZ			43213
9		Appealing Calculator Corporation Total		38275	1817	43213
10		Best Vegetable Company	DEF			
11		Best Vegetable Company Total				
12		Bright Eggbeater Corporation	ABC			
13			DEF			
14		Bright Eggbeater Corporation Total				
15		Bright Hairpin Company	ABC		11922	
16			DEF	2257		
17			XYZ			

Figure 10.2 *This dataset is not suitable for a pivot table.*

Pivot Table Limitations

As incredibly powerful as pivot tables are, they do have a few limitations:

- Only 1 million rows are allowed, despite the 1,048,576 rows on a sheet.
- Only 16,000 columns are allowed, despite the 16,384 columns on a sheet.
- Only 1 million unique items per field are allowed.
- You cannot add a calculated item to a grouped field.
- If a field is grouped by days, grouping by months, quarters, or years will undo the group by days.
- Changing the source data does not automatically update the pivot table. You must click the Refresh button.

- Blank cells confuse Excel. A single blank cell in a numeric column will make Excel think the column contains text values, changing the default behavior for that column.

- You cannot insert rows or columns in a pivot table.

Pivot Table Compatibility

Pivot table compatibility between Excel 2010 and the legacy versions is a bit tricky.

- If you open an xlsx file with a converter in a legacy version, the pivot tables will not work.

- If you create pivot tables in an xlsx file and then save the file as an xls, the pivot tables will not work. The compatibility checker dialog will appear when you save the file, warning of the incompatibilities, such as Show Values As.

- To get a pivot table created in 2010 to work in legacy Excel, save the file as an xls before creating the pivot table. Close and reopen the file, and then create the pivot table. Any options not compatible with older versions of Excel, such as slicers (which you can read more about later in this chapter), will not be available. Strangely enough, you can apply Show Values As and save the file. Excel will not warn of compatibility issues and the pivot table will open fine in legacy versions.

PivotTable Field List

There are two parts to a pivot table report—the pivot table itself and the PivotTable Field List, which appears only when a cell in the pivot table is selected. The PivotTable Field List consists of a list of the column headers in the dataset (the *fields*) and the four areas of a pivot table.

Figure 10.3 shows a basic pivot table, using all four areas of a pivot table to summarize product revenue by month on a regional basis. The four areas are as follows:

- **Report Filter**—Limits the report to a specific criteria; in this case, we are looking at only the West region's revenue. Instead of creating a separate report for each region, use the Report Filter to view the desired region.

- **Column Labels**—The headers going across the top of the pivot table—in this case, the monthly breakdown.

- **Row Labels**—The labels going down the left side of the pivot table—in this case, the Products. If there is more than one field, the fields will appear in a hierarchical view, with the second field under the first field.

- **Values**—The data being summarized—in this case, Revenue. The data can be summed, counted, and many other calculation types.

Not all four areas must be used. Each area can have more than one field.

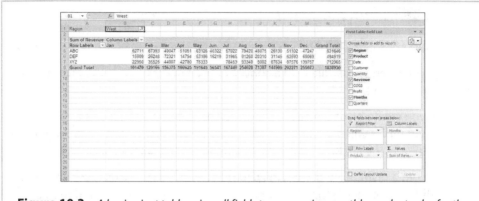

Figure 10.3   *A basic pivot table using all fields to summarize monthly product sales for the West region.*

Creating a Pivot Table

Creating a pivot table is simple if the dataset is suitable for pivot tables. It can be quickly created by selecting the desired fields in the field list. Based on the data in a field, Excel will place the selected field in the area it thinks it should go. Text fields will be placed in the Row Label area. Numeric fields will be placed in the Values area and summed. If a field needs to be moved, see the section "Moving Fields in a Pivot Table."

SHOW ME   Media 10.1—Creating a Pivot Table
Access this video file through your registered web edition at my.safaribooksonline.com/9780132182287/media.

LET ME TRY IT

Creating a Pivot Table

To create a pivot table from data on another sheet in the workbook, follow these steps:

1. Make sure the dataset is set up properly, as explained in the section "Data Preparation.

2. Select a cell in the dataset.

3. Go to Insert, Tables, and click the PivotTable button (not the drop-down arrow).

4. The Create Pivot Table dialog, shown in Figure 10.4, will appear where Excel will select the dataset. If the selection is correct, continue to step 5. If the selection is not correct, return to step 1.

Create PivotTable ? ☒

Choose the data that you want to analyze
◉ Select a table or range
    Table/Range: `Pivot Table'!$A$1:$H$564`
○ Use an external data source
    Choose Connection...
    Connection name:

Choose where you want the PivotTable report to be placed
◉ New Worksheet
○ Existing Worksheet
    Location:

OK   Cancel

Figure 10.4 *Use the Create Pivot Table dialog to identify the source data and where the pivot table should be created.*

5. Select the location where the pivot table is to be placed. The default location is always a new sheet. If using an existing sheet, ensure there is enough room on the sheet.

6. Click OK. The pivot table template and field list will appear, as shown in Figure 10.5.

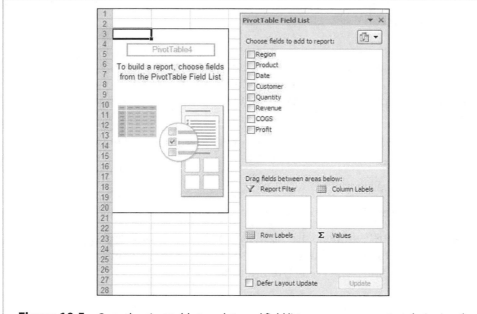

Figure 10.5   *Once the pivot table template and field list appear, you can start designing the report.*

7. Select the fields that should be the row labels. Select them in the order they should appear in, left to right on the report.

8. Select the fields the report should summarize.

9. If a field needs to be a column label, click and drag the field from the list to the Column Labels area.

10. If a field needs to be a filter, click and drag the field from the list to the Report Filter area.

11. If any of the fields in steps 7 and 8 didn't appear where you wanted them to or if the values were counted instead of summarized, see the section "Moving Fields in a Pivot Table."

TELL ME MORE   **Media 10.2—Using Other Data Sources**

To listen to a free audio recording about using other data sources to create pivot tables, log on to my.safaribooksonline.com/9780132182287/media.

Moving Fields in a Pivot Table

When you select fields in the field list and add them to an area that already contains fields, the new fields are placed below the existing fields. The up/down layout in the area corresponds to a left/right layout of the fields in the pivot table, except for the Report filter, which also goes up/down.

The order of the fields and the area in which they're located can be changed by clicking the field and dragging it to a new location. You can also drag fields from the field list to an area, instead of selecting them and letting Excel choose their locations.

You can reorganize the layout by clicking and dragging the headers in the pivot table itself. The new location is signified by a semisolid line, as shown in Figure 10.6.

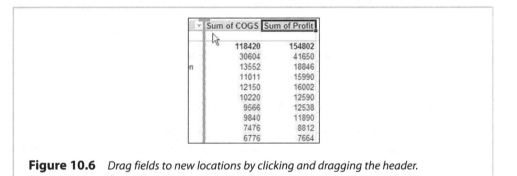

Figure 10.6   *Drag fields to new locations by clicking and dragging the header.*

Remove a Field

To remove a field from a pivot table, deselect it from the field list or click it in the area and select Remove Field. You can also click and drag the field from the area to the sheet until an X appears by the cursor. When the X appears, release the mouse button.

Rename a Field

You can rename the field as it appears in the pivot table by typing a new name directly in the cell. The name must be unique and cannot be the same as the field's original name before it was placed in the pivot table.

Change Calculation Type

When Excel identifies a field as numeric, it automatically sums the data. If it cannot identify the field as numeric, it will count the data. No matter which calculation type Excel appoints to a value field, it can be changed by going to PivotTable Tools, Options, Calculations, Summarize Values By, and selecting an option from the drop-down.

 **LET ME TRY IT**

Change the Calculation Type of a Field Value

To change the calculation type used on a field value, follow these steps:

1. Select a cell in the value field to change.

2. Go to PivotTable Tools, Options, Calculations, Summarize Values By.

3. Select a new calculation type from the drop-down.

Show Values Based on Other Items

Go to PivotTable Tools, Options, Calculations, Show Values As to change the way the data is viewed—for example, in comparison to another field as shown in Figure 10.7. The following options do not require additional information:

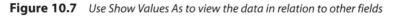

No Calculation

Sum of Revenue	Column		
Row Labels	2008	2009	Grand Total
⊟West	810984	1027946	1838930
ABC	267136	364510	631646
DEF	255506	239413	494919
XYZ	288342	424023	712365
⊞Central	1248944	1126935	2375879
⊞East	1347625	1145378	2493003
Grand Total	3407553	3300259	6707812

% Of Grand Total

Sum of Revenue	Column		
Row Labels	2008	2009	Grand Total
⊟West	12.09%	15.32%	27.41%
ABC	3.98%	5.43%	9.42%
DEF	3.81%	3.57%	7.38%
XYZ	4.30%	6.32%	10.62%
⊞Central	18.62%	16.80%	35.42%
⊞East	20.09%	17.08%	37.17%
Grand Total	50.80%	49.20%	100.00%

Rank Smallest To Largest In Product

Sum of Revenue	Column		
Row Labels	2008	2009	Grand Total
⊟West			
ABC	2	2	2
DEF	1	1	1
XYZ	3	3	3
⊞Central			
⊞East			
Grand Total			

% Of West Region

Sum of Revenue	Colum		
Row Labels	2008	2009	Grand Total
⊞West	100.00%	100.00%	100.00%
⊞Central	154.00%	109.63%	129.20%
⊞East	166.17%	111.42%	135.57%
Grand Total			

Figure 10.7 *Use Show Values As to view the data in relation to other fields*

- **No Calculation**—The default selection that shows the actual numbers.

- **% of Grand Total**—Displays values as a percentage of the grand total of all the values in the report.

- **% of Column Total**—Displays values as a percentage of the column total.

- **% of Row Total**—Displays values as a percentage of the row total.

- **% of Parent Row Total**—Displays values based on the following calculation: (value for the item)/(value for the parent item on rows).

- **% of Parent Column Total**—Displays values based on the following calculation: (value for the item)/(value for the parent item on columns).

- **Index**—Displays values based on the following calculation: ((value in cell) x (Grand Total of Grand Totals))/(((Grand Row Total) x (Grand Column Total)).

The following options require that a base field be specified:

- **% of Parent Total**—Displays values based on the following calculation: (value for the item)/(value for the parent item of the selected Base field).

- **Running Total In**—Displays values for successive items in the selected Base field as a running total.

- **% Running Total In**—Calculates the value for successive items in the selected Base field that are displayed as a running total as a percentage.

- **Rank Smallest to Largest**—Displays the rank of the values in the specified field, with 1 representing the smallest item.

- **Rank Largest to Smallest**—Displays the rank of the values in the specified field, with 1 representing the largest item.

The following options require that a base field and base item be specified:

- **% Of**—Displays values as a percentage of the value of the selected Base item in the Base field.

- **Difference From**—Displays values as the difference from the value of the selected Base item in the Base field.

- **% Difference From**—Displays values as the percentage difference from the value of the selected Base item in the Base field.

Pivot Table Sorting

Excel automatically sorts text data alphabetically when building a pivot table. Any record or field in a pivot table can be dragged to a new location, the same way a header can be as shown in Figure 10.6, but this is a temporary measure. After you pivot the table, the sort will be lost.

Another option is to sort using one of the methods in the following sections. When a sort is applied in a pivot table, it remembers the settings, so as you pivot the table, the sort sticks.

Pivot Table Quick Sort

The quick sort buttons offer one-click access to sorting cell values. There are four entry points to the quick sort buttons.

- On the Home tab, select Editing, Sort & Filter, Sort A to Z[1] or Sort Z to A[1].

- Data, Sort & Filter, select either the AZ or ZA quick sort buttons to sort the active field

- Right-click a cell in the pivot table, select Sort, and choose from Sort A to Z[1] or Sort Z to A[1].

- From a pivot label drop-down, select Sort A to Z[1] or Sort Z to A[1].

Unlike sorting outside pivot tables, it doesn't matter if you have more than one cell selected during the sort. Excel will automatically sort the entire pivot table. If multiple columns are selected Excel will sort only the leftmost column in the selection.

To quick sort a field, select a cell in the field and apply the desired quick sort method outlined previously. The data will re-sort based on the selected field. The sort dialog, discussed in the following section, will be updated for the selected field.

Pivot Table Sort (*Fieldname*) Dialog

To bring up the pivot table Sort (*fieldname*) dialog shown in Figure 10.8, select a

---

[1]*The actual button text may change depending on the type of data in the cell. For example, if the column contains values, the text will be Sort Smallest to Largest. If the column contains text, it will be Sort Z to A.*

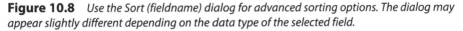

Figure 10.8 *Use the Sort (fieldname) dialog for advanced sorting options. The dialog may appear slightly different depending on the data type of the selected field.*

cell and use one of the following methods:

- Select a cell in the desired field, and then go to the Home tab, select Editing, Sort & Filter, Custom Sort.

- Select a cell in the desired field, and then go to Data, Sort & Filter, Sort.

- Right-click a cell in the desired field in the pivot table, select Sort, and select More Sort Options.

- From a pivot label drop-down, select More Sort Options. You can select the field to sort at the top of the drop-down.

The Sort (*fieldname*) dialog provides additional sorting options, which the pivot table will remember as the table layout is changed.

- **Manual**—The default sort, clearing, but not undoing, any previous settings.

- **Ascending/Descending**—These options sort the selected column based on the original field or a value field selected from the drop-down.

If you click the More Options button, the following options are revealed:

- **AutoSort**—Select to have the sort updated when the pivot table is updated.

- **First Key Sort Order**—Available when AutoSort is deselected, allowing the field to be sorted by a custom list.

- **Sort by Grand Total**—Available when either Ascending or Descending is selected with another field; this option sorts the data using the Grand Totals.

- **Sort by Values In Selected Column**—Available when either Ascending or Descending is selected with another field; this option sorts the data using the column of the selected cell.

LET ME TRY IT

Create a Sort Rule

To create a sort rule for one field based on another, as shown in Figure 10.9, follow these steps:

	Total Sum of COGS	Total Sum of Profit
Sum of Profit 2008	2009	
154802	154183	239173	308985

Sort (Customer)

Sort options
- ○ Manual (you can drag items to rearrange them)
- ⊙ Ascending (A to Z) by:
  - Sum of Profit
- ○ Descending (Z to A) by:
  - Sum of Profit

Summary
Sort Customer by Sum of Profit in ascending order using values in this column: 2008

| 1379 |
| 7441 |
| 7664 |
| 8812 |
| 11890 |
| 12538 |
| 12590 |
| 15990 |
| 16002 |
| 18846 |
| 41650 |
| 174287 |
| 149095 |
| 156325 |
| 183231 |

More Options...   OK   Cancel

Figure 10.9 *Create a rule to sort data on a specific column using More Options. In this case, customer names will be sorted by 2008 profits.*

1. Select a row or column label cell in the field to apply the rule to.

2. Go to PivotTable Tools, Options, Sort & Filter, Sort.

3. Make sure the field name in the Sort (*fieldname*) dialog is the field the rule will be applied to. If not, repeat steps 1 and 2.

4. Select the sort direction option.

5. From the now active drop-down, select the field to be sorted.

6. Select More Options

7. Select the AutoSort option if the report should re-sort automatically.

8. Select Grand Total to base the sort on the Grand Total of the column selected in step 5, and continue to step 9. Otherwise, skip to step 11.

9. Select Values in Selected Column to base the sort on a specific column.

10. If the cell address in the Values does not reflect the correct column, high-light it and then select a cell in the desired column on the sheet.

11. Click OK twice.

Expanding and Collapsing Fields

Individual groups in a pivot table can be quickly expanded and collapsed by click-ing the + and - icons. Additional methods, including the capability to expand or collapse all the groups in a fields are the following:

- Select a cell in the field and go to Data, Outline, Show Detail or Hide Detail, which affects all the groups in the field.

- Select a cell in the field and go to PivotTable Tools, Options, Active Field, Expand Entire Field or Collapse Entire Field, which affects all the groups in the field.

- Right-click a cell in the field and choose one of the following:
  - **Expand or Collapse**—Affects the selected group.
  - **Expand Entire Field** or **Collapse Entire Field**—Affects all the groups in the field.
  - **Collapse to (fieldname)** or **Expand to (fieldname)**—One or more menu options, depending on the number of grouped fields available, affects the selected group.

If you try to expand a data item instead of the field itself, Excel will open a Show Detail dialog allowing you to add a new field within the selected data item.

Drill Down

Double-clicking a data item, or right-clicking and selecting Show Details, will create a new sheet with a table showing the records from which the data item was derived. This can be useful if you notice a value in a pivot table that stands out and you need to investigate it in more detail.

The new table is not linked to the original data or the pivot table. If you need to make corrections to the data, make them to the original source and refresh the pivot table. You can then delete the sheet that was created for the drill down.

Grouping Dates

A common issue with pivot tables occurs when someone tries to group a date field and receives the error Cannot Group That Selection. The reason may be that the dates are not real dates, but instead text that looks like dates. If that's the case, see the "Using Text to Columns" section in Chapter 3, "Entering Data in Excel" to convert the text dates to real dates.

The Grouping dialog allows dates to be grouped by number of days, months, quarters, and years. When dates are grouped into more than one type, such as month and year, virtual fields are added to the pivot table, which can be used just like the regular fields.

To access the Grouping dialog, do one of the following:

- Right-click a date and select Group.

- Select a date cell and go to PivotTable Tools, Group, Group Selection or Group Field.

- Select a date and go to Data, Outline, Group.

When grouping dates, if Months is the only selection, multiple years will be combined into the month. To get the months grouped into their respective years, also select Years from the dialog.

To return the dates to normal, you have to ungroup the field. Unselecting the original or virtual field will not ungroup the dates. To ungroup the dates, do one of the following:

- Right-click a grouped date and select Ungroup.

- Select a date cell and go to PivotTable Tools, Options, Group, Ungroup.

- Select a date and go to Data, Outline, Ungroup.

SHOW ME   Media 10.3—Grouping Dates into Months and Years

Access this video file through your registered web edition at
my.safaribooksonline.com/9780132182287/media.

LET ME TRY IT

Group a Date Field into Months and Years

To group a date into months and years, follow these steps:

1. Select a cell in the pivot table with a date value.

2. Go to Tools, Group, Group Field. If you receive the error Cannot Group That Selection, see the "Using Text to Columns" section in Chapter 3 to convert the text dates to real dates. Otherwise, continue to step 3.

3. The date range found by Excel will appear in the Group dialog. Make changes if needed.

4. Select Months and Years.

5. Click OK. The data will be grouped into months and years, and a Years field will be added to the field list.

Summarize Weeks

At first glance, there does not appear to be a way of creating a weekly report. But by using the Days option in the Group dialog, seven days can be grouped together to create a week, 14 days for a biweekly report, and so on. Excel will group the selected number of days based on the range in the dialog, so if the weeks need to represent a normal week, such as Sunday to Saturday, change the starting date to be a Sunday that will include the first date in the dataset, as shown in Figure 10.10.

Row Labels	Sum of COGS
12/27/2007 - 1/2/2008	11204
1/3/2008 - 1/9/2008	31964
1/10/2008 - 1/16/2008	22078
1/17/2008 - 1/23/2008	16230
1/24/2008 - 1/30/2008	30168
1/31/2008 - 2/6/2008	26045
2/7/2008 - 2/13/2008	11858
2/14/2008 - 2/20/2008	50694
2/21/2008 - 2/27/2008	41649
2/28/2008 - 3/5/2008	28185
3/6/2008 - 3/12/2008	13938
3/13/2008 - 3/19/2008	38080
3/20/2008 - 3/26/2008	29405
3/27/2008 - 4/2/2008	27942
4/3/2008 - 4/9/2008	29476
4/10/2008 - 4/16/2008	20209
4/17/2008 - 4/23/2008	22943

Grouping dialog: Auto — Starting at: 12/27/2007, Ending at: 12/29/2009. By: Seconds, Minutes, Hours, Days, Months, Quarters, Years. Number of days: 7. OK / Cancel.

Figure 10.10 *Create a weekly report by selecting the Days option in the Grouping dialog.*

LET ME TRY IT

Group Dates into Weeks

To group dates into seven-day weeks, follow these steps:

1. Select a cell in the pivot table with a date value.

2. Go to Tools, Group, Group Field. If you receive the error Cannot Group That Selection, see "Using Text to Columns" in Chapter 3 to convert the text dates to real dates. Otherwise, continue to step 3.

3. The date range found by Excel will appear in the Group dialog. Make changes if needed.

4. Select Days.

5. Deselect Months if needed.

6. Change the Number of Days to 7.

7. Click OK. The data will be grouped into weeks, showing the first and last day of each week, as shown in Figure 10.10.

Filtering Options

This section reviews several filtering methods available for viewing only specific records. These methods can be accessed with one of the following steps:

- In the PivotTable Field List, highlight a field and click the drop-down arrow to open the filter listing.

- In the pivot table, click the label drop-down.

- Right-click a label in the pivot table and select Filter.

Filter Listing for Listed Items

The filter listing is probably the most obvious filter tool when you open the drop-down. If the pivot table area contains more than one field, a Select Field dropdown will appear at the top, allowing another field to be selected if the incorrect one is active, as shown in Figure 10.11. All items in the filter listing will be selected, because they are all visible the first time you open the drop-down, but you can select just the items that should appear in the data. Any item that no longer bears a check mark will be hidden.

Figure 10.11 *A drop-down at the top of the filter window allows the correct field to be selected.*

 LET ME TRY IT

Filter a Field for Specific Items

To filter a field for specific items, follow these steps:

1. Open the drop-down of the area to filter.

2. If needed, select the correct field from the drop-down at the top of the window, as shown in Figure 10.11.

3. Deselect the Select All item to clear all the check marks in the list.

4. Select the item(s) to be viewed in the dataset.

5. Click OK. The pivot table will update, showing only the item(s) selected.

Search Function for Listed Items

If you have a long list of items in the filter listing, you can search for items to include or exclude from the filter. Searches are done on the entire data list, not just the items currently filtered on. Use an asterisk (*) as a wildcard for one or more characters before, after, or in between any of the search terms.

Search for Items to Include in Filter

When a search term is entered in the search field, the filter listing updates with all matches selected. You can deselect the items you want to filter out, check Add Current Selection to Filter if you do **not** want to lose any items you previously filtered for, and click OK.

You should keep two things in mind when using the search function:

- The search looks through the entire column, including items you may have already filtered out.

- The search function is additive when the Add Current Selection to Filter is selected. If it's not selected, each search's results are treated as a new filter.

 **LET ME TRY IT**

Use the Search Function to Filter Items

To perform multiple searches to filter items, follow these steps:

1. Open the drop-down of the area to filter.
2. If needed, select the correct field from the drop-down at the top of the window.
3. Enter the first term, or partial term, to filter by.
4. If you want to filter by all the resulting terms, skip to step 7. Otherwise, continue to step 5.
5. Deselect Select All Search Results.
6. Select the desired items from the search results
7. Click OK.
8. Open the drop-down of the column to filter again.
9. Enter the second term, or partial term, to filter by.
10. If you want to filter by all the resulting terms, click OK and skip to step 13. Otherwise, continue to step 11.
11. Deselect Select All Search Results.

12. Select the desired items from the search results.

13. Select Add Current Selection to Filter.

14. Click OK.

Search for Items to Exclude from Filter

The search function can also be used to exclude items from the filter. This is done by entering a search term, deselecting the items to exclude from the results, and then selecting the Add Current Selection to Filter.

You should keep three things in mind when using the search function to exclude items:

- The search looks through the entire column, including items you may have already filtered out.

- To exclude items from the listing, deselect them from the result.

- The search function is additive when the Add Current Selection to Filter is selected. If not selected, each search's results are treated as a new filter.

 LET ME TRY IT

Use the Search Function to Exclude Items from Results

To exclude items from a list of filtered results, as shown in Figure 10.11, follow these steps:

1. Open the drop-down of the area to filter.

2. If needed, select the correct field from the drop-down at the top of the window.

3. Enter the first term, or partial term, to filter by.

4. If you want to filter by all the resulting terms, skip to step 7. Otherwise, continue to step 5.

5. Deselect Select All Search Results.

6. Select the desired items from the search results.

7. Click OK.

8. Open the drop-down of the column to filter again.

9. Enter the exclusion term.

10. If you want to filter out all the resulting terms, skip to step 13. Otherwise, continue to step 11.

11. Deselect Select All Search Results.

12. Select the desired items from the search results.

13. Select Add Current Selection to Filter.

14. Click OK.

Special Filters

Special filters are available in the filter drop-down and also by right-clicking a label and going to Filter. If the selected field is a date field, Date Filters will appear. If the selected field is anything other than a date, Label Filters will appear. In both cases, Value Filters will be included. All the special filters, except for ones that take action immediately, open a filter dialog in which specifics for the filter are entered.

Selection of any of the Label Filters opens the Label Filter (*fieldname*) dialog in which text can be entered. Wildcards can also be used in the text fields. Use an asterisk (*) to replace multiple characters or a question mark (?) to replace a single character.

Value Filters includes various options that will bring up the Value Filter (*fieldname*) dialog in which values can be entered. There is also a Top 10 option, described in more detail in the section "Top 10 Filtering."

Date Filters offers a wide selection of options, including additional options under All Dates in the Period, as shown in Figure 10.12. The Custom Filter (*fieldname*) dialog for dates includes calendars to aid in date entry. The options dealing with quarters refer to the traditional quarter of a year, January through March being the first quarter, April through June being the second quarter, and so on.

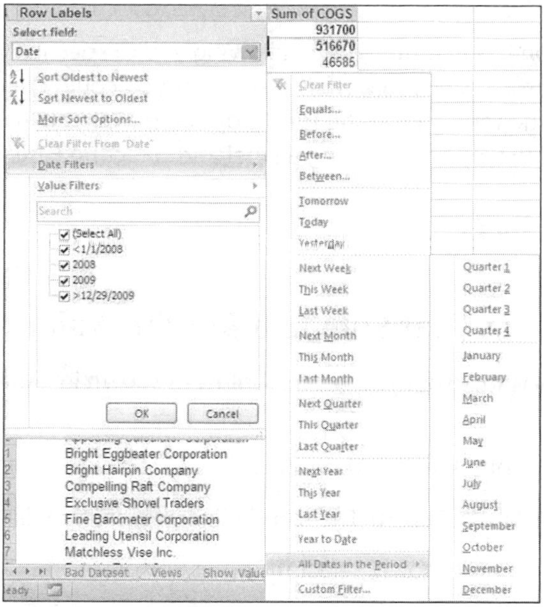

Figure 10.12   *Numerous methods are available in the Date Filters option.*

LET ME TRY IT

Filter a Value Field for a Range of Values

To filter a value field for a range of values, follow these steps:

1. Open the pivot table filter drop-down.

2. Go to Value Filters, Between.

3. From the first drop-down, select the value field to filter.

4. The second drop-down should show the text *Is Between*. Note that other selections can be made.

5. In the third field, enter the minimum value of the range to be shown.

6. In the fourth field, enter the maximum value of the range.

7. Click OK. The pivot table will update, showing only the records with grand totals that fell within the selected range.

Top 10 Filtering

The Top 10 option has a flexible dialog allowing you to specify the top or bottom items, percentages, or sums to view. For example, you could choose to view the bottom 15% or the top 7 items. The Top 10 option is available under the Values Filter listing and also by right-clicking a label and selecting Filter, Top 10.

 LET ME TRY IT

Filter for Records That Sum to a Specific Value

To filter for records that sum to a specific value, as shown in Figure 10.13, follow these steps:

1. Open the pivot table filter drop-down.

2. Go to Value Filters, Top 10. The Top 10 Filter (*fieldname*) dialog will appear.

3. From the first drop-down, select to Top or Bottom.

4. In the second field, enter the value to sum for. The actual summed value may surpass this.

3. Select sum from the third drop-down.

4. Select the value field to sum.

5. Click OK. The pivot table will filter to the records that meet the entered criteria.

Sum of Revenue	Column Labels		
Row Labels	2008	2009	Grand Total
Compelling Raft Company		358089 346270	704359
Exclusive Shovel Traders		195554 427240	622794
Remarkable Meter Corporation		331862 515114	846976
Safe Flagpole Supply		439390 430064	869454
Grand Total		1324895 1718688	3043583

Top 10 Filter (Customer)

Show

| Top | 2500000 | Sum | by | Sum of Revenue |

OK   Cancel

Figure 10.13 *Use the Top 10 option to create a report of top customers who account for a specific amount of revenue.*

Filter By Selection

One or more labels can be manually selected and filtered by right-clicking the selection and going to Filter. From the right-click context menu that appears, select Keep Only Selected Items or Hide Selected Items, as shown in Figure 10.14.

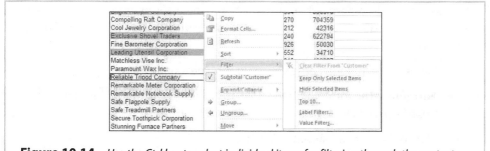

Figure 10.14   *Use the Ctrl key to select individual items for filtering through the context menu.*

 **LET ME TRY IT**

Filter by Manual Selection

To manually select items and apply a filter, follow these steps:

1. Select the first item.

2. While holding down the Ctrl key, select another item. Continue to hold down the Ctrl key as you select additional items. When all the items are selected, continue to step 3.

3. Right-click over a selected item.

4. Go to Filter and choose either Keep Only Selected Items or Hide Selected Items.

Clearing Filters

To clear all filters applied to a pivot table, go to PivotTable Tools, Actions, Clear, Clear Filters.

You can use two ways to clear a filter from a specific field:

- Right-click the field, go to Filter, and select Clear Filter from *fieldname*.

- Open the label's filter drop-down, select the field from the drop-down at the top, and select Clear Filter from *fieldname*.

Calculated Fields

A calculated field is a field you create by building a formula using existing fields and constants. Go to PivotTable Tools, Options, Calculations, Fields, Items, & Sets, and select Calculated Field. The entry fields in the dialog, shown in Figure 10.15, are the following:

- **Name**—The unique name you assign the new field.

- **Formula**—The formula for the field. It should consist of one or more selections from the Fields listing, operators, and constants.

- **Fields**—A list of all available fields.

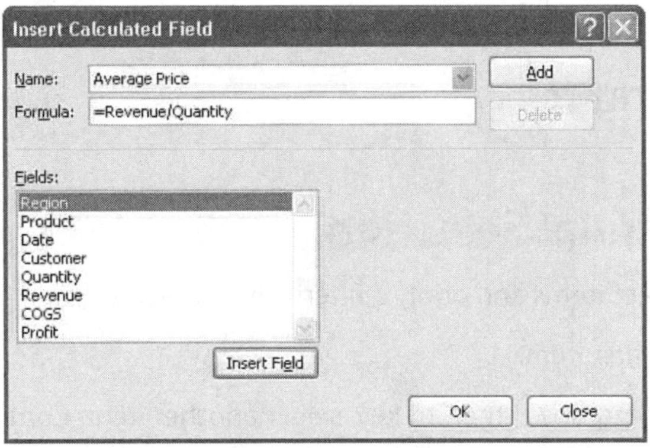

Figure 10.15 *Create a Calculated Field to do calculations with fields.*

Creating the formula isn't that different from building one in the formula bar, but instead of cell references, use the fields. Double-click or highlight and select Insert Field to insert a field in the formula. When the formula is complete, click Add to accept it. When you return to the pivot table, the new field will appear in the field list and can be used in the same way as the existing fields.

 **LET ME TRY IT**

Create a Calculated Field

To create a calculated field, follow these steps:

1. Go to PivotTable Tools, Options, Calculations, Fields, Items, & Sets and select Calculated Field.

2. In the Name field, enter the name of the field as it will appear in the field list.

3. Highlight the 0 in the Formula field.

4. Enter the formula in the Formula field. Double-click or highlight and click Insert Field to insert fields into the formula. Type any operators, constants or parentheses as needed directly in the Formula field.

5. Click Add to accept the formula.

6. Click OK. The new field is added to the field list and can now be arranged and formatted as needed in the pivot table.

Adding Color and Lines to a Pivot Table

PivotTable Tools, Design, PivotTable Styles consists of various designs that can be applied to the active pivot table. As the cursor is moved over the selections, the pivot table will update. When you find a style you like, click the style and it will be applied to the pivot table.

Hiding Totals

By default, subtotals and grand totals are automatically added to the pivot table as the fields are arranged. To hide grand totals, do one of the following:

- Right-click a specific grand total field and select Remove *fieldname*.

- Right-click the header of a specific grand total field and select Remove Grand Total.

- Right-click the pivot table and select PivotTable Options or go to PivotTable Tools, Options, PivotTable, Options. From the dialog that appears, go to the Totals & Filters tab and deselect Show Grand Totals for Rows and Show Grand Totals for Columns.

- Go to PivotTable Tools, Design, Layout, and click the Grand Totals dropdown. From there you can turn all grand totals on or off, or turn on only row grand totals or column grand totals.

To hide subtotals:

- Right-click a specific subtotal field and unselect Subtotal *fieldname*.

- Select a cell in the specific field. Go to PivotTable Tools, Options, Active Field, Field Settings. From the Field Settings dialog that appears, on the Subtotals & Filters tab, select None.

- Go to PivotTable Tools, Design, Layout, and click the Subtotals drop-down. From there you can turn all subtotals off or choose where they appear in respect to their data.

Formatting Values

If you right-click a cell in a pivot table, select Format Cells, and apply formatting to the cell, only the one cell will be formatted. To apply formatting to an entire field, the formatting must be applied through the pivot tables Format Cells dialog, shown in Figure 10.16. The dialog is similar to the normal Format Cells dialog, except only the Number tab is available. To access this dialog, do one of the following:

- Right-click a cell in the field and select Number Format

- Right-click a cell in the field and select Value Field Settings. From the dialog that appears, click Number Format.

- Select a cell in the field and go to PivotTable Tools, Options, Active Field, Field Settings. From the dialog that appears, click Number Format.

Refer to "Using Number Formats in Excel and Excel Starter" in Chapter 4, "Data Formatting," for details on the various number formats.

The selected format will be applied to the entire field. In Figure 10.16, the Currency format was applied to the Revenue field, which is represented by the columns 2008, 2009, and Grand Total.

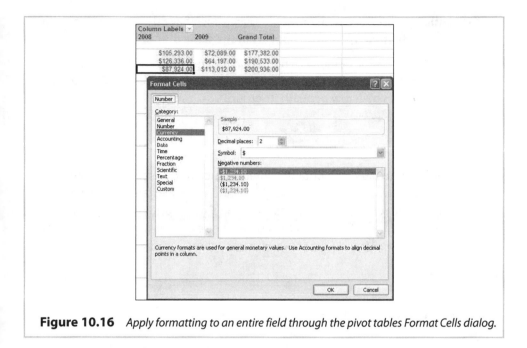

Figure 10.16   *Apply formatting to an entire field through the pivot tables Format Cells dialog.*

Pivot Table Views

There are three ways the pivot table report will appear, as shown in Figure 10.17. The view can be changed by going to PivotTable Tools, Design, Report Layout, and selecting one of the desired layouts:

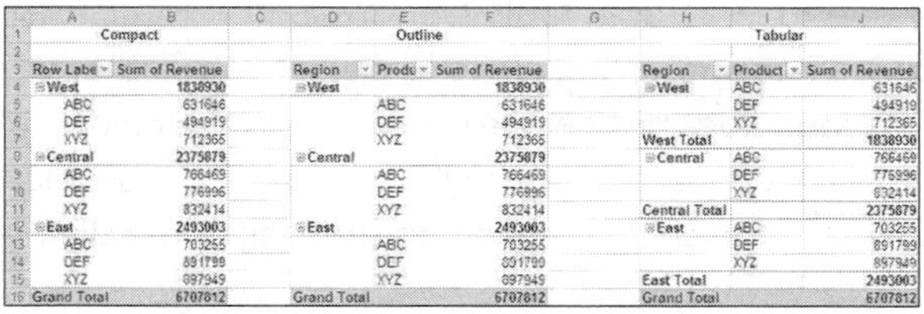

Figure 10.17   *Excel offers three ways of viewing and working with a pivot table report.*

- **Compact**—This is the default configuration for xlsx or xlsm files. All the fields in the row labels area share the same column. The Total, such as the West Total, appears in the same row as the field.

- **Outline**—The fields in the row labels area each have their own column. The Total, such as the West Total, appears in the same row as the field.

- **Tabular**—This the default configuration for an xls file. The fields in the row labels area each have their own column. The Total, such as the West Total, appears in its own row beneath its group.

Slicers

Slicers allow you to filter a pivot table, but in a much more user-friendly way. Unlike the filter drop-down, slicers are always visible and you can change their dimensions to better fit your sheet design, as shown in Figure 10.18. There are three filters—Year, Decade, and Genre—in the figure. The selections update the three pivot tables—Top 20, Top 10 and First Loser—beneath them.

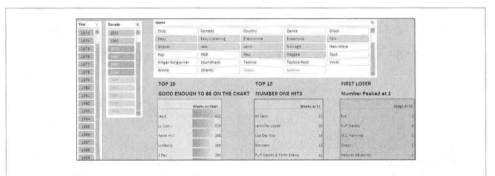

Figure 10.18 *The three slicers offer a more visually pleasing and user-friendly way of filtering the pivot tables.*

To insert a slicer, go to PivotTable Tools, Options, Sort & Filter, Insert Slicer. The Insert Slicers dialog appears, listing all fields except calculation fields. The field for which a slicer is added does not need to be visible in the pivot table. Slicers can be sized and placed as needed. The Slicer Tools will now be available, from which you can modify many settings, such as changing the look of the slicers and attaching the slicer to multiple pivot tables.

 SHOW ME   Media 10.4—Adding Slicers to a Pivot Table
Access this video file through your registered web edition at my.safaribooksonline.com/9780132182287/media.

 **LET ME TRY IT**

Add a Slicer to a Pivot Table

To add slicers to a pivot table, follow these steps:

1. Go to PivotTable Tools, Options, Sort & Filter, Insert Slicer.

2. Select the field(s) to create slicers for.

3. Click OK. The slicers will be added to the sheet.

4. Click and drag any corner of the slicer to resize it.

5. To set up multiple columns in the slicer, right-click the slicer and select Size and Properties. In the dialog that appears, go to Position and Layout. Under Layout, change the number of columns. Click Close.

6. To change the header that appears at the top of the slicer, right-click the slicer and select Slicer Settings. In the Caption field of the Slicer Settings dialog, enter a new caption. For example, you can use the caption to instruct users to "Hold down Ctrl to select multiple customers."

> For an in-depth look at slicers, refer to *Pivot Table Data Crunching: Microsoft Excel 2010* (ISBN 0-7897-4313-2) by Bill Jelen and Michael Alexander.

Making Data Suitable for Pivot Tables

Figure 10.2 displays data unsuitable for a pivot table. If you have a dataset with any of the issues shown in that figure, this section may have the steps to help you clean up the data.

1. Make a copy of the dataset.
    a. Right-click the sheet tab.
    b. Select Move or Copy.
    c. From the To Book drop-down, select New Book.
    d. In the Move or Copy dialog, select Create a Copy, as shown in Figure 10.19.

2. Ensure there are no formulas in the dataset.
    a. Select the entire sheet by clicking the light gray triangle above and to the left of cell A1.
    b. Press Ctrl+C to copy the data.
    c. Go to the Home, Clipboard, Paste drop-down and choose Paste Values.

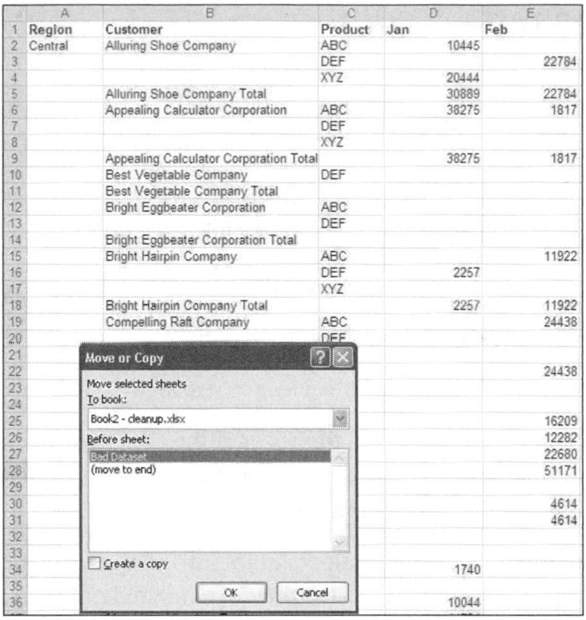

Figure 10.19   *Make a copy of the dataset in case you make a mistake.*

3. Review the data for patterns in your dataset similar to the patterns in Figure 10.19. The data contains total rows, such as row 5, where column C (Product) is blank.

4. The region and customer information in columns A and B are not repeated in every row. The data will need to be filled in. Select the last cell in column B and then press Ctrl+Shift+Home to select all the data up to column A1.

5. Select only the blank cells.
    a. Press F5 to bring up the Go To dialog.
    b. Click the Special button in the lower-left corner of the dialog.
    c. In the Go To Special dialog, select Blanks and click OK. All the blank cells in the original selection are now the only cells selected. *Do not* use the keyboard to navigate at this point or you will lose the selection.

6. Enter the following formula. Note that instead of cell references, just key strokes are used, so the formula is easily entered no matter what your actual column selections are. Press the =, the up-arrow key, and Ctrl+Enter. All the previously blank cells will be filled with a formula that points to the cell above the current cell, as shown in Figure 10.20.

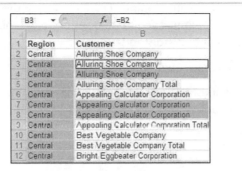

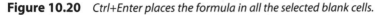

Figure 10.20 *Ctrl+Enter places the formula in all the selected blank cells.*

7. Convert the formulas to values.
   a. Select a cell in column B.
   b. Press the End key and then the down-arrow to select the last cell in the column.
   c. Hold down Ctrl+Shift+Home to select up to cell A1.
   d. Press Ctrl+C to copy the selection.
   e. Go to Home, Paste, Paste Values.

8. If your dataset contains total rows as discussed in step 3, you can now sort them out of the way and delete them. If your dataset does not contain total rows, skip to step 9.
   a. Select cell C1.
   b. Go to Home, Editing, Sort & Filter, Sort A to Z.
   c. The dataset will be re-sorted with any blank cells in column C moved to the bottom.
   d. With C1 still selected, press the End key and then the down-arrow twice. This will select the first empty cell in column C.
   e. Visually verify that from the selected cell to the bottom of the dataset, all the values in column B are total rows. These are the rows you want to delete.
   f. Move over one cell to the right so you're now in column B.
   g. Hold down the Shift key and press End then the down-arrow to select the rest of the rows.
   h. Right-click over the selection and choose Delete.
   i. From the Delete dialog, select Entire Row and press OK. The dataset now consists of only records, without any total rows.

9. The next issue is the dates going across the top of the data. They should be in their own column. If your data does not have this issue, skip to step 16. Otherwise, continue to step 10.

10. Insert a new column D with the heading Month.

11. Open a new workbook and copy cells A1:E1 from the original workbook to the new workbook.

12. Rename the new cell E1 to Revenue.

13. In the original workbook, copy cell E1 to column D from row 2 to the end of the dataset, as shown in Figure 10.21.

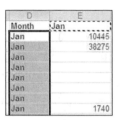

Figure 10.21   *Fill in the first data column's date in column D.*

14. Copy columns A:E of the original workbook to the next available blank row in the new workbook.

15. Return to the original workbook. At this point, all the Jan data has been copied to the new workbook, so the Jan column can be deleted. To delete the column
    a. Select the entire column by clicking the E heading.
    b. Right-click over the selection and select Delete.

16. Repeat steps 13–15 for the rest of the month columns.

17. After all the months are copied over to the new workbook, sort the data so the blank revenue columns are at the bottom of the dataset. You can then delete them.

18. The dataset is now suitable for pivot tables.

This chapter will show you how to insert and modify charts. It will also introduce you to a new type of mini-chart called sparklines.

11

Creating Charts

Charts are a great way to graphically portray data. They're a quick and simple way to emphasize trends in data. People prefer to look at them instead of trying to make sense of rows and columns of numbers. This chapter will show you how to create charts to supplement your data reports.

Excel's charting abilities discussed in this chapter are also available in Excel Starter. The Web App doesn't allow new charts to be inserted, but updating existing data, or, if the data is in a Table, adding new rows or columns will update any linked charts.

Components of a Chart

A chart is a graphical representation of numerical data. Behind every chart, there is a range on a sheet. This range is called the *source data*.

A *series* is a row or column from the source data represented on the chart as a line, a bar, or other component used to portray the data. A typical series consists of the following:

- **Series Name**—The cell with the name of the series that will appear in the legend.

- **Series Values**—The row or column containing the data to be charted.

- **Category Labels**—The range containing the label that will appear along the axis, identifying the series value.

The *axes* consist of major and minor gridlines that go usually below and to the left of the charted data (except for pie charts), labeling or marking intervals of the data. An axis may also have an Axis Title or Display Units Title.

The *legend* is the color code for the chart series, identifying each series by the name assigned it.

Data labels are text that appears in the chart by the series, identifying the value of the points being charted.

Put together, a chart has two areas:

- **Plot Area**—Consists of the series and inner gridlines
- **Chart Area**—Consists of the area surrounding the plot area, including the frame of the chart

The column chart in Figure 11.1 has three series, one for each row of data. The series names are East, Central, and West. The series values are presented by the thick-shaded vertical columns. The category labels are the dates, Jan-08 through May-08, along the horizontal or x-axis. Each series has a slightly different color. The legend across the top is used to identify the color for each series.

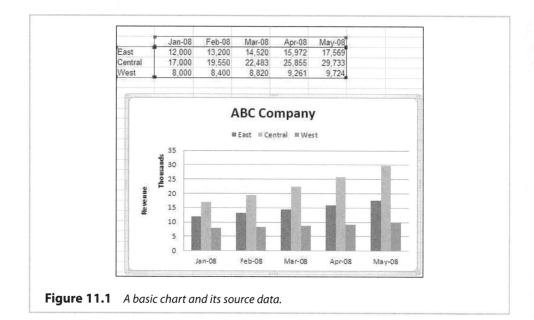

Figure 11.1   *A basic chart and its source data.*

Preparing Data

The first step in creating a chart is ensuring that the data is set up properly. While these rules aren't going to prevent a chart from being created, following them will allow Excel to help you quickly create a chart by identifying the chart components.

- Ensure that there are no blank rows or columns.
- Ensure that headers along the left column and top row identify each series.

If the headers consist of numbers or dates, leave the upper-left corner of the chart blank (see cell A2 in Figure 11.1). If the cell isn't blank, Excel will be confused when it tries to help you create the chart and it will assume there are not category labels.

Types of Charts

There are 11 chart groups, each with several types, giving a total of 73 charts you can select from in Excel. Further manual changes, such as mixing chart types, provide even more variations. The Charts group on the Insert tab shows six of the types, with the other five available under the Other Charts drop-down.

> In a chart, a marker is the graphic (for example a bar or pie slice) representing a data point being charted.

- **Column**—Includes 2D Column, 3D Column, Cylinder, Cone, and Pyramid chart types that feature markers relating the vertical height to size. They are useful for showing data changes over a period of time or comparing items.

- **Line**—Includes 2D Line and 3D Line chart types. They are useful for displaying continuous data over time against a common scale.

- **Pie**—Includes 2D Pie and 3D Pie chart types. Pie charts are most suitable for single series datasets. They are useful for showing how an item is proportional to the sum of all items.

- **Bar**—Includes 2D Bar, 3D Bar, Cylinder, Cone, and Pyramid chart types that feature markers relating the horizontal width to size. They are useful for comparing items.

- **Area**—Includes 2D Area and 3D Area chart types. They are similar to line charts except that the area underneath the line is filled with color. Area charts emphasize the magnitude of change over time.

- **Scatter (XY)**—Includes Scatter chart types of just markers, just lines, or combined markers and lines. They show the relationships among numeric values in several data series or can be use to plot two groups of numbers as one series of x,y coordinates.

- **Stock**—Used to illustrate the fluctuation of the data, such as stocks or temperatures.

- **Surface**—Useful for finding the optimum combinations between two sets of data.

- **Doughnut**—Similar to a pie chart in that it shows how an item is proportional to the whole, but unlike a pie chart, can include more than one series.

- **Bubble**—Used to plot data points with the size of a bubble suggesting its relationship to the other bubbles.

- **Radar**—Useful for comparing the total values of several data series.

Most of the chart types have three basic patterns available:

- **Clustered**—In a clustered chart, the markers are plotted side by side, making it easier to compare markers. The downside is that it is more difficult to tell if the data is increasing or decreasing in comparison to the next cluster. When viewing the chart types, clustered chart types show a light blue marker next to dark blue marker.

- **Stacked**—In a stacked chart, the markers are plotted on top of each other, making it easier to see how the sum of data changes, but making it more difficult to see how a specific series changes over time. When viewing the chart types, stacked charts show a dark blue marker on top of a light blue marker. The stacks are of differing heights.

- **100% Stacked**—In a 100% stacked chart, the markers are plotted on top of each other. All stacks are scaled to have a height of 100%, allowing you to see which data points make the largest percentage of each stack. When viewing the chart types, stacked charts show a dark blue marker on top of a light blue marker. The stacks are of the same heights.

TELL ME MORE   Media 11.1—The Importance of Choosing the Right Chart Type

To listen to a free audio recording about choosing the right type of chart, log on to my.safaribooksonline.com/9780132182287/media.

Creating a Chart

To create a chart, select a cell in your contiguous dataset and go to Insert, Charts. You can either make a chart selection from the drop-downs, or click the dialog pop-up in the lower-right corner of the group to open the Create Chart dialog shown in Figure 11.2.

SHOW ME   Media 11.2—Creating a Chart

Access this video file through your registered web edition at my.safaribooksonline.com/9780132182287/media.

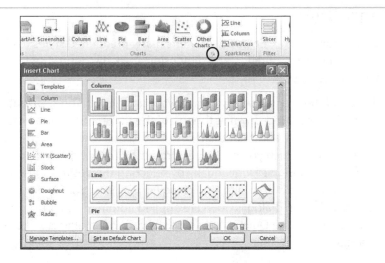

Figure 11.2   *Use the Create Chart dialog pop-up (circled) to bring up a dialog showing all the available chart types.*

 **LET ME TRY IT**

Creating a Chart

To create a chart, follow these steps:

1. Ensure the dataset abides by the rules in the "Preparing Data" section.

2. Select a cell in the dataset.

3. Go to Insert, Charts and select any chart type. Unless you already know the prerequisites for stock and bubble charts, do not select any of those.

4. Excel will add the chart to the sheet. Excel will decide whether to use the rows or columns as headers based on which there are more of. For example, if there are more columns, the rows will be used for the series, with the row headers in the legend and the column headers as the category labels across the horizontal axis (except for pie, bubble, donut, and radar charts).

Chart Styles

Chart Tools, Design, Chart Styles offers many predefined styles to choose from, ranging in colors, outlines, and dimension. Click the desired style and your chart will update.

If none of the predefined styles suits you, go to Chart Tools, Layout, and from the chart elements drop-down at the top of the Current Selection group, select Chart Area or Plot Area, and then click Format Selection. The Format Selection dialog appears, from which you can apply formatting to the selected area. Each series in a chart can be designed individually by selecting the desired series from the chart elements drop-down and then clicking Format Selection. Changes made while the Format Selection dialog is open are applied automatically, but you can click the Undo button in the Quick Access toolbar while the dialog is still open to undo the change.

 **LET ME TRY IT**

Manually Modifying the Look of a Chart

To manually modify the chart area, plot area, or series of a chart, follow these steps:

1. Select the desired area to modify by going to Chart Tools, Layout, Current Selection, and selecting Chart Area, Plot Area, or a series from the chart elements drop-down. If a series is selected, the markers of that series will have selection circles around them.

2. From the Current Selection group, click Format Selection.

3. The selected area/series will update automatically as changes are made. Click the Undo button in the Quick Access toolbar to reverse the last change.

4. If you need to make changes to other areas or series, select the area/series from the chart elements drop-down, as shown in Figure 11.3. There is no need to close the Format Selection dialog.

5. Click Close.

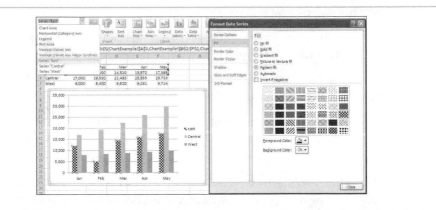
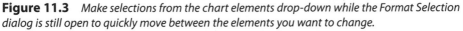

Figure 11.3 *Make selections from the chart elements drop-down while the Format Selection dialog is still open to quickly move between the elements you want to change.*

Chart Layouts

From Chart Tools, Design, Chart Layouts up to 12 chart layouts are available, depending on the type of chart selected. These predefined layouts offer combinations of the chart elements: legend, chart title, axis title, data labels, and data table. Unlike other selection drop-downs, the active chart does not automatically update as you move your cursor over the options. You will need to make a selection by clicking the item before the chart updates. If none of the predefined combinations is what you want, you can manually modify each element, as shown in the following sections.

Adding a Chart Title

To add a chart title, go to Chart Tools, Layout, Labels, Chart Title. Click in the title box added to the chart to change the text, or use the formatting tools on the Home tab to change the font as desired. You can also move the title's box around the chart. There are more formatting options, such as Word Art options, available under More Title Options, found under the Chart Title drop-down or on the Format tab under Chart Tools.

 LET ME TRY IT

Adding a Chart Title

To add a title to the selected chart, follow these steps:

1. Go to Chart Tools, Layout, Labels, Chart Title.

2. Select one of the predefined chart locations.

3. Select the default text and type in your title.

4. Select the title's box. The box lines will become solid, showing the box is selected, instead of its contents.

5. Go to Home, Font, and select a different font style from the font style drop-down. You can also make other selections, such as font size, bold, and so on.

6. To make changes to the box itself, such as a border or fill, with the box still selected, go to Chart Tools, Format, Shape Styles, and select an effect to apply to the box.

7. To move the title, place your cursor along the box edge until it turns into four arrows, as shown in Figure 11.4. At this point, hold down the mouse button and drag the box to a new location.

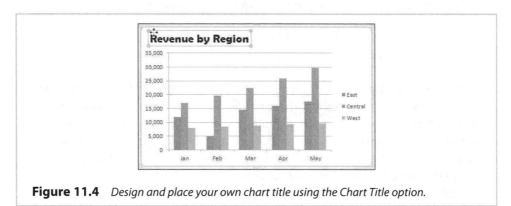

Figure 11.4   *Design and place your own chart title using the Chart Title option.*

Adding an Axis Title

To add an axis title, go to Chart Tools, Layout, Labels, Axis Titles, and select whether you want to add the title to the horizontal or vertical axis. The Vertical Axis Title can be a Rotated Title, Vertical Title, or Horizontal Title. The Horizontal Title can be placed only horizontally along the axis.

Click in the title box added to the chart to change the text, or use the formatting tools on the Home tab to change the font as desired. You can also move the title's box around the chart. More formatting options, such as Word Art options, are available under the more options selections for each axis or on the Format tab under Chart Tools.

Adding or Moving the Chart Legend

Go to Chart Tools, Layout, Labels, Legend to see the predefined options for locating the legend. It can be manually sized by clicking and dragging any circle in the corner of its selection frame or the squares on the edge.

To relocate the legend, place your cursor on its frame until it turns into a four-arrow cursor, then click and drag it to a new location. If you want the legend to overlap the chart, go to Chart Tools, Layout, Current Selection, Format Selection, and from the dialog that appears, on the Legend Options tab, deselect Show the Legend Without Overlapping the Chart.

Moving or Resizing a Chart

To resize a selected chart, place the cursor at any of the four corners or midway along any of the edges of the frame. When the cursor changes to a two-sided arrow, click and drag the chart to the desired size.

To move a chart elsewhere on the same sheet, click anywhere in the Chart Area and drag the chart to the new location.

To relocate the chart to another sheet, select the chart and go to Chart Tools, Design, Location, Move Chart. From the dialog that appears, select the new sheet from the Object In drop-down.

A chart sheet is a special type of sheet in Excel used to display only charts. To relocate the chart to its own chart sheet, select the chart and go to Chart Tools, Design, Location, Move Chart. From the dialog that appears, select the New Sheet option. Charts on a chart sheet cannot be resized, except by zooming in and out on the sheet.

Changing a Chart's Type

You don't have to re-create a chart from scratch if you want to change the chart type. Just select the chart, go to Insert Charts, and select a new chart type in the same way you created the original. Any formatting that can transfer over will be included in the new chart type.

 LET ME TRY IT

Changing an Existing Chart's Type

To change the chart type in an existing chart, follow these steps:

1. Right-click over the chart.

2. Select Change Chart Type.

3. Select a new chart type from the Change Chart Type dialog.

4. Click OK.

Mixing Chart Types

Some of the chart types can be used together in a single chart, as shown in Figure 11.5. For example, one series can be a bar chart and another series a line chart. To combine chart types, select the series you want to change and either use your preferred insert chart method or right-click the series and select Change Series Chart Type.

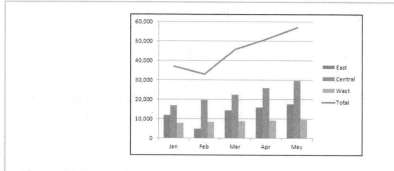

Figure 11.5   *Combine chart types, such as columns and lines, to create a more meaningful chart.*

 **LET ME TRY IT**

Creating a Chart with Multiple Chart Types

To create a single chart consisting of multiple chart types, follow these steps:

1. Select a cell in the dataset.

2. Go to Insert, Charts and select one of the chart types you want to appear in the chart. Excel will add the new chart to the sheet.

3. Select a data series to change by going to Chart Tools, Layout, Current Selection, and selecting the data series from the Chart Elements.

4. Go to Insert, Charts and select the new chart type to apply to the selected series.

5. Repeat steps 3 and 4 for any other series to change.

Showing Numbers of Different Scale

If the data to chart consists of a series with numbers of vastly different scales, it may be nearly impossible to see all the series in the chart, as shown in Figure 11.6. In this figure charting Revenue and Profit, the Revenue is in thousands whereas the Profits are less than 10 (remember 39% is also 3.9) and are not visible in the chart.

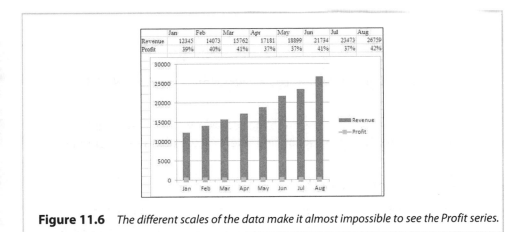

Figure 11.6 *The different scales of the data make it almost impossible to see the Profit series.*

To correct this, the Profit needs to be plotted against a second vertical axis. A chart can have two scales, one for each vertical axis. A series can be assigned to the secondary axis through the Format Data Series dialog, as shown in Figure 11.7.

Figure 11.7 *The Revenue columns are plotted to the left vertical axis, whereas the Profit line is plotted to the secondary axis on the right. Note that the dialog may be slightly different for different chart types.*

SHOW ME   Media 11.3—Assigning a Series to the Secondary Axis
Access this video file through your registered web edition at
my.safaribooksonline.com/9780132182287/media.

 **LET ME TRY IT**

Chart Data of Vastly Different Scales

To assign a series to the secondary axis, allowing for a different scale, follow these steps:

1. Select the data series to assign to the secondary axis by going to Chart Tools, Layout, Current Selection and selecting the data series from the Chart Elements.

2. Click Format Selection.

3. In the Series Options category, choose Secondary Axis in the Plot Series On frame. A second vertical axis with a scale suitable to the data series will be added to the chart, as shown in Figure 11.7.

Updating Chart Data

Unless the source data is a Table, the chart won't automatically update as new data is added to the source. To manually update the data source of a chart, do one of the following:

- Go to Chart Tools, Design, Data, Select Data, or right-click the chart and choose Select Data. Update the Chart Data Range in the Select Data Source dialog, shown in Figure 11.8.

- When the chart is selected, the data source is highlighted with a colored border. The borders can be manually modified, changing the source range, by clicking and dragging to include the new rows. If using this method, be careful to not move the range when trying to expand it.

In addition to the two previous methods, the existing series on a chart can be updated by copying the new data and pasting it into the chart.

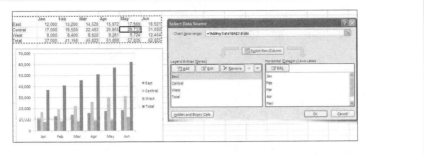

Figure 11.8   *Update the source data range to include the new series in the chart.*

   LET ME TRY IT

Pasting New Data onto Existing Series

To update existing series with new data using the copy/paste method, follow these steps:

1. Ensure that the new data has a header similar to the existing data. It is especially important that a heading entered as a Date is still a Date and not Text.

2. Select the new data, including the header.

3. Right-click over the selection and choose Copy.

4. Select the chart.

5. Go to Home, Clipboard, Paste. The chart will update with the new data.

Switching Rows and Columns

Excel does its best in figuring out what you want a chart to look like, but it can make mistakes. If the data source looks like the one in Figure 11.9, you would get a chart like the left one. But instead of reorganizing the data, use the Switch Row/Column button in the Select Data dialog to switch the range used for the series and the range used for the category labels, creating the chart on the right.

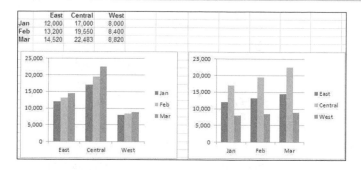

Figure 11.9 *Instead of reorganizing the data, use the Switch Row/Column button on the Select Data Source dialog to correct the series of the chart.*

Trendlines

Use a trendline to predict trends in the data or how data will progress if the data continues at the same pace, as shown in Figure 11.10. To add a trend to the selected chart, go to Chart Tools, Layout, Analysis and select a trend from the Trendline drop-down. To create a forecasting trendline, choose More Trendline Options.

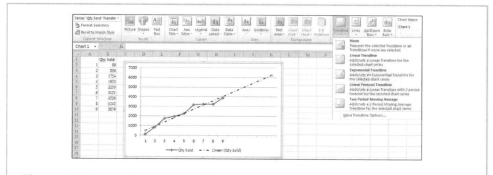

Figure 11.10 *Use the More Trendline Options of the Trendline drop-down to create a trendline that predicts the future.*

You can choose from four predefined trendlines in the drop-down:

- **Linear Trendline**—Adds a linear trendline.

- **Exponential Trendline**—Adds an exponential trendline.

- **Linear Forecast Trendline**—Adds a linear trendline based on a two-period forecast.

- **Two Period Moving Average**—Adds a Two-Period Moving Average Trendline.

If the predefined trendlines do not fit your requirements, you can design your own through the Format Trendline dialog, using one of the following Trend/Regression Types:

- **Exponential**—A curved line used when values rise or fall at constantly increasing rates. Cannot be used if the data contains zero or negative values.

- **Linear**—A best fit straight line, usually showing that something is increasing or decreasing at a steady rate.

- **Logarithmic**—A best fit curved line used when the rate of change of the data increases or decreases quickly and then levels out.

- **Polynomial**—A curved line used when data fluctuates. Enter the Order to determine the number of fluctuations in the data.

- **Power**—A curved line used to compare measurements that increase at a specific rate. Cannot be used if the data contains zero or negative values.

- **Moving Average**—Smoothes out fluctuations in the data by averaging a specific number of data points and using that average as a point in the line.

More than one trendline may be added to a chart by making different selections from the drop-down. To modify an existing trendline, you will need to select it from the Chart Elements drop-down and choose Format Selection.

 LET ME TRY IT

Adding a Forecasting Trendline

To add a forecasting trendline to an existing chart, follow these steps:

1. Select the chart.

2. Go to Chart Tools, Layout, Analysis, Trendlines, and choose More Trendline Options.

3. In the Trendline Options category, in the Trend/Regression Type frame, select the type of trendline to add to the chart.

4. In the Forecast frame, enter the number of periods to forecast in the Forward field.

5. In the Line Style category, select a dashed line from the Dashed Type drop-down so the trendline will stand out from a normal series.

Stock Charts

There are four types of stock charts that you can create using historical stock data. Each type has specific requirements for included columns and their order. If the order of the data is not met, the chart will not be created. The charts and their required columns and order are as follows:

- **High-Low-Close**—Requires four columns of data: date, high, low, close.

- **Open-High-Low-Close**—Requires five columns of data: date, open, high, low, close.

- **Volume-High-Low-Close**—Requires five columns of data: date, volume, high, low, close.

- **Volume-Open-High-Low-Close**—Requires six columns of data: date, volume, open, high, low, close.

After the data is in the correct column order, the chart can be selected from the Other Charts drop-down, as shown in Figure 11.11.

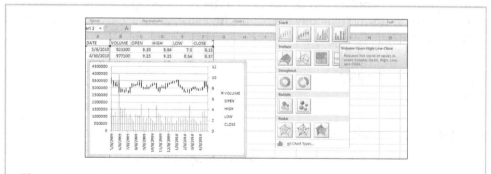

Figure 11.11   *The column order for a stock chart must match the ToolTip exactly.*

LET ME TRY IT

Creating a Stock Chart

To create a stock chart, follow these steps:

1. Decide which stock chart you want by going to Insert, Charts, Other Charts and moving the cursor over each stock chart. Note the required columns and their order for the desired chart.

2. Ensure that the columns in the dataset are in the correct order. If not, refer to "Rearranging Columns" in Chapter 7, "Sorting."

3. Sort the data by date, oldest to newest.

4. Select a cell in the dataset.

5. Return to the drop-down of stock charts and this time click the desired chart.

Bubble Charts

You may want to use a bubble chart because they are unusual, but there is a practical reason for using one. With a bubble chart, you can display a relationship among three variables. The x,y coordinates represent two variables and the size of the bubble is the third.

In Figure 11.12, Miles and Age are charted along the x and y axes, respectively. The Price becomes the size of the bubble at the intersection of the x,y coordinate.

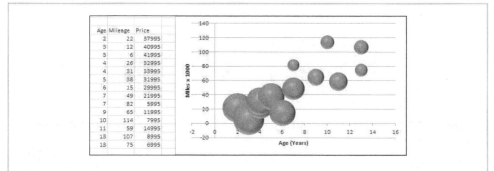

Figure 11.12   *The size of the bubble at the intersection represents the relative price.*

Pie Chart Issue: Small Slices

When creating a pie chart, you may end up with slices that are very difficult to see. Two possible ways of dealing with this are to rotate the pie or create a Bar of Pie chart.

Rotating the Pie

Rotating the pie works best if the chart is 3D. By rotating the chart so the smaller slices are toward the front, they are easier to see, as shown in Figure 11.13. To rotate the pie:

1. Select the chart.

2. Go to Chart Tools, Layout, Current Selection, and select the series from the chart elements drop-down.

3. Select Format Selection.

4. From the Series Options category, in the Angle of First Slice frame, move the slider to the right, toward Full Rotation. The chart will update when you let go of the mouse button, so you can see how far you need to move the slider.

5. When the chart is rotated satisfactorily, click Close.

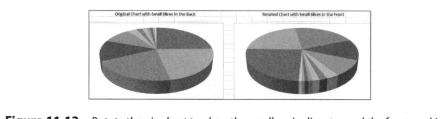

Figure 11.13   *Rotate the pie chart to place the smaller pie slices toward the front, making them easier to see.*

Create a Bar of Pie Chart

Bar of Pie is one of the options listed under Insert, Chart, Pie. It's used to explode out the smaller pie slices into a stacked bar chart, as shown in Figure 11.14, making the smaller slices more visible. Excel will create a new slice called Other, which is a grouping of the slices now in the bar. But the default explosion may not be adequate to your needs. This can be changed by going into the Format Data Series dialog and changing the number of values included in the bar.

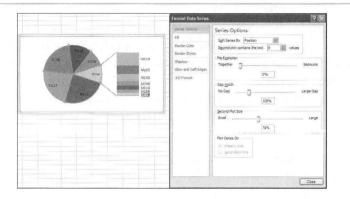

Figure 11.14 *Use a Bar of Pie chart to group smaller slices into a stacked bar chart, making the smaller slices more visible.*

 **LET ME TRY IT**

Change to a Bar of Pie Chart

To change an existing pie chart to a bar of pie chart and modify the number of slices used in the stacked bar in the chart, follow these steps:

1. Right-click over the chart.

2. Select Change Chart Type.

3. In the Change Chart Type dialog, go to Pie and select Bar of Pie.

4. Click OK. The chart will change to a bar of pie chart. If you're happy with the default selection for the number of slices moved to the stacked bar, you're done. Otherwise, continue to step 5 to change the number of slices used in the bar.

5. With the chart still selected, go to Chart Tools, Layout, Current Selection, and select the series from the Chart Elements drop-down.

6. Click Format Selection.

7. From the Series Options category, change the number of values in the Second Plot Contains the Last *x* Values field. As the value is changed using the spin buttons, the chart will update.

8. When satisfied with the chart, click Close.

Sparklines

A *sparkline* is a tiny chart inside of a cell. It can be placed right next to the data it's charting. And because the sparkline is in the background of the cell, you can still enter text in that cell. There are three types of sparklines available: Line, Column and Win/Loss. Different colors can be applied to them and various settings affect how the sparkline will be designed.

To add a sparkline to your data, select either where you want the sparkline to go or the dataset (not including the headers) and go to Insert Sparklines. Fill in the fields of the Create Sparklines dialog and the sparklines will be added to the sheet.

 SHOW ME　Media 11.4—Creating Sparklines
Access this video file through your registered web edition at my.safaribooksonline.com/9780132182287/media.

 **LET ME TRY IT**

Creating Sparklines

To create sparklines for a dataset, follow these steps:

1. Select the range where you want the sparklines to be placed.

2. Go to Insert, Sparklines, and select the desired sparkline type.

3. In the Create Sparklines dialog that appears, place your cursor in the Data Range field.

4. Highlight the data range on the sheet, making sure not to include any row or column headers.

5. Verify the Location Range. It should be the same range you selected in step 1.

6. Click OK. The sparklines will be added to the cells.

Adding Points to a Sparkline

After you've created a sparkline, you can choose to show the High Point, Low Point, Negative Points, First Point, Last Point, and Markers (line charts only), as shown in the first two examples in Figure 11.15. To add points to a sparkline, select the sparkline and then go to Sparkline Tools, Design, Show, and select the desired points. Each point can be assigned its own color by going to the Marker Color drop-down in the Style group.

	A	B	C	D	E	F	G	H
Column Chart with High Point Indicators (Dark Columns)								
		Q1	Q2	Q3	Q4			
East		9,853	7,141	2,339	634			
Central		6,826	6,599	7,594	1,839			
West		6,411	260	755	2,074			
Line Chart with Markers								
		Jan	Feb	Mar	Apr	May	Jun	
East		2,689	1,332	3,233	1,369	2,970	21	
Central		1,028	1,931	1,894	2,089	1,279	1,388	
West		121	3,101	3,415	4,007	3,545	1,313	
Win/Loss Chart								
		Jan	Feb	Mar	Apr	May	Jun	
East		84	67	-26	43	3	-97	
Central		96	-70	-14	-26	-4	88	
West		42	-45	15	-28	-50	90	
Column Chart with Date Axis								
		1/1/2010	1/4/2010	1/5/2010	1/6/2010	1/7/2010	1/8/2010	
East		9,853	7,141	2,339	634	2,689	2,970	
Central		6,826	6,599	7,594	1,839	1,028	1,279	
West		6,411	260	755	2,074	121	3,545	

Figure 11.15 *Use Sparklines to add in-cell charts to your data.*

Spacing Markers in a Sparkline

The fourth chart in Figure 11.15 uses the Date Axis Type option to space the columns out in respect to the date of the dataset. Note the space in the sparkline between the first and second columns. This is parallel to the date difference between the first two columns of data. The setting is available in the sparklines Axis drop-down.

The date range must include real dates. For example, Jan, Feb, Mar, and the like won't work because these are not actual dates, but if the actual dates are 1/1/10, 2/1/10, 3/1/10 and they are simply formatted to just show the month, they will work to space out the data in the sparkline.

LET ME TRY IT

Spacing Sparklines Based on Date

To space out sparklines based on the dates in the dataset, follow these steps. If you've already created the sparklines, skip to step 7:

1. Select the range where you want the sparklines to be placed.

2. Go to Insert, Sparklines, and select the desired sparkline type.

3. In the Create Sparklines dialog that appears, place your cursor in the Data Range field.

4. Highlight the data range on the sheet, making sure not to include any row or column headers.

5. Verify the Location Range. It should be the same range you selected in step 1.

6. Click OK. The sparklines will be added to the cells, in the default configuration close together. You will begin spacing them out in the next step.

7. Select a cell in the sparkline group.

8. Go to Sparkline Tools, Design, Group, Axis, and select Date Axis Type from the drop-down.

9. The Sparkline Date Range dialog appears. Select the date range to apply to the sparklines.

10. Click OK. The sparklines will update to accommodate the spacing in the selected date range.

Delete Sparklines

You cannot simply highlight a sparkline and delete it. Instead, to delete a sparkline, go to Sparkline Tools, Design, Group, Clear, and choose either Clear Selected Sparklines or Clear Selected Sparkline Groups.

Saving a Chart as a Template

If you have a chart design you want to apply to multiple charts, you can save the design as a template. All the settings for colors, fonts, effects, and chart elements are saved and can be applied to other charts. Because the template is saved as an external file, you can share it with other users.

To create the template, build and customize a chart as necessary. Then select the chart and go to Chart Tools, Design, Type, Save as Template. Give the template a name and click Save. The template is now available in the Templates option of the Insert Chart dialog.

 LET ME TRY IT

Creating a Chart Using a User-Created Template

To use a custom template to create a chart, follow these steps:

1. Select a cell in the dataset.

2. Go to Insert, Charts, and from any of the drop-downs, select All Chart Types to open the Insert Chart dialog.

3. In the Insert Chart dialog, choose Templates.

4. Select the desired template.

5. Click OK. The chart will be created with the saved settings from the template.

This chapter will show you how to insert SmartArt, WordArt and Pictures onto your sheets.

12

SmartArt, WordArt, and Pictures

You can add a little pizzazz to your workbooks by using graphic text and images. This chapter introduces you to SmartArt, which combines graphics and text to depict ideas, WordArt to twist colorful text, and the Picture tools you can use to manipulate imported images.

SmartArt

SmartArt is a collection of similar shapes, arranged to imply a process, groups, or a hierarchy. You can add text to SmartArt shapes, and for some shapes, include a small picture or logo. Excel 2010 has more than 130 available diagrams, grouped into eight categories of SmartArt:

- **List**—Designs for nonsequential lists of information.
- **Process**—Designs for sequential lists of steps.
- **Cycle**—Designs for steps that repeat.
- **Hierarchy**—Designs for organization charts, decision trees, and other hierarchical relationships.
- **Relationship**—Designs for showing the relationships between items.
- **Matrix**—Designs to show four quadrants of a list.
- **Pyramid**—Designs to show overlapping, proportional, containment, or interconnected relationships.
- **Picture**—Designs for use with pictures in either sequential or nonsequential layouts. The picture tools can be used to adjust the imported images.

You can't insert SmartArt in Excel Starter, but you can edit the text; editing options are available by right-clicking a component and selecting Format Shape.

SmartArt diagrams are removed when you open a workbook in the Excel Web App. In legacy versions of Excel, SmartArt will be turned into Pictures.

Inserting SmartArt

To insert a SmartArt diagram, go to Insert, SmartArt, and select the desired layout. Excel places the diagram in the middle of the screen with the Text pane to the left, as shown in Figure 12.1. When you're done entering text, click any cell on the sheet and the Text pane will disappear.

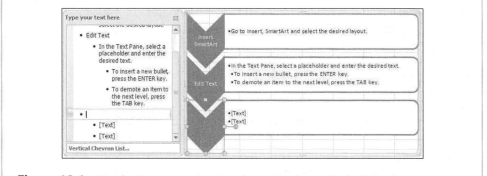

Figure 12.1 *Use the Text pane to insert and organize the text in the SmartArt.*

Do not click the x in the upper-right corner of the Text pane to close it or the next time you place SmartArt, the Text pane will not automatically appear. If this happens, you can manually open the Text pane by going to SmartArt Tools, Design, Create Graphic, and selecting Text Pane.

You should keep a few things in mind concerning the Text pane:

- Click a placeholder to enter the text.
- Navigate between bulleted items by using the mouse or arrow keys.
- The Tab key will not work to move between the placeholders. Instead, use the Tab key to demote an item.
- Press Enter to add a new item beneath the currently selected item.
- Deleting a bullet will promote the ones beneath it if they are of a lower level.

SHOW ME   Media 12.1—Inserting SmartArt

Access this video file through your registered web edition at
my.safaribooksonline.com/9780132182287/media.

LET ME TRY IT

Inserting SmartArt

To insert a SmartArt layout and enter text, follow these steps:

1. Go to Insert, SmartArt, and select the desired layout.

2. In the Text pane, select a placeholder and enter the desired text.

3. Use the mouse to select the next placeholder or use the down-arrow key
   to move to the next placeholder for entering text.
   - To insert a new bullet, press the Enter key.
   - To demote an item to the next level, press the Tab key.
   - To add a new graphic, select the last bullet, press the Enter key to insert a
     new bullet, and then click Promote, found under Tools, Design, Create
     Graphic, as many times as necessary to make the bullet a level 1 item.

4. Repeat step 3 as many times as necessary.

5. When you are done entering information, click any cell on the sheet.

Inserting SmartArt Images

This section covers the specifics of working with images in SmartArt. If this is the
first time you've entered SmartArt, refer to "Inserting SmartArt" for instruction
on entering text, adding new graphics, and promoting or demoting the bulleted
items.

Some SmartArt layouts include image placeholders, as shown in Figure 12.2. To
insert an image, click the image placeholder and browse to the desired image.
When an image in the SmartArt is selected, the Picture Tools tab becomes visible
and you can use any of the picture tools on the image.

- To change the image, select it and go to Picture Tools, Format, Change Picture.

- You cannot delete the accompanying text placeholder, but if you do not need it, enter a space in the field.

Figure 12.2   *Use images in SmartArt to create a business organization chart.*

The picture tools are reviewed in the later section "Inserting Pictures."

SHOW ME   Media 12.2—Inserting SmartArt That Includes Images
Access this video file through your registered web edition at
my.safaribooksonline.com/9780132182287/media.

   **LET ME TRY IT**

Inserting SmartArt with Images

To insert a SmartArt layout that includes images, follow these steps:

1. Go to Insert, SmartArt, and select a layout that includes image placeholders.

2. Click the image placeholder and the Insert Picture dialog opens. Browse to the desired image and click Insert.

3. Use the options on the Picture Tools tab to make any required changes to the image.

4. If you do not want any text in the image's accompanying text placeholder, enter a space in the text's placeholder.

5. Repeat steps 2 through 4 as many time as required.

Selecting SmartArt

Selecting SmartArt must be done carefully. If you have the incorrect frame selected, you will move the component instead of the entire SmartArt frame. You can tell if a component is selected because the frame around it will become visible. Only the frame around the entire SmartArt diagram is visible when you've selected the entire diagram. Also, nothing will be selected in the Text pane when the entire diagram is selected.

If a component is selected, move your cursor over the frame until it turns into four arrows, then click on the frame and the entire diagram will be selected. When the frame is selected, you can move it to a new location, resize it, or delete it.

- When moving or resizing the diagram, the Text pane will momentarily disappear.

- To move the diagram, place the cursor on the frame until it turns into four arrows; then click and drag it to a new location.

- To resize the diagram, place the cursor in any corner or place it in the center of any edge until it turns into a double arrow. You can then click and drag the diagram to a new size.

Adding and Deleting Shapes

Use Add Shape to add a new shape to the SmartArt diagram. The new shape will be added above the selected shape or at the bottom if the entire diagram is selected.

To delete a shape, select it so you see the frame around it and press the Delete key.

 **LET ME TRY IT**

Adding a Shape in the Middle of the Diagram

To add a new component shape in the middle of the diagram, follow these steps:

1. Select the component where you want the new shape.

2. Go to SmartArt Tools, Design, Create Graphic, and select Add Shape.

3.   The component selected in step 1 will be moved down and the new shape inserted in its location.

4.   If the new shape is not in the correct location, select level 1 of the component and go to SmartArt Tools, Design, Create Graphic, and choose Move Up or Move Down.

Reorder Components

To move a component to a new location, use Move Up and Move Down found under SmartArt Tools, Design, Create Graphic. Move Up and Move Down refer to the order of the items as shown in the Text pane, not their actual configuration in the diagram. To move an item to a new component, it must be cut from its current location and pasted to the new location.

*   Any customized formatting of a component will move with the component.

*   Each level can be moved individually, with any sublevels moving with their parent level.

*   A level can be moved only within its group, it cannot be moved beyond its group. So if an item is level 2, it cannot be moved past its level 1 parent.

 LET ME TRY IT

Reordering Components in a Diagram

To change the order of components, follow these steps:

1.   In the Text pane, place your cursor in the text of the level to be moved. Any children of the selected level will move with the parent. So if you're moving an entire component, select level 1. If a level 2 item includes level 3 items, place your cursor at level 2 and the level 3 items will also move.

2.   Go to SmartArt Tools, Design, Create Graphic, and choose Move Up to move the select item up the Text pane or Move Down to move the item down the Text pane.

3.   If an item needs to be moved to an entirely different component group, highlight the text in the Text pane.

4.   Press Ctrl+X to cut the text out of the Text pane.

5.   Place your cursor in the new location for the text.

6.   Press Ctrl+V to paste the text to the new location.

Formatting the Selected Layout

The text formatting options found in the Font group of the Home tab can be applied to any selected item in SmartArt. If you select a component, the formatting will be applied to all text entries in the component. If you select a single word, the formatting will apply to just that word.

The exception to this formatting is font size. Selecting a single item in a component, such as just one word in a sentence, will have unexpected results, as shown in Figure 12.3. But you can change the font size of all the text in a selected component.

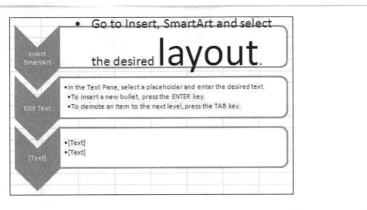

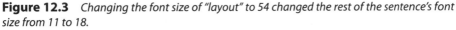

Figure 12.3   *Changing the font size of "layout" to 54 changed the rest of the sentence's font size from 11 to 18.*

Changing the Selected Layout

You can change the layout of the current diagram to a new layout by going to the Layouts group of the SmartTools, Design tab. The drop-down will show the available layouts of the current diagrams category, but you can access all the categories and their layouts by selecting the More Layouts option at the bottom of the drop-down. This will open the Choose a SmartArt Graphic dialog with all available categories and layouts. Existing levels and text will transfer over to the new layout.

Changing an Individual Component

You can change the shapes of individual components in a diagram by selecting the component and going to SmartTools, Format, Shapes, Change Shape, and selecting a new shape in the drop-down. Every component in the diagram can be replaced, as shown in Figure 12.4.

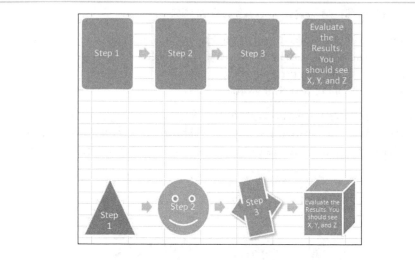

Figure 12.4   *You can replace every shape in a diagram to create your own custom SmartArt.*

Linking a Cell to Smart Art

Converted SmartArt diagrams will be removed when you open a workbook in the Excel Web App.

You can't actually link SmartArt text to a cell, but you can create the layout in SmartArt, convert it to shapes, and then replace the text with formulas linking the component to a cell. This allows the text in the layout to update automatically when the cell's text updates.

There are two reasons why it's important to make sure the SmartArt is designed perfectly before converting it. First, after you convert it, it's no longer SmartArt and you will not have access to the SmartArt tools to make changes. The second reason is that it is much easier to select the correct frames when they have text in them already.

SHOW ME   **Media 12.3—Linking SmartArt to Cells**
Access this video file through your registered web edition at my.safaribooksonline.com/9780132182287/media.

LET ME TRY IT

Linking SmartArt to Cells

To link SmartArt to a cell, follow these steps:

1. Set up the sheet as needed, including the cells with dynamic text that you will link the SmartArt components to.

2. Completely design the SmartArt, including the placement of sample text.

3. Select the diagram.

4. Go to SmartArt Tools, Design, Reset, Convert to Shapes. This will convert the SmartArt to individual shapes.

5. Go to Drawing Tools, Format, Arrange, Selection Pane. The Selection pane opens on the right side of the window.

6. Many components in SmartArt consist of layers of shapes, which are all now visible in the Selection pane. Select one of the components called Freeform. The corresponding shape will be selected on the sheet. If this is not the desired shape, select another in the Selection pane until the shape you want is highlighted. Freeform is usually the shape used to hold text.

7. After the desired shape is selected, place your cursor in the formula bar, type an equal sign and then the cell address of the cell you want to link the shape to, as shown in Figure 12.5.

8. Repeat steps 6 and 7 until all components are linked.

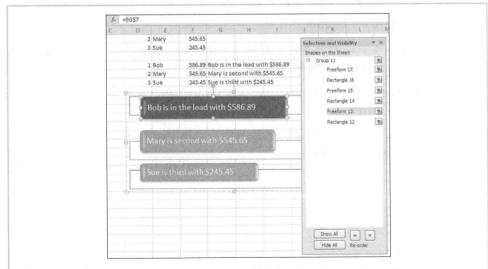

Figure 12.5 *Insert the formula in the formula bar to link the shape to a cell.*

Inserting WordArt

WordArt is removed when you open a workbook in the Excel Web App. In Excel Starter and legacy versions of Excel, WordArt may not appear as designed.

WordArt allows you to design text beyond the capabilities of the normal font settings on the Home tab, as shown in Figure 12.6. After inserting the WordArt, go to the Drawing Tools, Format tab to access the various tools for modifying the color and shape.

Figure 12.6   *Use WordArt to bend and twist text.*

 **LET ME TRY IT**

Inserting and Formatting WordArt

To insert WordArt and customize it, follow these steps:

1. Go to Insert, Text, WordArt, and select a text style from the drop-down. The WordArt will be added to the active sheet.

2. Excel adds generic text in the preset WordArt. Select the default text and type your own text.

3. To change the font style, select the text and choose a new font style from the Font group of the Home tab.

4. To add effects to the WordArt, such as the curve in Figure 12.6, go to Drawing Tools, Format, WordArt Styles, Text Effects. An option from Transform was used in the figure.

Inserting Pictures

After you've inserted a picture onto a sheet, the picture tools become available, which you can use to crop and add many effects to the image.

 LET ME TRY IT

Inserting a Picture

To insert a picture, follow these steps:

1. Select the cell where you want the top-left corner of the picture to be.

2. Go to Insert, Illustrations, Picture.

3. Select the image to import and click Insert.

Resizing and Cropping Pictures

Cropped images are removed when you open a workbook in the Excel Web App.

To resize the selected image, click and drag one of the handles along the edge or in the corners of the picture. For more specific sizing, enter the size in the Shape Height or Shape Width fields of the Size group on the Picture Tools, Format tab.

You can manually crop an image or crop it to a specific shape, as shown in Figure 12.7. To crop the selected image, go to Picture Tools, Format, Size, and select an option from the Crop drop-down. If you later decide you've made a mistake, go to Picture Tools, Format, Adjust, Reset Picture, Reset Picture & Size, and the image will return to its original state.

The Crop option is for a manual crop. On the image, black cropping handles appear that you can use to outline the area to crop. The part of the picture you are cropping away will appear grayed out.

Figure 12.7 *Use the cropping tools to crop the image to a particular object or place the image in a shape.*

 LET ME TRY IT

Choose Crop to Shape to crop the image to one of the shapes available in the drop-down. The image will be recut to the selected shape. To nudge the image within the shape, right-click the image and select Format Picture. From the Format Picture dialog, go to the Crop category and under the Picture Position options, change the values in the Offset X and Offset Y fields. Adjusting the Offset X value will move the image left or right in the shape; Adjusting the Offset Y value will move the image up or down in the shape.

Cropping a Picture to a Shape

To crop an inserted picture to a shape, follow these steps:

1. Select the picture to crop.

2. Go to Picture Tools, Format, Size, and from the Crop drop-down, select Crop to Shape and select the desired shape.

3. If the image needs to be moved within the shape, right-click the image and select Format Picture.

4. Go to the Crop category.

5. Under the Picture Position options, adjust the Offset X and Offset Y values as needed until the image is placed properly in the shape.

Corrections, Color, and Artistic Effects

You can correct the brightness and contrast, change a color image to a black-and-white image, or apply artistic effects to the selected image through the options in the Adjust group of the Picture Tools, Format tab. As you select an option in a drop-down, the image automatically adjusts, providing a preview of the option. Click the option to accept the change.

 TELL ME MORE   Media 12.4—Applying Styles

To listen to a free audio recording about the various picture styles, log on to my.safaribooksonline.com/9780132182287/media.

Corrections

The Corrections drop-down consists of options to Sharpen and Soften the image and to adjust Brightness and Contrast. If none of the predefined options are what you want, you can manually make the adjustments by selecting Picture Corrections Options, which will open the Format Picture dialog to the Picture Corrections category. Changes made in the dialog will apply automatically to the image. To undo a change, click the Undo button in the Quick Access toolbar.

Color

The Color drop-down includes options for adjusting Color Saturation, Color Tone, or recoloring the image. The More Variations option at the bottom of the drop-down is part of the Recolor group. The Set Transparent Color allows you to select a pixel in the image, and all pixels of the same color will become transparent, showing whatever is behind the image. For more control of saturation, tone, and recolor options, select Picture Color Options, which opens the Format Picture dialog to the Picture Color category. Changes made in the dialog will apply automatically to the image. To undo a change, click the Undo button in the Quick Access toolbar.

Artistic Effects

Artistic effects include Glow Edges, Film Grain, Light Screen, and many other effects that will change the way an image looks, as shown in Figure 12.8. After you select an effect, you can fine-tune it through the Artistic Effects category of the Format Picture dialog. The fine-tuning options differ depending on the effect chosen. Changes made in the dialog will apply automatically to the image. To undo a change, click the Undo button in the Quick Access toolbar.

Figure 12.8 *The Pencil Grayscale effect was used to change a photograph into an image that looks like a sketch.*

Arranging Pictures

The Arrange group of the Picture Tools, Format tab consists of several options for arranging imported images:

- **Bring Forward**—Brings the selected image forward, placing it on top of other images it is stacked with. Includes Bring to Front, which places the selected image as the topmost image.

- **Send Backward**—Send the selected image backward, placing it below other images it is stacked with. Includes Send to Back, which places the selected image behind all other images.

- **Selection Pane**—Opens a side pane that lists all the shapes on the active sheet. You can use this pane to select a specific shape.

- **Align**—Includes various alignment options, as shown in Figure 12.9, to quickly line up the selected images.

- **Group**—Includes the options to group and ungroup the selected images. Grouping images allows you to move them together without losing their alignment or order. If selective images were grouped together at one point and then ungrouped, Regroup will re-create the group without your having to reselect all the images.

- **Rotate**—Rotates or flips the selected image.

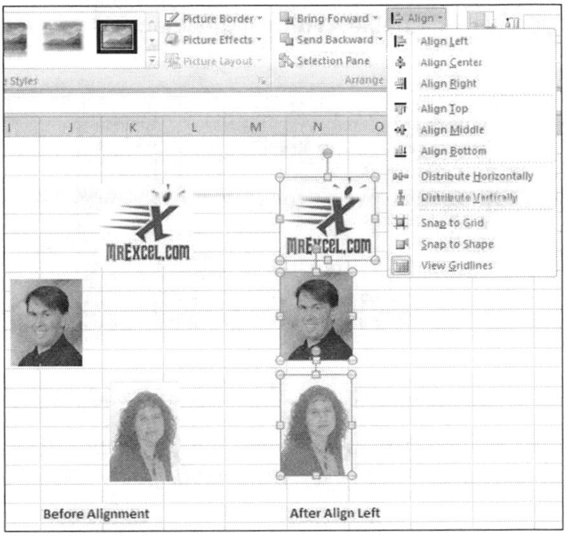

Figure 12.9   *Align Left lines up the selected images based on the left edge of the topmost image.*

  LET ME TRY IT

Aligning Selective Images

To align selective images, follow these steps:

1. Place the images approximately how you want them. For example, if you want to align the images left, place them in a vertical layout. If you want to line them up by their centers, place them in a horizontal layout. Each command's icon provides an example of how the images should be laid out.

2. Select the images by holding down the Ctrl key and clicking each image in turn.

3. Go to Picture Tools, Format, Arrange, and select the desired alignment from the Align drop-down.

Reducing a Picture's File Size

Importing a picture into a workbook can dramatically increase the file size. The Compress Pictures option offers multiple options for compressing images based on how you will be using the workbook, as shown in Figure 12.10. You can further reduce the file size by selecting the Delete Cropped Areas of Pictures option, but this means that you will be unable to return the image to its original state.

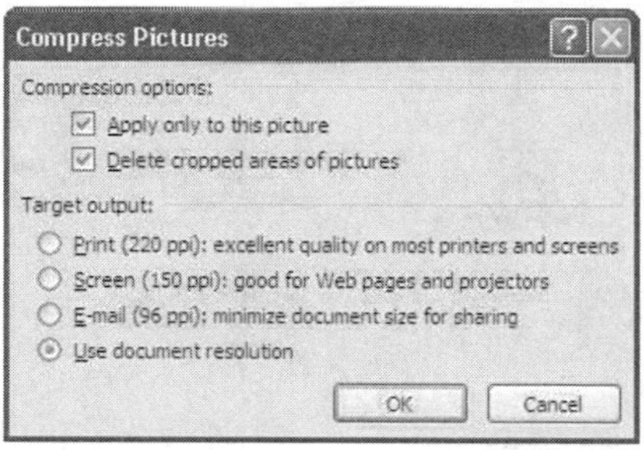

Figure 12.10   *The Compress Pictures dialog offers multiple options for how much the image resolution should be reduced based on how you will be using the workbook.*

You don't need to be a programmer to record macros or create UDFs. This chapter will teach you how to get the most out of the macro recorder and how to create custom functions.

13

Macros and UDFs

VBA macros enable you to automate any process in Excel. The macro recorder is provided to help create macros, but there are undocumented rules that must be followed to have the macro recorder work successfully. This chapter teaches you how to successfully record a simple macro that can deal with datasets of any size. It also introduces you to user-defined functions (UDF), which are useful when a built-in function doesn't exist for your needs.

To really get beyond the macro recorder and write your own code, check out *VBA and Macros for Microsoft Excel 2010* by Bill Jelen and Tracy Syrstad from Que Publishing (ISBN 0789743140).

Enabling VBA Security

Security settings can be set for all workbooks or for specific, trusted locations. Workbooks stored in a folder that is marked as a trusted location will automatically have its macros enabled.

Macro settings are found under File, Options, Trust Center, Trust Center Settings, Macro Settings. The four macro setting options are

- **Disable All Macros Without Notification**—Prevents all macros from running. With this setting, only macros in the Trusted Locations folders can run.

- **Disable All Macros with Notification**—The recommended setting. A message is displayed in the Message Area that macros have been disabled. You can choose to enable the content by clicking that option, as shown in Figure 13.1.

- **Disable All Macros Except Digitally Signed Macros**—Requires you to obtain a digital signing tool from VeriSign or another provider. Appropriate if you are going to be selling add-ins to others, but a bit of a hassle if you just want to write macros for your own use.

- **Enable All Macros (Not Recommended: Potentially Dangerous Code Can Run)**—Although this option requires the least amount of hassle, it opens your computer to attacks from malicious Melissa-like viruses. Microsoft suggests that you do not use this setting.

The recommended macro setting is Disable All Content with Notification. With this setting, if you open a workbook that contains macros, you'll see a Security Warning in the area just above the formula bar, as shown in Figure 13.1. Assuming you were expecting macros in this workbook, click Enable Content.

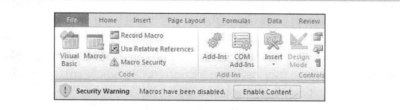

Figure 13.1   *The Disable Macros with Notification settings gives you control over whether to allow macros to run.*

If you do not want to enable macros for the current workbook, dismiss the Security Warning by clicking the X at the far right of the message bar.

If you forget to enable the macros and attempt to run a macro, a message informs you that you cannot run the macro because all macros have been disabled. You will need to close the workbook and reopen it to access the message bar again and enable the macros.

After you enable macros for a workbook stored on a local hard drive and then save the workbook, Excel will remember that you previously enabled macros in this workbook. The next time you open this workbook, macros will be automatically enabled.

TELL ME MORE   Media 13.1—Creating a Trusted Location

To listen to a free audio recording about creating a trusted location for your workbooks, log on to my.safaribooksonline.com/9780132182287/media.

Developer Tab

By default, the Developer tab is hidden in Excel. The Developer tab contains useful tools, such as buttons for recording macros and adding controls to sheets. To access it, do the following:

1. Go to File, Options, Customize Ribbon.

2. In the right list box, select the Developer tab, which is near from the bottom.

3. Click OK to return to Excel. Excel displays the Developer tab shown in Figure 13.2.

Figure 13.2   *You'll need the Developer tab to access tools specific to macros.*

The buttons in the Code group on the Developer tab are used for recording and playing back macros:

*   **Visual Basic**—Opens the Visual Basic Editor (VB Editor or VBE).

*   **Macros**—Displays the Macro dialog, where you can choose to run or edit a macro from the list of macros.

*   **Record Macro**—Begins the process of recording a macro.

*   **Use Relative Reference**—Toggles between using relative or absolute recording. With relative recording, Excel will record that you move down three cells. With absolute recording, Excel will record that you selected cell A4.

*   **Macro Security**—Shortcut to access the Trust Center, where you can choose to allow or disallow macros to run on this computer.

Introduction to the Visual Basic Editor

Click the Visual Basic button in the Code group of the Developer tab. This will open the VB Editor, shown in Figure 13.3, which is the interface used for writing and editing macros. On the left side is the Project Explorer, which lists all the workbooks and add-ins and their components. On the right side is the Code pane where you view and edit the macros you create.

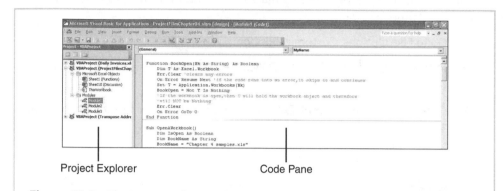

Project Explorer   Code Pane

Figure 13.3   *The Project Explorer on the left side of the screen is the primary method of navigating through the components of the workbook in the editor.*

Project Explorer

The Project Explorer lists any open workbooks and add-ins that are loaded, as shown in Figure 13.3. If you click the + icon next to the VBA Project, you will see a folder with Microsoft Excel objects. There can also be folders for forms, class modules, and standard modules. Each folder includes one or more such components. If the Project Explorer is not visible, select View, Project Explorer from the menu.

A *module* is a component that in the Project Explorer where you enter code. A *userform,* or *form,* is a popup window, for example a window that asks you to type in more information, which also includes code.

Right-clicking a component, such as Module1, and selecting View Code or just double-clicking the desired component brings up any code in the module in the Code pane. The exception is userforms, where double-clicking displays the userform in Design view.

Inserting Modules

A project consists of sheet modules for each sheet in the workbook and a single ThisWorkbook module. Code specific to a sheet, such as controls or sheet events, is placed on the corresponding sheet. Workbook events, code that runs automatically when something happens, for example when the workbook is opened or text is entered in a cell, are placed in the ThisWorkbook module. The code you record and the UDFs you create will be placed in standard modules.

LET ME TRY IT

Inserting a Standard Module

To insert a standard module, follow these steps:

1. Right-click the project you need to insert the module into.

2. From the context menu, select Insert, Module.

3. The module is placed in the Modules folder.

Understanding How the Macro Recorder Works

This section is about the difference between recording a macro that will run successfully on a new dataset and one that will make you cry in frustration when it fails on a new dataset. You'll rarely be able to record 100 percent of your macros and have them work on different datasets, but with the tips in the following subsections, you'll greatly improve your chances.

The macro recorder is very literal, especially with the default settings. For example, if you have cell A1 selected, then begin the macro recorder and use the mouse to select your entire dataset in range A1:B10, this is what will be recorded:

Range("A1:B10").Select

If the next time you run the macro the dataset is A1:B20, your macro won't run on all the rows. There are two things you need to change to make the recorded macro work properly. First, don't use the mouse when selecting ranges. Second, don't use the default settings of the macro recorder.

SHOW ME   Media 13.2—Getting the Most Out of the Macro Recorder by Using the Keyboard
Access this video file through your registered web edition at my.safaribooksonline.com/9780132182287/media.

Navigating While Recording

To get the most out of the macro recorder, you should use the keyboard shortcuts to navigate the sheet, not the mouse. The reason is that some of the keyboard shortcuts translate to commands instead of specific cell selections. For example, if you record pressing Ctrl+down-arrow to jump to the last row in a column, you will get

Selection.End(xlDown).Select

If your dataset changes in size the next time you run the macro, the preceding line of code will be much more useful than if you'd recorded the macro by using the mouse.

Relative References in Macro Recording

The second rule to successful macro recording is to know when to turn relative referencing on and off. By default, it is off, which has it uses, but you'll often want it on.

For more information on relative referencing, refer to "Relative Versus Absolute Formulas" in Chapter 5, "Using Formulas."

You can turn Relative Referencing on and off as needed while recording a macro.

When relative referencing is off, the macro records specific cell addresses. Imagine you have a list of addresses similar to Figure 13.4. Each address is exactly three rows, and a blank row separates each address. To transpose an address to a single row, you would follow these steps:

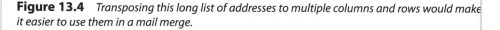

	A
1	HARRY SANTIAGO
2	248 MILL LANE
3	RIVERSIDE, VA 74720
4	
5	WHITNEY HARRIS
6	1292 PINE HIGHWAY
7	ST JOSEPH, ME 93197
8	
9	VELMA TALLEY
10	1845 HILL AVENUE
11	GREENWOOD, VI 24124
12	
13	KATHRYN PRATT
14	411 RAILROAD CIRCLE
15	ROCHESTER, NY 73115
16	

Figure 13.4 *Transposing this long list of addresses to multiple columns and rows would make it easier to use them in a mail merge.*

1. Start in cell A1.

2. Press the down-arrow key.

3. Press Ctrl+X to cut the address.

4. Press the up-arrow key and then the right-arrow key (to move to cell A2, remember, use the keyboard to navigate).

5. Press Ctrl+V to paste the address next to the name.

6. Press the left-arrow key once and the down-arrow key twice to move to the cell containing the city, state and ZIP Code.

7. Press Ctrl+X to cut the city.

8. Press the up-arrow key twice and the right-arrow key twice to move to the right of the street cell.

9. Press Ctrl+V to paste the city.

10. Press the left-arrow key twice and the down-arrow key once to move to the new blank row just beneath the name.

11. Hold down the Shift key while pressing the down-arrow key twice to select the three blank cells.

12. Press Ctrl+- to bring up the Delete dialog.

13. Press R to select the Entire Row option and then press Enter to accept the command.

If you record these steps with relative referencing off, you will get code that is cell specific, as shown in the text box in Figure 13.5. The results of running this code repeatedly on the data from Figure 13.4 is shown in Figure 13.5. A couple of repetitions of the code overwrites the first address line, ruining the record.

If this example was your first recorded macro, you might despair, as many before you have, at the uselessness of the recorder. But there is a way to make it work, and that's to turn on the Use Relative References option found in the Code group on the Developer tab. Performing the same steps with relative referencing on returns the results in Figure 13.6. As the active (or selected) cell moves down the column, the correct fields are cut and pasted to the proper row and column.

 SHOW ME   Media 13.3—Recording a Macro Using Relative Referencing
Access this video file through your registered web edition at
my.safaribooksonline.com/9780132182287/media.

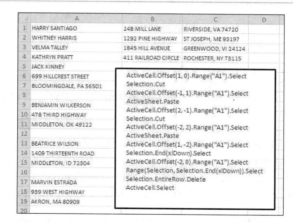

Figure 13.5 *Recording the macro with relative referencing off recorded the specific cell address for processing the first address, making the code useless for subsequent addresses.*

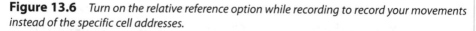

Figure 13.6 *Turn on the relative reference option while recording to record your movements instead of the specific cell addresses.*

Avoid the AutoSum Button

If you use the AutoSum button while recording a macro, Excel will record the actual formula entered in the cell in R1C1 notation. It doesn't record that you wanted it to select the range above or to the left of the formula. It's just not that flexible. So, instead of using the AutoSum button, manually type in the formula mixing relative and absolute referencing.

For more information on relative referencing, refer to "Relative Versus Absolute Formulas" in Chapter 5, "Using Formulas."

For example, if you want to sum G2:G13, the AutoSum function will create the formula =SUM(G2:G13), or in R1C1 notation, =SUM(R[-12]C:R[-1]C). When viewed in R1C1 notation, you see how fixed the formula is. Although it will work in any column that it's placed in, it specifically includes the cells 12 cells above (row 2) and directly above (row 13) the formula cell. The problem is if you add more rows, then the first cell is no longer 12 rows above—it's more. The solution is to type in the formula manually, fixing the row for the first argument, as shown in Figure 13.7.

	f_x	=SUM(G$2:G13)	
D	E	F	G
ustomerⁿ	ProductRe	ServiceRe	ProductCost
8754	639600	12000	325438
7874	964600	0	435587
4844	988900	0	587630
4940	673800	15000	346164
7969	513500	0	233842
8468	760600	0	355305
1620	894100	0	457577
3238	316200	45000	161877
5214	111500	0	62956
3717	747600	0	444162
7492	857400	0	410493
7780	200700	0	97937
			3918968

Figure 13.7   *Instead of using the AutoSum button, type in SUM formulas manually, making sure to fix the row of the first argument.*

Recording a Macro

To begin recording a macro, select Record Macro from the Code group of the Developer tab. Before recording begins, Excel displays the Record Macro dialog box shown in Figure 13.8.

 **LET ME TRY IT**

Filling in the Record Macro Dialog

To begin recording a macro and fill in the record macro dialog, follow these steps:

  1. Go to Developer, Code, Record Macro. The Record Macro dialog appears.

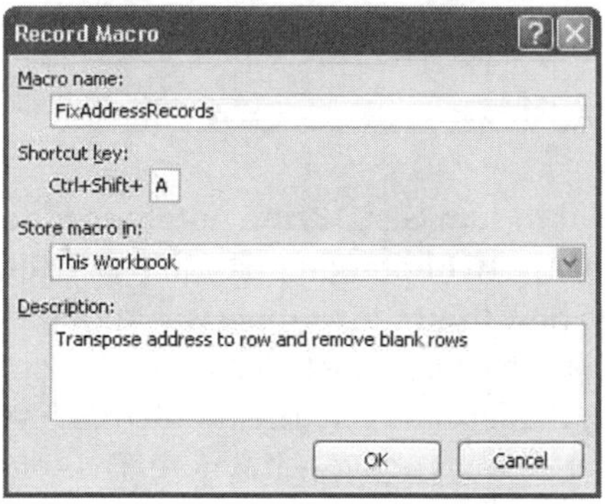

Figure 13.8 *Provide details for the macro you're about to record.*

2. In the Macro Name field, type a name for the macro, making sure not to include any spaces. Use a meaningful name for the macro, such as FormatReport.

3. The Shortcut Key field is optional. If you type J in this field, and then press Ctrl+J, this macro runs. Note that most of the lowercase shortcuts from Ctrl+a through Ctrl+z already have a use in Excel. Rather than being limited to the unassigned Ctrl+j, you can hold down the Shift key and type Shift+A through Shift+Z in the shortcut box. This will assign the macro to Ctrl+Shift+A.

4. From the Store Macro In drop-down, choose where you want to save the macro: Personal Macro Workbook, New Workbook, This Workbook. It is recommended that you store macros related to a particular workbook in This Workbook.

    The Personal Macro Workbook (Personal.xlsb) is not a visible workbook; it's created if you choose to save the recording in the Personal Macro Workbook. This workbook is used to save a macro in a workbook that will open automatically when you start Excel, thereby allowing you to use the macro. After Excel is started, the workbook is hidden.

5. Enter a description of the macro in the optional Description field. This description is added as a comment to the beginning of your macro.

6. Click OK and record your macro. When you are finished recording the macro, click the Stop Recording icon in the Developer tab.

Running a Macro

If you assign a shortcut key to your macro, you can play the macro by pressing the key combination. Macros can also be assigned to the Ribbon, the Quick Access toolbar, forms controls, drawing objects, or you can run them from the Macros button in the Code group on the Developer tab.

Running a Macro from the Ribbon

You can add an icon to a new group on the Ribbon to run a macro. This is appropriate for macros stored in the Personal Macro Workbook.

 LET ME TRY IT

Adding a Macro Button to the Ribbon

Follow these steps to add a macro button to the Ribbon:

1. Go to File, Options, Customize Ribbon.

2. In the right list box, choose the tab name where you want to add the macro button.

3. Click the New Group button below the right list box. Excel adds a new entry called New Group (Custom) to the end of the groups in that ribbon tab.

4. To move the group to the left in the ribbon tab, click the up-arrow icon on the right side of the dialog several times.

5. To rename the group, click the Rename button. Type a new name, such as Report Macros, and click OK.

6. Open the upper-left drop-down and choose Macros from the list. Excel displays a list of available macros in the left list box.

7. Choose a macro from the left list box.

8. Click the Add button in the center of the dialog. Excel moves the macro to the right list box in the selected group. Excel uses a generic VBA icon for all macros, which you can change in step 9.

9. To rename or change the icon used for the macro:
   a. Select the macro in the right list box.
   b. Click the Rename button.

c. Excel displays a list of possible icons. Choose an icon or type a new name for the macro in the Display Name field, such as Format Report, as shown in Figure 13.9.

Figure 13.9 *Create a custom group on the ribbon to add buttons for your macros.*

d. Click OK to return to the Excel Options dialog.

10. Click OK to close the dialog. The new button appears on the selected Ribbon tab.

Running a Macro from the Quick Access Toolbar

You can add a button to the Quick Access toolbar to run your macro. If your macro is stored in the Personal Macro Workbook, you can have the button permanently displayed in the Quick Access toolbar. If the macro is stored in the current workbook, you can specify that the icon should appear only when the workbook is open.

LET ME TRY IT

Running a Macro From the Quick Access Toolbar

Follow these steps to add a macro button to the Quick Access toolbar:

1. Go to File, Options, Quick Access Toolbar.

2. If the macro should be available only when the current workbook is open, open the upper-right drop-down and change For All Documents (Default) to For *FileName.xlsm*. Any icons associated with the current workbook are displayed at the end of the Quick Access toolbar.

3. Select Macros from the list in the upper-left drop-down. Excel displays a list of available macros in the left list box.

4. Choose a macro from the left list box and click the Add button in the center of the dialog to move the macro to the right list box. Excel uses a generic VBA icon for all macros, which you can change by following steps 5 and 6.

5. To rename and change the icon used for the macro:
   a. Select the macro in the right list box.
   b. Click the Modify button.
   c. Excel displays a list of possible icons. Choose an icon or type a new name for the macro in the Display Name field, such as Format Report, as shown in Figure 13.10. The name will appear as the ToolTip when you place your cursor over the button.

Figure 13.10   *Add a button to the Quick Access toolbar to run the macro saved to a specific workbook.*

6. Click OK to close the Modify Button dialog.

7. Click OK to close Excel options. The new button appears on the Quick Access toolbar.

Running a Macro from a Form Control, Text Box, or Shape

You can create a macro specific to a workbook, store the macro in the workbook, and attach it to a form control or any object on the sheet to run it. Macros can be assigned to any worksheet object such as clip art, a shape, SmartArt graphics, or a text box. To assign a macro to any object, right-click the object and select Assign Macro.

LET ME TRY IT

Running a Macro from a Button on a Sheet.

Follow these steps to attach a macro to a button on a sheet:

1. In the Controls group of the Developer tab, click the Insert button to open its drop-down list. Excel offers 12 form controls and 12 ActiveX controls.

2. Click the Button (Form Control) icon in the upper-left corner in the drop-down.

3. Move your cursor over the worksheet; the cursor changes to a plus sign.

4. To draw a button, click and hold the left mouse button while drawing a box shape. Release the button when finished.

5. Choose the macro from the Assign Macro dialog and click OK. The button is created with generic text such as Button 1. To customize the text or the button's appearance, refer to steps 6 and 7.

6. To give the button a new caption:
    a. Right-click over the button and select Edit Text. The cursor within the button will become visible.
    b. Replace the current caption with your own text.
    c. When finished, click anywhere outside the button

7. For further text and button formatting options, right-click over the button and select Format Control.

8. Click the button to run the macro.

User-Defined Functions

Excel provides many built-in formulas, but sometimes you need a custom formula not offered in the software. You can create functions in VBA that can be used just like Excel's built-in functions, such as SUM, VLOOKUP, and MATCH, to name a few. After the user-defined function (UDF) is created, a user needs to know only the function name and its arguments.

A few things to keep in mind when you create a UDF:

*   UDFs can only be entered into standard modules. Sheet and ThisWorkbook modules are a special type of module; if you enter the function there, Excel won't recognize that you are creating a UDF.

*   A variable is a word used to hold the place of a value, similar to an argument. Variables cannot have any spaces or unusual characters, such as the back-

slash (\) or hyphen (-). Make sure any variables you create are unique. For example, if your function is called BMI, you cannot have a variable with the same name.

- A variable type describes the variable as string, integer, long, and so on. This tells the program how to treat the variable—for example, integer and long—though both numbers have different limitations. The type also tells the program how much memory to put aside to hold the value.

- A simple UDF formula is not that different from a formula you write down on a sheet of paper. For example, if asked how to calculate the final cost of a store item, you would explain that it's the sale price *(1 + tax rate). Similarly, in a FinalCost UDF, you might enter FinalCost = SalePrice* (1+ TaxRate).

- A UDF can only calculate or look up and return information. It cannot insert or delete rows or color cells. The UDF has the same limitations as built-in functions.

Structure of a UDF

Like a normal function, a UDF consists of the function name followed by arguments in parentheses. To help you understand this, follow these steps to build a custom function to add two values in the current workbook. It is a function called ADD that will total two numbers in different cells. The function has two arguments:

Add(Number1,Number2)

Number1 is the first number to add; Number2 is the second number to add. After the UDF has been created, it can be used on a worksheet.

 SHOW ME   Media 13.4—Creating a Simple UDF
Access this video file through your registered web edition at
my.safaribooksonline.com/9780132182287/media.

1. Open the VBE by going to Developer, Code, Visual Basic.

2. Find the current workbook in the Project Explorer window.

3. Right-click over the current workbook and select Insert, Module. A new module will be added to the Modules folder.

4. Double-click the new module to open it in the Code pane.

5. Type the following function into the module's Code pane, as shown in Figure 13.11.

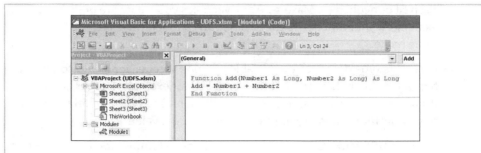

Figure 13.11 *A UDF's code must be entered in a standard module.*

```
Function Add(Number1 As Long, Number2 As Long) As Long
Add = Number1 + Number2
End Function
```

Let's break this down:

- Function name: ADD.

- Arguments are placed in parentheses after the name of the function. This example has two arguments: Number1 and Number2.

- As Long defines the variable type as a whole number between -2,147,483,648 to 2,147,483,647. Other variable types include
  - As Integer if you were using a whole number between -32,768 and 32,767.
  - As Double if you were using decimal values.
  - As String if you were using text.

- ADD =Number1 + Number2: The result of the calculation is returned to the function, ADD

Not all the variable types in the function have to be the same. You could have a string argument that returns an integer—for example, *FunctionName(argument1 as String) as Long*.

When computers were slower and every bit of memory mattered, the difference between Integer and Long was crucial. But with today's computers, in most cases memory doesn't matter and Long is becoming preferred over Integer because it doesn't limit the user as much.

How to Use a UDF

After the function is created in the code, follow these steps to use it on a sheet:

1. Type any numbers into cells A1 and A2.

2. Select cell A3.

3. Press Shift+F3 to open the Paste Function dialog box (or from the Formulas tab, choose Insert Function).

4. Select the User Defined category.

5. Select the ADD function and click OK.

6. Place your cursor in the first argument box and select cell A1.

7. Place your cursor in the second argument box and select cell A2.

8. Click OK. The function will return the calculated value, as shown in Figure 13.12.

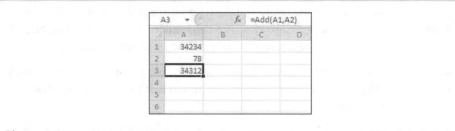

Figure 13.12   *Using your UDF on a sheet is no different from using one of Excel's built-in functions.*

Sharing UDFs

Where you store a UDF affects how you can share it:

- **Personal.xlsb**—If the UDF is just for your use and won't be used in a workbook opened on another computer, you can store the UDF in the Personal Workbook.

- **Workbook**—If the UDF needs to be distributed to many people, you can store it in the workbook in which it is being used.

- **Template**—If several workbooks need to be created using the UDF, and the workbooks are distributed to many people, you can store it in a template.

- **Add-in**—If the workbook is to be shared among a select group of people, you can distribute it via an add-in. For more information on add-ins, refer to the VBA book mentioned at the beginning of this chapter.

Using Select Case to Replace Nested IF

A really useful application of a UDF is with a Select Case statement. A Select Case statement is similar to a nested IF statement, but much easier to read. Also, since the new 64 nested IF statements allowed in 2010 are not compatible in legacy versions of Excel, using a UDF with Select Case statements ensures compatibility.

For more information on nested IF statements, refer to "Nested IF Statements" in Chapter 6, "Using Functions."

The statement begins with Select Case and then the variable you want to evaluate. Next, follow the Case statements, which are the possible values of the variable, each including the action you want to take when the variable meets the Case value. You can also include a Case Else, as a catch-all for any variable that doesn't fall within the predefined cases. The statement ends with End Select.

Within the Case statements, you have the option of using comparison operators with the word Is, such as Case Is <5 if the variable is less than 5. You also have To, used to signify a range, such as Case 1 to 5.

Example: Calculate Commission

Imagine you have the following formula on a sheet. For the different type and dollar of hardware, there's a different commission percentage to use in the commission calculation. It's rather difficult to read and also to modify.

```
=IF(C2="Printer",IF(D2<100,ROUND(D2*0.05,2),ROUND(D2*0.1,2)),IF(C2="Scanner",
IF(D2<125,ROUND(D2*0.05,2),ROUND(D2*0.15,2)),IF(C2="Service
Plan",IF(D2<2,ROUND(D2*0.1,2),ROUND(D2*0.2,2)),ROUND(D2*0.01,2))))
```

Instead take the same logic, make it a Select Case Statement, and see the commission percentage breakdown for each hardware item. You can easily make changes, including adding a new Case statement. And because in the original formula the commission calculation for each hardware type is the same (price*commission percentage), that formula doesn't need to be repeated in each Case statement. Use the Select Case statements to set the commission percentage and have a single formula at the end to do the calculation. You can also provide more flexibility in case users enter a different hardware description, for example "Printers" instead of just "Printer."

In the code below, there is text following an apostrophe ('). For example: 'If Hardware is Printer or Printers, do the following.

Any text following an apostrophe is called a comment and not treated as code. Use comments to leave yourself notes about what the line of code is for. Comments do not have to be after the corresponding line of code. They can be anywhere within the Sub or Function, except directly inline before code - because then you are also turning the code into a comment.

```
Function Commission(Hardware As String, HDRevenue As Long) As Double
Select Case Hardware 'Hardware is the variable to be evaluated
    Case "Printer", "Printers" 'If Hardware is Printer or Printers, do the
following
        If HDRevenue < 100 Then 'If Hardware is less than 100
            ComPer = 0.05 'then ComPer is 5%
        Else 'else, ComPer is 10%
            ComPer = 0.1
        End If
    Case "Scanner", "Scanners"
        If HDRevenue < 125 Then
            ComPer = 0.05
        Else
            ComPer = 0.15
        End If
    Case "Service Plan", "Service Plans"
        If HDRevenue < 2 Then
            ComPer = 0.1
        Else
            ComPer = 0.2
        End If
    Case Else
            ComPer = 0.01
End Select
'Once a value is assigned to ComPer, do the calculation and return it to
'the function
        Commission = Round(HDRevenue * ComPer, 2)
End Function
```

Example: Calculate BMI

This example takes the user input, calculates the BMI (body mass index), then compares that calculated value to various ranges to return a BMI descriptive, as shown in Figure 13.13. When creating a UDF, think of the formula in the same way you would write it down, because this is very similar to how you will enter it in the UDF. The formula for calculating BMI is as follows:

BMI=(weight in pounds*703)/height in inches(squared)

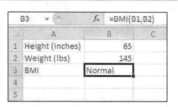

Figure 13.13   *A UDF can perform calculations based on user input and return a string.*

The table for returning the BMI descriptive is as follows:

Below 18.5 = underweight
18.5-24.9 = normal
25-29.9 = overweight
30 & above = obese

The code for calculating the BMI then returning the descriptive is the following:

```
Function BMI(Height As Long, Weight As Long) As String
'Do the initial BMI calculation to get the numerical value
calcBMI = (Weight * 703) / (Height ^ 2)
Select Case calcBMI 'evaluate the calculated BMI to get a string value
    Case Is < 18.5 'if the calcBMI is less than 18.5
        BMI = "Underweight"
    Case 18.5 To 24.9 'if the calcBMI is a value between 18.5 and 24.9
        BMI = "Normal"
    Case 25 To 29.9
        BMI = "Overweight"
    Case Is > 30 'if the calcBMI is greater than 30
        BMI = "Obese"
End Select
End Function
```

index

Symbols

¢ (cent) symbol, 82

100% stacked charts, 233

A

absolute formulas, 100-102

accessing SkyDrive, 34

Accounting format (numbers), 76

Advanced Filter
  criteria range, 174
  filtering datasets with, 175
  filtering for unique items, 176
  overview, 173-177
  removing duplicates from single column, 176-177

alignment, 69-70

Analysis Toolpak, 142-144

AND function, 133

Anova tools, 143

applying themes, 89

area charts, 233

Arrange Windows dialog, 23

arranging
  pictures, 268-269
  windows, 23

array formulas
  deleting, 115
  editing, 114-115
  examples, 112-113
  overview, 111-112

artistic effects, 267-268

Auto Outline option, 196-197

AutoFitting column data, 88-87

AutoSum function, 125-127, 278-279

Average function, 126

averaging ranges, 126-127

axis titles, 238

B

bar charts, 233

Bar of Pie charts, 248-249

blank rows, inserting after subtotals, 192-196

BMI (body mass index), calculating, 290

BMI() function, 290

body mass index (BMI), calculating, 290

bold, 66

borders, 66-67

bubble charts, 233, 247

built-in rules, 94

buttons
  adding to groups, 10
  quick sort buttons, 151-153

C

calculated fields, 222

calculating. *See also* formulas
  BMI (body mass index), 290
  calculated fields, 222
  calculation settings, 100
  commission, 288-289
  date calculation functions, 138-139
  overtime, 141-142
  pivot table field calculation types, 206

case-sensitive sorts, 151

cells
  cell references
    changing, 103-104
    names, 107-109
  controlling cell selection, 55-57
  entering functions into
    with Formula Wizard, 122-124
    typing directly into cells, 124-125
  formatting, 65-72
    alignment, 69-70
    borders, 66-67
    fill, 67-68
    font color, 69
    fonts, 65-66
    indents, 71
    text orientation, 72
    text wrap, 71
  linking to SmartArt, 262
  merging, 70-71
  names, 107-109
  styles, 74
  unlocking, 27

cent (¢) symbol, 82

changing chart type, 239

charts
  100% stacked charts, 233
  area charts, 233
  axis titles, 238
  bar charts, 233
  bubble charts, 233, 247
  changing chart type, 239
  chart data of different scales, 241
  chart styles, 236
  clustered charts, 233
  column charts, 233
  components of, 231-232
  creating, 233-235
  data preparation for, 232-233
  doughnut charts, 233
  layouts, 237

legends, 238-239
line charts, 232
mixing chart types, 240
modifying, 236-237
moving, 239
overview, 230-231
pie charts, 233
  Bar of Pie charts,
    248-249
  rotating, 248
radar charts, 233
resizing, 238
saving as templates,
  252-253
scatter charts, 233
sparklines
  adding points to,
    250-251
  creating, 250
  overview, 250
  spacing based on date,
    251-252
stacked charts, 233
stock charts, 233, 246-247
surface charts, 233
switching rows/columns,
  243-244
titles, 237-238
trendlines, 244-245
updating, 242-243
CHOOSE function, 127
clearing
  conditional formatting, 98
  filters, 160
  groups, 197
clustered charts, 233
Collapse Dialog button, 20
collapsing
  pivot table fields, 211
  subtotals, 184-185
color
  adding to pivot tables,
    223
  filtering by, 171
  font color, 69
  in number formats, 81
  in pictures, 267
  sorting by, 149-150
column charts, 233

columns
  adjusting width of, 87
  AutoFitting data in, 88-87
  column breaks, changing,
    17
  copying formulas down,
    49
  filtering single column,
    161-162
  freezing, 21
  inserting, 24
  quick sorting, 151-152
  randomizing data in,
    152-153
  rearranging, 155-157
    with mouse, 156-157
    with Sort dialog, 155-
      156
  removing duplicates from,
    176-177
  sorting. See sorting
  subtotals. See subtotals
  summing values with
    SUMIFS function,
    128-129
  switching rows/columns,
    243-244
  Text to Columns option,
    51-55
combining rules, 97
commands
  adding to Quick Access
    toolbar, 11-13
  removing from Quick
    Access toolbar, 15
comments, 289
Commission() function,
  288-289
commission, calculating,
  288-289
Compact view (pivot tables),
  225
comparison operators, 134
compatibility of pivot tables,
  201
Compress Pictures dialog,
  270
conditional formatting
  clearing, 98

custom icon sets, 92-93
overview, 91-98
rules, 93-98
  built-in rules, 94
  combining, 97
  custom format for top n
    items in range, 94-95
  custom rules, 94-97
  stopping rules from
    being checked, 97-98
conditions in number
  formats, 81
Consolidate tool, 178-179
consolidating data, 178-179
controls, running macros
  from, 283-284
Convert Text to Columns
  Wizard, 51-55
Convert to Number option,
  47-48
converting
  date conversion func-
    tions, 136-137
  formulas to values, 50
  text case, 48-49
  text to dates, 140-141
  text to numbers, 55
  time conversion
    functions, 138
Copy Here as Values Only
  command, 50
copying
  formulas, 49, 104-106
  range formatting, 86
  sheets to new workbooks,
    25
  subtotals, 185-186
corrections to pictures, 267
Correlation tool, 143
Count Numbers function,
  126
Covariance tool, 143
Create Sparklines dialog, 250
criteria range (Advanced
  Filter), 174
cropping pictures, 265-266
custom lists, sorting with,
  153-154

Customize the Quick Access Toolbar dialog, 11-15

Customize the Ribbon dialog, 7-11

customizing
cell styles, 74
icon sets, 92-93
lists, 44-45
number formats, 78-84
cent (¢) symbol, 82
color and conditions, 81
dates and times in, 82-84
decimals and thousands separator, 80
significant and insignificant digits, 80-81
symbols, 81-82
text and spacing, 79-80
Quick Access toolbar, 11-15
adding commands, 11-13
for current workbook, 14-15
Ribbon, 7-11
rules, 94-97
tabs, 9
views, 22

D

data analysis tools, 142-144

data entry
controlling cell selection, 55-57
converting text case, 48-49
data validation, 61-63
criteria, 61-62
limiting user entry to selection from list, 62-63
fixing numbers as text, 47-48
formulas
converting to values, 50
copying, 49
joining dates and text, 46-47

joining text, 45-46
overview, 41-43
series
creating, 44-45
extending by dragging fill handle, 43-44
tables
adding totals to, 60
capabilities, 57
defining, 57-59
expanding, 59-60
Text to Columns option, 51-55

data formatting. *See* formatting

data ranges, preselecting, 56

data validation, 61-63
criteria, 61-62
limiting user entry to selection from list, 62-63

Data Validation dialog, 61-63

datasets, 175

date formats (numbers), 76

DATE function, 137

dates
converting text to, 140-141
date/time functions, 136-142
date calculation functions, 138-139
date conversion functions, 136-137
overview, 136
troubleshooting, 140-142
filtering for, 164-165
filters, 169-171
grouped dates filter listing, 162-165
grouping in pivot tables
grouping dates into months and years, 213
grouping dates into weeks, 214-213
overview, 212
summarizing weeks, 213-214

inserting into headers, 18-19
joining dates and text, 46-47
in number formats, 82-84
spacing sparklines based on, 251-252

DATEVALUE function, 137

DAY function, 137

decimals, 80

Decrease Decimal button, 85

defining tables, 57-59

deleting
array formulas, 115
shapes, 259-260
sparklines, 252

delimited text, separating into multiple columns, 51-53

Descriptive Statistics, 143

Developer tab, 273

dialog launchers, 15-16

dialogs. *See* specific dialogs

Disable All Macros Except Digitally Signed Macros setting, 271

Disable All Macros with Notification setting, 271

Disable All Macros Without Notification setting, 271

documents, viewing recent, 27

doughnut charts, 233

downloading workbooks, 37-38

dragging fill handle, 43-44

drilling down pivot tables, 211-212

duplicates
consolidating data, 178-179
removing from datasets, 177-178
removing from single column, 176-177

E

EDATE function, 137

editing
  array formulas, 114-115
  column breaks, 17
  multiple worksheets, 25-26
  simultaneous editing, 40-41

Enable All Macros setting, 272

Enter key, 55-56

entering
  formulas, 100, 104
  functions
    directly into cells, 124-125
    with Formula Wizard, 122-124

EOMONTH function, 137

error messages, formula errors, 116-117

Evaluate window, 119-120

evaluating formulas, 119-120

Excel 2000, 2

Excel 2002, 2

Excel 2003, 2

Excel 2007, 2

Excel 2010, 1

Excel 97, 2

Excel options, troubleshooting, 29

Excel Starter, 1

Excel WebApp, 1
  filtering in, 161
  navigation methods, 41
  number formatting, 84-85
  overview, 29-31
  sorting in, 147
  system requirements, 31
  Windows Live ID, 31-33
  workbooks
    sharing, 38-41
    uploading/downloading, 33-38

excluding items from results, 166

expanding
  pivot table fields, 211
  subtotals, 184-185
  tables, 59-60

Exponential Smoothing, 143

F

FALSE function, 134

Field List (pivot tables), 201-202

fields (pivot table)
  calculated fields, 222
  calculation type, 206
  collapsing/expanding, 211
  moving, 205
  removing, 205
  renaming, 205

File menu commands, Recent, 27

filenames, inserting into headers, 18-19

files
  reducing file size, 270
  saving to local drive, 37-38

fill, applying to cells, 67-68

Fill Effects dialog, 68

fill handle, dragging to extend series, 43-44

filtered data
  Advanced Filter, 173-177
    criteria range, 174
    filtering datasets with, 175
    filtering for unique items, 176
    overview, 173
    removing duplicates from single column, 176-177
  applying filters to datasets, 159-162
  clearing filters, 160
  creating custom view of, 22
  data preparation, 159
  filtering by selection, 172

filtering in WebApp, 161

filtering on protected sheets, 172-173

filtering options, 162-171
  excluding items from results, 166-167
  filter listing for listed items, 162
  filtering by color or icon, 171
  filtering for specific dates, 164-165
  filtering items with search function, 165-166
  grouped dates filter listing, 162-165
  search function for grouped dates, 167-169
  searching for items to exclude from filter, 166
  searching for items to include in filter, 165
  searching functions for listed items, 165
  text, number, and date special filters, 169-171

filtering single column, 161-162

overview, 157-159

pivot table filtering options, 214-220
  filter by selection, 221
  filter listing for listed items, 214-215
  search function for listed items, 215-218
  special filters, 218-220

reapplying filters, 161

removing duplicates
  from datasets, 177-178
  from single columns, 176-177

Report Filter, 201

finding functions, 121-122

fixed width text, separating into multiple columns, 54-55

folders
  creating, 38-39
  permissions, 39-40
fonts
  color, 69
  formatting, 65-66
forecasting trendlines, 245
Format Cells dialog, 224
  See formatting, cells
Format Data Series dialog, 242
Format Painter, 85-86
formatting
  cells
    alignment, 69-70
    borders, 66-67
    fill, 67-68
    font color, 69
    fonts, 65-66
    indents, 71
    overview, 65-72
    styles, 74
    text orientation, 72
    text wrap, 71
  conditional formatting
    clearing, 98
    custom icon sets, 92-93
    overview, 91-92, 91-98
    rules, 93-98
  Format Painter, 85-86
  numbers
    Accounting format, 76
    Currency format, 75
    custom formats, 78-84
    date formats, 76
    in Excel WebApp, 84-85
    Fraction format, 77
    General format, 75
    Number format, 75
    overview, 74-75
    Percentage format, 76
    Scientific format, 77
    special formats, 78
    Text format, 77
    time formats, 76-77
    troubleshooting, 84
  overview, 63-65
  pivot table values, 224
  rows/columns, 87
  subtotals, 186-187

text justification, 72-73
themes
  applying, 89
  creating, 89-90
  overview, 88-89, 88-90
  sharing, 90
WordArt, 264
forms, running macros from, 283-284
Formula Wizard, 122-124
formulas
  array formulas
    deleting, 115
    editing, 114-115
    examples, 112-113
    overview, 111-112
  calculation settings, 100
  cell references
    changing, 103-104
    names, 107-109
  compared to values, 100-101
  converting to values, 50
  copying, 49, 104-106
  entering, 100, 104
  evaluating, 119-120
  formatting data with, 96-97
  importance of laying out data properly, 99-100
  inserting into tables, 109-110
  mathematical operators, 106-107
  order of operations, 107
  overview, 98-99
  R1C1 notation, 102
  relative versus absolute, 100-102
  table references in, 110-111
  troubleshooting, 145-146
    error messages, 116-117
    trace precedents and dependents, 116-117
    Watch Window, 118-119
Fourier Analysis, 143
Fraction format (numbers), 77
Freeze Panes options, 20-21

freezing panes, 20-21
F-Test Two-Sample for Variances, 143
functions
  AutoSum, 125-127, 278-279
  Average, 126
  Count Numbers, 126
  data analysis tools, 142-144
  date/time functions, 136-142
    date calculation functions, 138-139
    date conversion functions, 136-
    overview, 136
    time conversion functions, 138
    troubleshooting, 140-142
  entering
    directly into cells, 124-125
    with Formula Wizard, 122-124
  finding, 121-122
  function wizard, troubleshooting formulas with, 145-146
  Goal Seek, 144-145
  logical functions, 133-135
    AND, 133
    comparison operators, 134
    FALSE, 134
    IF, 133
    IFERROR, 133, 135-136
    NOT, 133
    OR, 133
    TRUE, 134
  lookup functions, 127-131
    CHOOSE, 127
    INDEX, 129-130
    INDIRECT, 130-131
    MATCH, 129-130
    VLOOKUP, 127-129
  Max, 126
  Min, 126
  nested IF statements, 135-136

overview, 120-121
RAND, 152-153
SUBTOTAL, 181
SUMIFS, 131-132
SUMPRODUCT, 132-133
syntax, 121
UDFs (user-defined functions)
  adding to sheets, 287
  BMI(), 290
  comments, 289
  Commission(), 288-289
  overview, 284-285
  sharing, 287-288
  structure of, 285-286

G

General format (numbers), 75
Goal Seek, 144-145
Group option, 196-197
grouped dates filter listing, 162-165
Grouping dialog, 212
groups
  adding buttons to, 10
  adding to existing tab, 9
  adding to Ribbon, 9
  clearing, 197
  creating, 196-197
  grouping dates in pivot tables
    into months and years, 213
    overview, 212
    summarizing weeks, 213-214
    into weeks, 214-213
  removing from Ribbon, 8
  of worksheets, 26

H

headers
  inserting dates into, 18-19
  inserting filenames into, 18-19
  repeating, 20

hiding
  tabs, 7-8
  totals, 223-224
HOUR function, 138

I

icons
  customizing icon sets, 92-93
  filtering by, 171
  sorting by, 149-150
IDs, Windows Live ID, 31-33
IF function, 133
IF statements
  nested IF statements, replacing with Select Case, 288
  nesting, 135-136
IFERROR function, 133, 135-136
images
  pictures
    arranging, 268-269
    artistic effects, 267-268
    color, 267
    corrections, 267
    inserting, 265
    reducing file size, 270
    resizing and cropping, 265-266
  SmartArt
    adding/deleting shapes, 259-260
    categories, 255
    changing individual components, 261-262
    changing selected layout, 261
    formatting selected layout, 261
    inserting, 255-259
    linking cells to, 262
    reordering components, 260
    selecting, 259
  WordArt, 264
Increase Decimal button, 85
indenting cell contents, 71

INDEX function, 129-130
INDIRECT function, 130-131
Insert Chart dialog, 253
Insert menu commands, SmartArt, 256, 258
inserting
  blank rows after subtotals, 192-196
  formulas into tables, 109-110
  modules, 274-275
  pictures, 265
  shapes, 259-260
  SmartArt, 255-259
  WordArt, 264
italic, 66

J-K

joining
  dates and text, 46-47
  text, 45-46
justifying text, 72-73

L

labels in pivot tables, 201
layouts
  chart layouts, 237
  importance of laying out data properly, 99-100
legacy version of Excel
legends, 238-239
limitations of pivot tables, 200-201
line charts, 232
lines, adding to pivot tables, 223
linking cells to SmartArt, 262
lists
  creating, 44-45
  custom lists, sorting with, 153-154
  filter listing for listed items, 162, 214-215
  limiting user entry to selection from list, 62-63

search function for listed items, 215-218

logical functions, 133-135
AND, 133
comparison operators, 134
FALSE, 134
IF, 133
IFERROR, 133, 135-136
NOT, 133
OR, 133
TRUE, 134

lookup functions, 127-131
CHOOSE, 127
INDEX, 129-130
INDIRECT, 130-131
MATCH, 129-130
VLOOKUP, 127-129

LOWER function, 49

M

macro recorder, 275-279
AutoSum button, 278-279
navigating while recording, 275-276
relative references in macro recording, 276-277

macros
adding for current workbook, 14-15
Developer tab, 273
overview, 271-272
recording
Record Macro dialog, 279-280
relative references in macro recording, 276-277
running
from form controls, text boxes, or shapes, 283-284
from Quick Access toolbar, 282-283
from Ribbon, 281-282
security settings, 271-273
Visual Basic Editor, 273-275

inserting modules, 274-275
macro recorder, 275-279
Project Explorer, 274

MATCH function, 129-130

mathematical operators, 106-107

Max function, 126

merging cells, 70-71

Min function, 126

MINUTE function, 134

mixing chart types, 240

modules, inserting, 274-275

MONTH function, 137

months, grouping dates into, 213

mouse, rearranging columns with, 156-157

Move or Copy dialog, 24-25

moving
cell pointer direction, 56
charts, 239
pivot table fields, 205
Quick Access toolbar, 11
sheets, 24
within workbook, 25
between workbooks, 25

Moving Average, 143

multiple columns
quick sorting, 151-152
subtotaling, 190-191

multiple subtotal function types, 187-190

multiple worksheets, changing, 25-26

N

named ranges, 56-57

names (cell), 107-109

navigation in Excel WebApp, 41

nested IF statements, 135-136

.NET Passport Wizard, 35

NETWORKDAYS function, 139

NETWORKDAYS.INTL function, 139

NOT function, 133

Number format, 75

numbers
charting numbers of different scale, 241
converting text to, 55
filters, 169-171
fixing numbers as text, 47-48
formatting
Accounting format, 76
Currency format, 75
custom formats, 78-84
date formats, 76
in Excel WebApp, 84-85
Fraction format, 77
General format, 75
Number format, 75
overview, 74-75
Percentage format, 76
Scientific format, 77
special formats, 78
Text format, 77
time formats, 76-77
troubleshooting, 84
numbering pages, 19
numerical series, extending by dragging fill handle, 44

O

opening
templates, 28-29
workbooks, 37

operators
comparison operators, 134
mathematical operators, 106-107

OR function, 133

order of operations, 107

orientation (text), 72

Outline view (pivot tables), 226

outlining, 196-197

overtime, calculating, 141-142

P

Page Break Preview, 17

Page Layout mode, 18-19

Page Setup dialog, 19

pages
- numbering, 19
- page breaks, previewing, 17

panes, freezing, 20-21

PDF, saving files as, 28

Percentage format (numbers), 76

permissions, 39-40

pictures
- arranging, 268-269
- artistic effects, 267-268
- color, 267
- corrections, 267
- inserting, 265
- reducing file size, 270
- resizing and cropping, 265-266

pie charts, 233
- Bar of Pie charts, 248-249
- rotating, 248

pivot tables
- color, 223
- column labels, 201
- compatibility, 201
- creating, 202-204
- data preparation, 199-200
- drilling down, 211-212
- Field List, 201-202
- fields
  - *calculated fields, 222*
  - *calculation type, 206*
  - *collapsing/expanding, 211*
  - *moving, 205*
  - *removing, 205*
  - *renaming, 205*
- filtering options, 214-220
  - *filter by selection, 221*
  - *filter listing for listed*

items, 214-215
- *search function for listed items, 215-218*
- *special filters, 218-220*
- formatting values, 224
- grouping dates
  - *into months and years, 213*
  - *overview, 212*
  - *summarizing weeks, 213-214*
  - *into weeks, 214-213*
- limitations, 200-201
- lines, 223
- making data suitable for, 227-230
- overview, 199
- Report Filter, 201
- row labels, 201
- showing values based on other items, 206
- slicers, 226-227
- sorting
  - *overview, 208*
  - *quick sort buttons, 208*
  - *Sort (fieldname) dialog, 208-210*
  - *sort rules, 210*
- totals, hiding, 223-224
- values, 202
- views, 225

points, adding to sparklines, 250-251

preselecting data ranges, 56

previewing page breaks, 17

Project Explorer, 274

PROPER function, 48

Protect Sheet dialog, 27

Protect Workbook command, 26

protected sheets, filtering on, 172-173

protecting
- sheets, 27
- workbooks, 26

Q

Quick Access toolbar
- commands
  - *adding, 11-13*
  - *removing, 15*
- customizing for current workbook, 14-15
- moving, 11
- running macros from, 282-283

quick sort buttons, 151-153, 208

R

R1C1 notation, 102

radar charts, 233

RAND function, 152-153

Random Number Generator, 143

random sort, 152-153

ranges
- averaging, 126-127
- copying formatting of, 86
- criteria range (Advanced Filter), 174
- data ranges, preselecting, 56
- filtering for, 219
- named ranges, 56-57

Rank and Percentile tool, 143

reapplying filters, 161

rearranging columns, 155-157
- with mouse, 156-157
- with Sort dialog, 155-156

Recent command (File menu), 27

recent documents, viewing, 27

Record Macro dialog, 279-280

recording macros
- Record Macro dialog, 279-280

relative references in macro recording, 276-277

reducing file size, 270

reflowing text, 73

Regression tool, 143

relative formulas, 100-102

relative references in macro recording, 276-277

Remove Duplicates command, 177-178

removing
  commands from Quick Access toolbar, 15
  duplicates
    from datasets, 177-178
    from single columns, 176-177
  groups from Ribbon, 8
  pivot table fields, 205
  subtotals, 184

renaming
  pivot table fields, 205
  sheets, 24

reordering components, 260

repeating headers, 20

Report Filter, 201

reports
  headers
    inserting dates into, 18-19
    inserting filenames into, 18-19
    repeating, 20
  pages. *See* pages

Resize Table dialog, 60

resizing
  charts, 238
  pictures, 265-266

Review menu commands, Protect Workbook, 26

Ribbon
  buttons, adding to groups, 10
  groups
    adding, 9
    adding to existing tab, 9
    removing, 8

minimizing, 10-11
running macros from, 281-282
tabs
  adding, 9
  adding groups to, 9
  hiding, 7-8

rotating pie charts, 248

Row Height dialog, 193

rows
  adjusting width of, 87
  blank rows, inserting after subtotals, 192-196
  freezing, 21
  grouping, 196-197
  inserting, 24-23
  switching rows/columns, 243-244
  total rows, adding to tables, 60

rules, 93-98
  built-in rules, 94
  combining, 97
  custom format for top items in range, 94-95
  custom rules, 94-97
  sort rules, 210
  stopping rules from being checked, 97-98

running macros
  from form controls, text boxes, or shapes, 283-284
  from Quick Access toolbar, 282-283
  from Ribbon, 281-282

S

Sampling tool, 143

Save As dialog, 28

saving
  charts as templates, 252-253
  files as PDF, 28
  to SkyDrive, 35-36
  workbooks to local drive, 37-38

scatter charts, 233

Scientific format (numbers), 77

search function for listed items, 215-218

SECOND function, 138

security
  macros, 271-273
  sheets, 27
  workbooks, 26

Select Case statement, replacing nested IF with, 288

Select Data Source dialog, 243-244

selecting SmartArt, 259

selection, filtering by, 172

series
  creating, 44-45
  extending by dragging fill handle, 43-44

shapes
  adding/deleting, 259-260
  cropping pictures to, 266
  running macros from, 283-284

sharing
  themes, 90
  UDFs (user-defined functions), 287-288
  workbooks, 38-41

sheets
  adding UDFs to, 287
  changing multiple, 25-26
  grouping, 26
  moving, 24
    within workbook, 25
    between workbooks, 25
  protected sheets, filtering on, 172-173
  protecting, 27
  renaming, 24

sizing
  fonts, 65-66
  rows/columns, 87

SkyDrive
  accessing, 34
  downloading workbooks from, 37-38

folders
creating, 38-39
permissions, 39-40
saving to, 35-36
slicers, 226-227
SmartArt
adding/deleting shapes,
259-260
categories, 255
changing individual
components, 261-262
changing selected layout,
261
formatting selected
layout, 261
inserting, 255-259
linking cells to, 262
reordering components,
260
selecting, 259
Sort (fieldname) dialog,
208-210
Sort dialog, 147-151
case-sensitive sorts, 151
rearranging columns,
155-156
sorting by color or icon,
149-150
sorting by custom list,
153-154
sorting by values, 148
sorting
case-sensitive sorts, 151
by color or icon, 149-150
with custom sequences,
153-154
data preparation, 147
in Excel WebApp, 147
overview, 146-147
pivot tables
overview, 208
quick sort buttons, 208
Sort (fieldname) dialog,
208-210
sort rules, 210
quick sort buttons,
151-153
random sort, 152-153
rearranging columns,
155-157
Sort dialog, 147-151

subtotals, 192
troubleshooting, 157
by values, 148
spacing
in number formats, 79-80
sparklines based on date,
251-252
sparklines
adding points to, 250-251
creating, 250
deleting, 252
overview, 250
spacing based on date,
251-252
special filters, 218-220
stacked charts, 233
statements, IF
nesting, 135-136
replacing nested state-
ments with Select
Case, 288
stock charts, 233, 246-247
stopping rules from being
checked, 97-98
strikethrough, 66
styles
cell styles, 74
chart styles, 236
subscript, 66
Subtotal dialog, 182-184
SUBTOTAL function, 181
subtotals
collapsing/expanding,
184-185
copying, 185-186
formatting, 186-187
increasing amount of
space after, 193-194
inserting blank rows after,
192-196
by multiple columns,
190-191
multiple subtotal function
types, 187-190
placing above data, 184
removing, 184
sorting, 192
Subtotal dialog, 182-184
SUBTOTAL function, 181

suitable data for pivot tables,
227-230
SUM function. See AutoSum
function
SUMIFS function, 131-132
summarizing weeks, 213-214
SUMPRODUCT function,
132-133
superscript, 66
surface charts, 233
switching rows/columns,
243-244
symbols in number formats,
81-82

T

tables
adding totals to, 60
capabilities, 57
cells. See cells
defining, 57-59
expanding, 59-60
inserting formulas into,
109-110
pivot tables. See pivot
tables
table references in
formulas, 110-111
tabs
adding, 9
adding groups to, 9
hiding, 7-8
Tabular view (pivot tables),
226
templates
opening, 28-29
saving charts as, 252-253
text
converting case, 48-49
converting to dates,
140-141
converting to numbers,
55
delimited text, separating
into multiple columns,
51-53
filters, 169-171

fixed width text, separating into multiple columns, 54-55

fixing numbers as text, 47-48

joining, 45-46

joining with dates, 46-47

justification, 72-73

in number formats, 79-80

orientation, 72

reflowing, 73

Text to Columns option, 51-55

text wrap, 71

WordArt, 264

text boxes, running macros from, 283-284

Text format (numbers), 77

TEXT function, 46-47

Text to Columns option, 51-55

themes
  applying, 89
  creating, 89-90
  overview, 88-89
  sharing, 90

thousands separator, 80

time formats (numbers), 76-77

TIME function, 138

times
  date/time functions, 136-142
    overview, 136
    time conversion functions, 138
  in number formats, 82-84
  overtime, calculating, 141-142

TIMEVALUE function, 138

titles
  axis titles, 238
  chart titles, 237-238

toolbar, Quick Access. See Quick Access toolbar

top 10 filtering, 220

totals
  adding to tables, 60
  formatting, 186-187

hiding, 223-224

subtotals. See subtotals

trace precedents and dependents, 116-117

trendlines, 244-245

troubleshooting
  date functions, 140-142
  Excel options, 29
  formulas, 143-146
    error messages, 116-117
    trace precedents and dependents, 116-117
  number formats, 84
  sort problems, 157
  VLOOKUP function, 128-129
  Watch Window, 118-119

TRUE function, 134

t-Test: Paired Two Sample for Means, 143

t-Test: Two-Sample Assuming Equal Variances, 143

t-Test: Two-Sample Assuming Unequal Variances, 143

U

UDFs (user-defined functions)
  adding to sheets, 287
  BMI(), 290
  comments, 289
  Commission(), 288-289
  overview, 284-285
  sharing, 287-288
  structure of, 285-286

underline, 66

ungrouping items, 26, 197

unique items, filtering for, 176

Unique Records Only option (Advanced Filter), 176

unlocking cells, 27

updating charts, 242-243

uploading workbooks, 34-35

UPPER function, 49

user-defined functions. See UDFs (user-defined functions)

V

validating data, 61-63
  criteria, 61-62
  limiting user entry to selection from list, 62-63

values
  compared to formulas, 100-101
  converting formulas to, 50
  in pivot tables, 202
  showing values based on other items, 206
  sorting by, 148

VBA security, 271-273

versions of Excel

View menu commands
  Page Break Preview, 17
  Page Layout, 18-19
  Zoom, 16

viewing
  Developer tab, 273
  recent documents, 27

views
  custom views, 22
  pivot table views, 225

Visual Basic Editor, 273-275
  macro recorder, 275-279
    AutoSum button, 278-279
    navigating while recording, 275-276
    relative references in macro recording, 276-277
  modules, inserting, 274-275
  Project Explorer, 274

VLOOKUP function, 127-129

W

Watch Window, 118-119

WebApp. See Excel WebApp

WEEKDAY function, 137

WEEKNUM function, 137

weeks
grouping dates into,
214-213
summarizing, 213-214
width, of rows/columns,
adjusting, 87
windows, arranging, 23
Windows Live ID, 31-33
wizards
Convert Text to Columns
Wizard, 51-55
Formula Wizard, 122-124
.NET Passport Wizard, 35
WordArt, 264
workbooks
creating, 35-36
customizing Quick Access
toolbar for, 14-15
downloading, 37-38
moving sheets between,
25
moving sheets within, 25
opening, 37
protecting, 26
saving
as PDF, 28
to SkyDrive, 34-35
sharing, 38-41
simultaneous editing,
40-41
uploading, 34-35
WORKDAY function, 139
WORKDAY.INTL function, 139
worksheets. *See* sheets

X-Y

YEAR function, 137
YEARFRAC function, 139
years, grouping dates into,
213

Z

Zoom Slider, 16-17
zooming in/out, 16-17
z-Test: Two Sample for
Means, 144